A WORLD OF
INFLATION

A World of Inflation

Geoffrey Maynard

(Professor of Economics, University of Reading)

and

W. van Ryckeghem

(Professor of Economics, Free University of Brussels)

B. T. BATSFORD LTD, LONDON

First published 1976
© Geoffrey Maynard and W. van Ryckeghem, 1976

Printed and bound in Great Britain by
Redwood Burn Ltd, Trowbridge & Esher
for the publishers,
B. T. Batsford Ltd, 4 Fitzhardinge Street, London W1H 0AH

ISBN: 0 7134 3068 0

Contents

Preface

The aim of this book is to provide a description and an analysis of the long inflation which has afflicted the Western capitalist world in the post second war years. The writing of it has taken its authors far longer than they had anticipated when they embarked on the task in 1970. Apart from natural dilatoriness and a general willingness to be diverted into doing other things at the same time, the main reason for this is that, during the course of writing, the rate of inflation throughout the world constantly accelerated: there was no time between 1970 and 1974 when we could finish the book, confident that our description and analysis were reasonably up-to-date. Moreover, the character of inflation appeared to undergo a significant change, forcing us continually to reappraise our ideas about its causes and consequences. Even now, it is not clear whether the deceleration which has set in (second half 1975) represents a return to the moderate inflation rates of the 1950s and 1960s, or whether it is no more than a lull in the general tendency towards ever higher inflation rates.

The appearance of faster inflation in the 1970s as compared with the 1950s and 1960s, brought about a significant reassessment of the theoretical explanations of inflation. For instance, the fact that faster inflation in the 1970s was associated with more, not less unemployment of labour, tended to discredit, perhaps prematurely, Phillips-curve type explanations of variations in inflation rates. Monetary explanations became more prominent: indeed, it could be said that the revival of 'monetarist' doctrine was largely due to the acceleration of inflation at the end of the 1960s: but the focus of attention shifted from domestic money supply to international money supply. Although we do not doubt that monetary factors *per se* played a more autonomous role in the inflation of the early 1970s than in the inflation of the 1950s and 1960s, we are far from convinced that monetary explanations in themselves are adequate to account for inflation in the advanced industrial countries of the world, or that the policy dilemmas facing policy makers can be appreciated without an understanding, not usually provided by 'monetarists', of the market forces which actually determine price and money wage behaviour. Hence, in our theoretical analysis of the inflationary process, we devote considerable attention to the behaviour of product and labour markets.

A substantial part of the empirical section of the book is devoted to the moderate inflation of the 1950s and 1960s. The justification for this is the conviction that the forces producing moderate inflation are likely to be a permanent feature of modern industrial societies, while those responsible for recent high inflation rates are ad hoc and in principle avoidable. Time will tell whether this is an optimistic view. Aside from this, the econometric analysis employed to bring out the underlying nature of the moderate inflation of the 1950s and 1960s also serves to bring out by contrast the different nature of the recent faster inflation, to the description and analysis of which a separate chapter is devoted. Our econometric analysis of the 1950-68 period convinces us that in these years, at least, there was a trade-off between inflation and unemployment, even taking into account that wage and price determination may have been affected by price anticipations. However, it is clear that differences among countries in average unemployment levels cannot explain why different countries experienced different average inflation rates in this period; and further econometric analysis is employed to test certain structural explanations which have been advanced.

The student of economics looking for a presentation of the various alternative theories of inflation now current will be disappointed by this book. Our purpose has been to describe the inflation actually experienced by the countries of the West, and to employ an eclectic theoretical approach to explain it: we have some doubt whether theoretical explanations emphasising one cause to the exclusion of others are really satisfactory. It is unlikely that our analysis and explanations will satisfy all, perhaps even the majority of professional economists: even so, we hope they and students of economics generally will find both useful and interesting the brief, but we believe reasonably comprehensive, statistical account of inflation in OECD countries, as well as the econometric analysis of the relation between unemployment and inflation and of the underlying structural factors operating. The non-professional may have difficulty with some aspects of the latter, but we believe there is sufficient non-technical matter in the book to make it of interest to him as well.

In the preparation of this book, we have been greatly assisted by Mr Graham Bird and Mr Leon De Koker. The former was responsible for assembling much of the statistical material of Chapter 5 and for the underlying calculations of Chapter 6: the latter supervised the laborious computation for Chapters 7 and 8. Mrs Meg Wells and Mrs Hilary Millar cheerfully undertook successive re-typings of the book, and in addition the latter accepted responsibility for the tedious task of reading and correcting the proofs. We are greatly indebted to all of them.

An author's name index is provided at the end of the book, but a subject index was thought to be unnecessary, given the contents of the book and the arrangement of the chapters. Readers should have little difficulty in tracing matters of particular interest to them if they refer to the contents page for chapter headings and sub-headings. However, we apologise in advance to those readers who find the absence of a subject index inconvenient.

G.W.M.
W.v R.

1
Introduction

Inflation: a worldwide phenomenon
The 30 years since the end of the Second World War have seen a
period of major economic advance throughout the world. They have
witnessed sustained and high rates of economic growth not often equalled
in earlier periods of economic history in countries already well developed
before the war began,[1] and they have seen the economic awakening of a
large number of countries which for centuries past had remained stagnant,
poor and under-developed. During these years, unlike the 1930s, widespread
and chronic unemployment ceased to be, in the developed countries at
least, a major economic and social problem; and under the stimulus of
dwindling barriers to trade, international trade expanded at an unpreced-
ently fast rate. At the same time, however, the quarter of a century witnessed the emergence of chronic inflation as a worldwide problem which
has displaced unemployment as the major concern of governments of
developed countries, and which in at least some less developed countries
has made economic development more difficult.

The extent to which post-war inflation was, and is, a worldwide phenomenon is revealed in detail in Table 1.1.

Table 1.1. RATES OF INFLATION IN INDUSTRIAL, OTHER DEVELOPED
AND LESS DEVELOPED COUNTRIES, 1949-73
(Annual average)

Industrial countries	1949-69	1949-53	1954-59	1960-65	1966-69	1970-73
Austria	5.85	14.28	1.95	3.77	3.07	5.70
Belgium	2.00	1.21	1.58	2.20	3.31	5.05
Canada	2.50	3.43	1.57	1.59	4.07	4.65
Denmark	4.46	4.28	2.91	4.68	6.67	7.10
France	5.74	11.30	4.29	3.73	4.01	5.90
Germany*	1.80	0.42	1.57	2.63	2.28	5.40
Italy	3.09	3.10	2.16	4.49	2.40	6.55
Japan	5.24	9.08	1.59	5.85	4.98	7.37
Netherlands	4.12	5.29	3.10	3.60	5.07	6.70
Norway	4.07	6.31	3.10	3.46	3.66	7.90
Sweden	3.93	5.44	3.13	3.62	3.70	6.72
Switzerland	1.85	0.70	1.05	2.97	3.34	5.79
United Kingdom	3.83	5.80	2.72	3.07	4.14	8.05
United States	2.07	2.35	1.39	1.28	3.90	4.90
Group average	3.61	5.29	2.29	3.35	3.90	6.27

Other developed
countries

Australia	4.89	12.58	2.50	2.18	2.94	6.40
Finland	4.69	4.25	4.71	4.82	5.03	6.60
Greece	4.71	9.69	5.14	1.73	2.34	6.41
Iceland	8.71	9.59	4.61	9.35	12.79	12.50
Ireland	3.78	4.88	2.56	3.53	4.60	9.30
New Zealand	3.98	6.21	3.42	2.28	4.59	8.31
Portugal	2.42	0.65	1.21	2.46	6.38	10.50
South Africa	3.15	5.39	2.52	2.05	2.94	6.41
Spain	6.06	4.99	7.15	6.58	5.00	8.40
Turkey	7.41	2.32	14.10	4.16	8.64	12.10
Group average	8.69	6.06	4.79	3.91	5.53	8.69

Less developed countries

Argentina	26.95	27.46	33.33	23.92	21.28	33.2
Bolivia	36.89	37.72	86.96	6.27	6.67	3.9
Brazil	31.45	11.34	21.97	58.04	30.94	11.8
Ceylon	1.70	1.99	0.52	1.14	3.93	6.3
Chile	30.96	20.22	49.86	25.20	24.61	75.7
Colombia	9.73	8.23	8.58	11.57	10.94	12.6
Costa Rica	2.69	4.75	1.97	2.22	1.90	3.7
Dominican Republic**	0.91	0.71	0.37	1.74	0.67	6.2
Ecuador	2.63	2.53	0.37	3.52	4.79	8.1
El Salvador	2.90	9.40	1.66	0.18	0.74	1.2
Ghana	6.13**	7.60	2.10	10.18	3.65	9.4***
Guatemala	1.41	4.08	0.86	− 0.16	1.24	3.5
Honduras	2.50	3.79	1.97	2.06	2.25	3.1
India	3.99	1.87	2.41	5.52	6.73	6.4
Iran	3.88	1.99	7.63	3.36	1.39	5.2
Iraq	0.17	− 5.59	1.47	1.47	3.44	4.6
Israel	8.35	17.55	5.86	6.35	3.60	8.1
Korea	45.67	134.90	25.62	14.43	11.05	10.0
Mexico	5.17	7.23	7.63	2.47	2.94	9.4
Morocco	4.92**	11.56	2.78	4.35	− 0.62	3.4
Nicaragua	4.58†	9.45	2.84	1.03	2.74	6.2
Pakistan	2.71	2.48	1.18	2.90	5.02	5.5
Panama	0.20	− 0.89	− 0.17	0.82	1.20	4.3
Peru	9.35	10.30	7.35	9.20	11.13	6.9
Phillippines	2.48	− 0.86	0.71	4.67	3.46	10.4
Thailand	3.30	6.44	3.16	1.02	3.02	4.1
Tunisia	4.69	11.76	2.47	1.87	3.43	3.4
United Arab Republic	1.95**	1.21	0.37	2.94	4.35	3.4
Uruguay	30.25	7.06	16.64	31.97	77.07	43.4
Venezuela	1.62	3.23	1.38	0.65	1.42	3.1
Group average	9.67	11.99	10.00	8.03	8.50	10.8

Group average (excluding high inflation countries; Argentina, Bolivia, Brazil, Chile, Korea, Uruguay).	3.67	5.04	2.73	3.38	3.47	5.04

Source: Joseph O. Adekunle, 'Rates of Inflation in Industrial, Other Developed and Less Developed Countries — 1949-65', IMF Staff Papers, November 1968, updated to 1974 from *International Financial Statistics,* amended to include Germany.

   * 1950-69
  ** 1949-68
  † 1949-67
*** 1970-72

It will be seen that with very few exceptions practically all countries have suffered from persistent inflation in some degree throughout the postwar period. Until the late 1960s with the exception of a small group of countries, mostly Latin American, which suffered from very high rates of inflation, in some cases exceeding over 25 per cent per annum, inflation was generally moderate. Between 1944 and 1969, annual rates of inflation (as measured by cost of living indices) in industrial countries as a whole averaged about 3.7 per cent per annum, with Austria, France and Japan at the top end of the scale and Belgium, United States and Switzerland at the bottom. In this period, inflation seems to have occurred at a somewhat faster rate in the non-industrialized developed countries in which it averaged about 4.8 per cent per annum; but contrary to general impression, and with the exception of the high inflation countries mentioned earlier to which special attention must clearly be given, the less developed countries as a whole do not appear to have suffered from more inflation than did developed countries. In fact, at any rate up to the end of the 1960s, a significant number of less developed countries experienced annual rates of inflation averaging less than 2 per cent per annum over the period. In two of them, Panama and Iraq, prices showed a tendency to fall rather than to rise.

In most countries prices were rising fast in the years 1949 to 1953 when the Korean war and general expectations of more widespread conflict between Russia and America caused emergency stock-piling of materials and commodities, forcing up their prices to very high levels. Inflation rates were much lower in the next decade, but it is an ominous feature of Table 1.1 that following the return to more stable prices in the 1950s and early 1960s, by the end of the latter decade inflation showed signs of accelerating once again. In 1973/4 inflation attained new dimensions. In many industrial countries prices rose by well over 10 per cent; and in some countries inflation rates were expected to approach 20 per cent in 1975. Far from there being signs that the problem of inflation is being handled successfully, there is every sign that it is becoming more serious.

Earlier history of price inflation

The 1946-74 period is, of course, not the only period in recent world economic history in which prices have shown a long-term tendency to rise. The long inflation in England and Europe in the sixteenth and seventeenth centuries and the shorter prolonged inflation which accompanied Britain's early industrial revolution in the latter half of the eighteenth century have attracted much attention from economists and economic historians. It is true that apart from the Napoleonic war years, and a short price boom in the 1850s, the general course of prices in the nineteenth century was generally downward: the value of money in England was probably higher in 1895 than it was immediately following the Napoleonic wars. But after 1895 prices began to rise again and continued to do so at a slow rate until the outbreak of the First World War when the rate of increase sharply accelerated. Following the First World War the general trend of prices was once again downward in most countries, although Germany and one or two other defeated countries experienced hyper-inflation in the 1920s. The Second World War saw the appearance of inflation once again, although at a much slower rate than in the First World War; but in contrast to the latter, prices continued to rise in all countries even when the war had ended.

Although, as Table 1.1. shows, inflation in much of the post Second War period, at any rate up to 1970, was generally moderate in most countries, with annual rates of price increase averaging less than four per cent, it nonetheless took place at a faster rate than at any other comparable period in history. For instance, the cost of living in England rose by not much more than about one per cent per annum in the 18 years prior to the First World War, and at about the same rate in the United States if we ignore the sharp price inflation that accompanied the massive boom in economic activity that took place in that country at the turn of the century. Moreover, it is of significance to note that even during the periods when prices showed a long term tendency to rise, as for instance between 1895 and 1914, there were years when prices actually fell (as in 1907 and 1908 in both the United Kingdom and the United States). Conversely, in periods when the secular or longer term tendency was for prices to fall, years can be found in which they rose. These shorter term fluctuations of prices that took place within the longer term trends were associated with (in fact they partly define) the so called trade or business cycle — that is, the short run expansions and recessions in economic activity during which prices, output and employment tended to rise and fall together — that characterized the economic development of England, the United States and many European countries in the nineteenth and early twentieth centuries.

There has been a good deal of recent speculation about whether the business cycle has continued to survive in the post Second War period, and if so, in what form.[2] Whatever the outcome of this speculation, it is clear from Table 5.1. of Chapter 5 that the period we are concerned with in this study is characterized by the virtual absence of the cycle in its nineteenth-century form. Economic instability there has certainly been, but it has largely taken the form of fluctuations in *rates of growth* of output rather than of fluctuations in absolute levels. Only a few countries experienced even minor recessions in GNP and then only for very short periods.[3] Moreover, the period has been characterized by the complete absence in practically all countries of any years in which prices actually fell, although clearly the rate at which prices rose fluctuated from time to time. Both of these features of the postwar period suggest that new forces were at work influencing price and output behaviour, and that the analysis developed for understanding the behaviour of capitalist economies in the nineteenth and early twentieth centuries, if not inappropriate today, is certainly inadequate.

It would be surprising if the disappearance of the business cycle in its nineteenth-century form and the postwar sustained rise in prices were unconnected with each other. Indeed, it is tempting to attribute the latter simply to the postwar disappearance of major recessions in which output and employment actually fell. But apart from leaving open the question — why have the recessions disappeared? — this explanation by itself throws no light on why some countries have experienced inflation at a faster rate than others even though their output may have risen less fast, or on why the rate of inflation has varied quite significantly over time in a way not necessarily related to variations in the rate of growth. In the U.K., for instance, prices usually tended to rise faster when output was expanding less fast. We cannot be sure that if economic forces had in fact operated in the postwar period to produce periodic declines in output and employment as they did earlier, money wages and prices would have behaved as they did in former times. It is possible that, in addition to the disappearance of the nineteenth-century-type business cycle, significant changes occurred in structural and other factors affecting prices and wages, making them less flexible in the downward direction and more flexible in the upward direction than was the case earlier.

Political and economic environment

Much of the research devoted to the nature and causes of inflation in the post Second War period has been concerned with the operation of the market forces that have produced a continuous rise in the price level; and a major but perhaps increasingly sterile debate has developed between those emphasizing the prior importance of costs and those emphasizing the prior role of demand. At the centre of the discussion lie first, the nature of the pricing decisions of firms operating in markets that are believed to be becoming less and less like the perfect competition model, and, second, the effect on wage determination of trade union bargaining power which is clearly stronger in the postwar period than it was in the nineteenth century.

Unfortunately, the discussion has been somewhat inconclusive, since it is by no means evident that conditions in respect of either of these elements in the inflationary process were so different in the postwar period as compared with periods before, or that they operated to prevent a business cycle of nineteenth century type, or, assuming that such a cycle had existed, they would have produced a different pattern of price and wage behaviour. In the absence of clear evidence to the contrary, it is plausible to believe that the fundamental nature of the private sector of capitalist market economies, defined in terms of profit motive, price determination, investment and financing decisions, were broadly the same in the postwar period as earlier, but that the overall economic environment in which firms and industries were operating was markedly different from what it was in earlier periods.[4]

It is not necessary to seek far to discover an obvious major difference in the economic environment in which the private sector now works. It is manifestly clear that governments now play a far more dominant economic role in practically all countries, whether they be capitalist, semi-capitalist or mixed, or non-market collectivized ones, than was the case earlier. Of prime importance is the responsibility accepted by all governments of 'managing the economy' with a view to maintaining a high level of employment, avoiding depressions and promoting and accelerating economic growth. Whatever view one might take about the acceptance of these responsibilities — and there are some who believe that it was unnecessary, even unfortunate, since most economies would have behaved at least as well without — it can hardly be denied that market behaviour and therefore price and wage determination have been affected. Nor has government influence been confined to a stabilization and growth promoting role; the operations and responsibilities of government go very much wider. In most countries government seek to redistribute income, and to a lesser extent wealth, in favour of the poor sections of the community; they provide the community with a large and growing proportion of its current consumption, in the form of community-type goods such as health, education, etc; they act as large insurance agencies providing security against ill-health, unemployment and old-age; they have become increasingly important as producers of goods, particularly in areas involving large investments in technology and research, they have become large direct employers of labour; and they have become concerned with regional distribution of production and income within the frontiers of their own countries, as well as accepting the international obligation of promoting development in the poorer, less developed countries of the world. All these activities are essentially economic and are additional to the more traditional roles of governments (such as the provision of defence and law and order) which also impose a claim on resources. It would be surprising if price and wage determination in both public and private sectors of capitalistic economies was not influenced by the expanded role of government.

Outline of book

In this book we describe and attempt to account for the worldwide inflation of the post Second World War years, focusing most attention on the experience of the major industrial countries of the West. We do not examine the price experience of Soviet Russia or other planned economies of Eastern Europe. Thus we are concerned with the nature and causes of inflation in free market economies in which price and wage determination remains largely a private enterprise decision. The manner in which governmental policies of the Western democracies, referred to in the previous paragraph, have affected market forces and influenced price behaviour will however become manifest in various parts of the book.

We begin in Chapter 2 with an analysis of actual price and wage determination in a free market economy, which then provides a basis for a description in general terms of the nature of the inflationary process. The operation of and interaction between both demand and cost factors are necessarily discussed at length. Chapter 3 then provides a theoretical discussion of a possible relationship between the level of employment and the rate of inflation; and Chapter 4 examines the process by which inflationary pressures are transmitted from one country to another. These three chapters provide an analytical framework for an understanding of why the inflation rate may vary over time; why it may differ in different countries; and why, despite differences in the degree of inflation affecting different countries, it tends to rise and fall in most countries roughly simultaneously.

The next five chapters are the empirical core of the book. Chapter 5 provides a descriptive, anatomical account of post Second War inflation in the major industrial countries of the O.E.C.D.[5] Chapter 6 attempts to measure the impact of government fiscal policy on aggregate demand in these countries, while Chapters 7 and 8 provide an empirical investigation of the relationship between the pressure of demand, as indicated by unemployment, and the rate of inflation, and of the contribution of structural factors. These two chapters concentrate on the period up to 1968. The post 1968 period, up to the present time, in which inflation rates in the Western World began to accelerate dramatically, is examined separately in Chapter 10 since there are reasons to believe that the nature and characteristics of inflation are significantly different from what had been the case earlier. Chapter 9 describes the nature of the inflationary forces operating in less developed countries, and looks briefly at the experience of one or two of the very high inflation countries of Latin America. Finally, Chapter 11 summarizes our findings and examines the problem which inflation poses for economic policy. However, this chapter does not pretend to offer concrete solutions for the acute inflationary problem now (1974) facing the western world.

Monetary explanation

Before concluding this brief introduction it is perhaps necessary to make a preliminary brief reference to an explanation of inflation which satisfied most economists in earlier times and still satisfies some at present. The explanation is based on the observable facts that in the past a sustained rise in the general price level has always been accompanied by a parallel sustained rise in the quantity of money, and further that there appears never to have been a sustained rise in the quantity of money which greatly exceeded the growth of output of goods and services in the same period which was not accompanied by an increase in the general price level. The conclusion can therefore be drawn that a sustained increase in the quantity of money is both a necessary and a sufficient condition for a sustained rise in the price level. The great price inflation in Europe in the sixteenth and seventeenth centuries and the secular movement of prices in the nineteenth and early twentieth centuries, which have been referred to earlier, have all been explained in these terms.[6]

If this explanation of inflation were accepted as complete in itself, without need of qualification or further consideration, there would be little point in carrying the analysis of inflation further. If it cannot take place without an increase in the quantity of money, and it cannot be avoided if the quantity of money increases relatively to the output of goods and services, the policy implications are then obvious.

The reason why the explanation does not satisfy all economists can be brought out by posing the question: What would have happened if the quantity of money had not been allowed to rise at a faster rate than the actual rise in output of goods and services?[7] The pure adherents to the explanation would argue that the only difference would have been that prices would not have risen, everything else happening as before. In particular, the output of goods and services would still have risen at the rate it actually did, quite independently of what happened to the quantity of money. Sceptical economists doubt this since they believe, with some evidence to support them, that a wide range of forces, including of course money supply itself, bear on prices and output simultaneously; and while the quantity of money may be an important determinant, within fairly close limits, of what happens to the *value* of output, it does not by itself determine what happens to prices independently of what happens to output. If other forces are operating to push up prices, limitation of the quantity of money may bear more heavily on output than on prices, forcing the community to 'trade-off' lower output, employment and perhaps economic growth for more price stability.

If the economy is faced with such a 'trade-off' problem, then it becomes necessary for analysis to delve further into the mechanism through which prices and wages are determined, and also into the connection between price and wage determination on the one hand and output, employment and investment decisions on the other. The purpose of such an analysis would be to throw light on the nature and determinants of the 'trade-off' and thereby to suggest how policy might minimize the sacrifice explicitly involved.

This view of the problem of inflation is accepted in this book, which accordingly devotes most attention to the behaviour of commodity and labour markets, and to the nature of the trade-off dilemma facing governments. The approach by no means implies, of course, that 'money does not matter' and the role of money is not ignored in the theoretical and empirical analysis of the book.[8]

2
The Nature and Causes of
Inflation in Industrial Countries [1]

In the real world prices do not rise as if lifted by an invisible hand: they are raised by formal and explicit managerial decisions. This very obvious fact leads us into a search for answers to three broad groups of questions. First, what is the nature of the considerations that induce an entrepreneur to change, and in particular to raise, the price of his product; and what are the constraints on his decision to do so? Second, since a decision by one entrepreneur to raise his price does not constitute inflation, which in this as in most other studies is defined as a process in which all or most prices are continuously rising at the same time, we must explain why most, if not all, entrepreneurs are being induced to raise their prices roughly simultaneously. What is the nature of the market forces conducive to all, or most prices broadly rising together? Third, since if the average price level is rising and total output is unchanged or increasing also (which has typically been the case in most countries in the postwar period), aggregate monetary expenditure must be sufficient to absorb the higher or unchanged level of output at the higher price level, we need to ask whether a level of aggregate monetary demand adequate to absorb unchanged or rising output at higher prices must have been already in existence before the general rise in price, or at any rate be a precondition of it. Or is it the case that the general rise in the price level automatically and as a direct consequence brings with it the necessary rise in aggregate monetary demand? Or is there some other element in the situation which produces this necessary rise, not as a direct inevitable consequence, but rather indirectly?

The nature of the answers that can be given to these questions is the subject matter of this chapter. First, we consider the market and other factors affecting the pricing decisions of individual firms, in particular the decisions to raise prices; we then go on to examine the conditions that are likely to be conducive to general and widespread decisions to raise prices by all or most producers roughly simultaneously; third, we examine the determinants of aggregate monetary demand or expenditure, relating these to the behaviour of prices. Finally, we pull the analysis together to describe the interaction of all the factors described above in the process of inflation — how it can start, how it continues and how it may come to an end.

Price determination by the individual firm

If a producer had at all times full and accurate knowledge of the demand curve for his product, and of the schedule of his total costs at all levels of output, and if there were no constraints on his ability to alter his price and/or output whenever, and as quickly as his demand curve and cost schedules changed, he could choose for each period during which cost and demand remained unchanged that combination of price and output that would maximize his profits (assuming that demand and costs were such that profits were possible at all). In other words, he could fix a price at which marginal revenue would be equal to marginal cost. If the demand curve shifted, or its elasticity at the existing price changed, marginal revenue at the existing price and output would also change, leading the producer to choose a different combination of price and output: so, too, would a change in his marginal costs of production. In these circumstances, prices would be responsive, or flexible, to short-run changes in both demand and cost.

In fact, individual firms do not typically possess such full and accurate knowledge of their demand and cost curves relating even to short periods of time; nor do demand and cost conditions remain unchanged sufficiently long for producers to arrive at their short run profit-maximizing combination by trial and error. It is true that decision making for producers or sellers operating in perfectly competitive markets is less complicated than suggested by the above considerations, for they can leave the market to determine the price for them, while concentrating their minds on the volume of output they should sell. But the conditions necessary for perfect competition to exist can be found nowhere in the real world, and, leaving aside financial markets, are only approximated in the markets for relatively few products, mainly of a primary character. But where they are approximated, prices tend to be very flexible and responsive to short run changes in demand relatively to short run market supply.

Most manufactured products of advanced industrialized countries at any rate are sold in imperfectly competitive markets in which producers do not have to accept market price as a datum for their output decisions. In general, industries are characterized by having fewer (often far fewer) firms than perfect competition would require. Moreover, products are differentiated and not homogeneous, and markets are broken up by transport and selling costs. In such conditions, owing to a less than infinite elasticity of the demand curve facing producers, both price and output decisions have to be explicitly and jointly made together. Furthermore, some producers are faced with the situation that the prices charged by some of their competitors are not independent of the prices they charge themselves and may be affected by it. But firms do not possess knowledge either of the precise nature of the interdependence between the firm's own price and the demand for its product, or of the repercussions that changes in the firm's own price will have on the prices charged by its competitors. Thus, since market demand and cost conditions are also far from static in the real world, it is clear that decision making is fraught with much uncertainty and risk; and while entrepreneurs are undoubtedly interested in high and growing profits, not only as the desired end result of productive activity but also as a means of self-financing or attracting outside finance for further expansions of productive capacity, it would be unrealistic to assume that in the pricing of their products they consciously and continuously aim at short run profit maximization. Indeed, even apart from uncertainty, it is probably unrealistic to believe that short term profit maximization provides the only, or even the main, objective of firms: while some minimum level of profits must be earned if shareholders are to be kept contented and takeovers are to be avoided, firms are likely to take a rather long run view of their future, aiming at survival and a satisfactory rate of growth. The pricing decision is only one element in a wide range of interlinked policy decisions, relating, for example, to the introduction of new products, advertising, relationships with actual and potential competitors, and to investment and growth. Thus it seems plausible to believe that pricing policy is aimed at expanding output and profit over time; and that the uncertainty which faces entrepreneurs at all times is handled by the application of fairly simple rule of thumb methods which can of course be amended in the light of changing circumstances.

In general, entrepreneurs have better knowledge of their costs and the way they are related to output than they have of market demand. Hence, it seems reasonable to believe that the rule of thumb pricing methods employed by entrepreneurs will be based on costs. If costs rise, entrepreneurs will have a strong incentive to raise prices: for them not to raise prices in such circumstances, strong evidence suggesting that a rise in price would reduce total revenue from sales would have to exist. Such conditions are not impossible; for instance, as suggested earlier, a firm may be operating in an oligopolistic market situation in which the response of its own sales to a change in its price depends very much on the reaction of a few major competitors. Unless these other firms also raise their prices, the first firm may well find its total sales revenue reduced by a rise in its own price. Much will depend, therefore, on whether the entrepreneur has reason to believe that the rise in costs afflicting him is also afflicting his major competitors. If he believes so, then he will have much less fear of the consequences of raising his own price.

On the other hand, when operating in a less than perfectly competitive environment, an entrepreneur is probably less likely to respond to an increase in the demand for his product with an immediate rise in his price than when faced by an increase in his costs. An increase in the demand for his product will be revealed to him by an increase in his sales at the existing price; with an unchanged volume of production his inventories will tend to decline. Lacking precise knowledge of the elasticity of his demand curve, the entrepreneur has a clear incentive to raise his output but not his price, provided his direct or marginal costs per unit of output remain broadly constant. In these circumstances, average cost per unit of output is likely to fall as output rises, so that increased output means higher profits than before, even if they are not necessarily maximized. If output cannot be expanded with existing plant or equipment, or can be expanded only with steeply rising direct costs per unit of output, the entrepreneur must clearly think more about his pricing policy, for in these circumstances an expansion of output may not be accompanied by an increase in profits. Even so, the more important question that will face him is whether to expand his whole scale of operations by increasing his plant and equipment. If he is to do this, he must be reasonably sure that the level of demand which is at present outstretching his capacity to produce will be a permanent, or at any rate long run, feature of the situation, warranting an expansion of his fixed costs and perhaps a radical change in his whole cost structure. If the longer term prospects are such as to encourage him to expand his scale of production, he may well be reluctant to cash in on a situation in which current demand for his product is in excess of current production by raising his price — at any rate by raising his price to the point where demand in excess of capacity output is eliminated — fearing that this may well have an adverse effect on demand in the longer run. Instead, he will prefer to allow queues to be formed and waiting lists to be developed, until such time as his scale of output can be raised.

This view of the pricing process, which implies that prices are determined, at any rate in the short run, by some rule of thumb procedure rather than be aimed at profit maximization, and which suggests that price changes are more likely to be related to prior cost changes than to demand, does not imply that demand and profits are irrelevant to pricing decisions in imperfect competition conditions. Demand still plays a crucial role and affects pricing decisions even in the short run. Thus, as we have indicated earlier, a firm faced with expanding demand for its product at the existing price may raise output rather than price if it can do so on the basis of existing plant and equipment with little or no rise in his direct cost; but in order to raise output it may have to increase its labour force. If this entails paying higher money wages per unit of labour and/or higher prices for necessary raw materials and intermediate goods, direct costs per unit of output may rise. Unless fixed costs per unit of output fall significantly as output expands, so that average costs per unit of output at the new higher level of output are no higher than they were at the lower level, entrepreneurs have a strong incentive to raise prices. From their point of view prices have been raised because costs in the form of higher money wages or higher material costs have gone up; but it is clear that in the circumstances postulated, the rise in the price level was primarily due to the expansion of demand for the firm's product which led it to expand its demand for labour and other inputs.

This example assumes that money wages per unit of labour paid by the firm rise as a result of the firm bidding for more of it. A firm, however, may be willing, on its own initiative, to pay higher wages to its existing employees, or be faced with a trade union demand for higher money wages, even when demand for its product is not such as to induce it to expand its existing labour force. A firm may be induced to act on its own initiative in this respect if its profits are demonstrably and embarrassingly high and/or if the productivity of its labour force is rising. The payment of higher money wages in these circumstances may seem preferable to lowering prices, since the latter could be construed by competitors as aggressive competition, entailing repercussions that cannot easily be estimated. There appears to be universal reluctance on the part of firms to cut prices except in the most extreme circumstances and prices are even less likely to be lowered in the face of excess supply than they are to be raised in the face of excess demand.[2]

High profits and rising labour productivity may also provide the motivation for trade union demands for higher money wages even when the employer does not act on his own initiative. But if excessive profits or rising productivity do provide the basis for money wage increases, there is no need for prices to rise; for either labour costs of production do not rise, or, if they do, they are absorbed by profits. On the other hand, a firm may be faced with a demand for wage increases clearly in excess of productivity increase, the conceding of which will raise labour costs and direct costs per unit of output to an extent that cannot be absorbed in profits. The reaction of the entrepreneur obviously depends on his assessment of the total market situation and of the extent to which his competitors are subject to similar wage pressures. If his assessment is that total market demand for the industry's product is presently buoyant and expanding, and that money wage demands are being pressed on the industry as a whole, wage pressures will be conceded to and prices will promptly be raised. Even if the current industry market situation is not particularly buoyant, but the outlook is good, a firm may still concede the wage increase and raise prices, particularly if the cost to it of a strike is high: this will be the case if only this firm and not others is likely to be faced with a strike, or if its production function is heavily capital intensive. On the other hand, the firm is more likely to resist wage demands if current and future demand prospects are poor, since the cost of raising price in terms of a restriction of the future growth of demand and revenue may then exceed the cost of accepting a strike.

The decisions to concede money wage demands and to raise prices are clearly not taken independently of each other. Unless its profits were initially excessive, a firm cannot pay higher money wages unless it can raise its price. For otherwise profits would be squeezed and the ability of the firm to expand its scale of output through extensions to plant and capacity would be reduced.[3] It cannot safely raise its price unless current, and particularly expected future demand for its product is high, since otherwise competitors may fail to respond in the short run, and the growth of demand and of the firm may therefore be prejudiced in the long run. Thus, although related rather closely to costs in the short run, the price charged by the firm, as well as the wages paid by it, are obviously affected by the state of demand, although less by its level in the current period than by its expected rate of growth in the longer run. The price level acts to create a balance between the rate of growth of demand in the long run and, because of its bearing on profits and on the firm's ability to raise finance, on the rate of growth of capacity to meet it.[4]

Factors bearing on prices in general

A decision by one producer to raise the price of his product does not constitute inflation. This occurs only when all or the majority of producers are induced to raise their prices altogether and are led to do so at repeated intervals of time. The factors outlined earlier which cause one producer to raise his price must be afflicting all or most producers roughly simultaneously. Appreciation of this obvious fact suggests that although each producer tends to raise his price because his costs have risen, rather than because his demand is in excess of his current production, excessive demand may still play the vital role in the inflationary process. As indicated earlier, a producer, when faced with an expansion of demand for his product, will tend to take steps to expand his output; these steps may result in his having to pay higher prices for his material and labour input, causing him to raise his price. But unless the firm is very large, or has a rather specialized demand for particular materials and labour which are in short supply, it is unlikely that the increase in its demand for inputs alone will force up their prices and, therefore, his costs. The matter is different if all or the majority of firms are experiencing buoyant and expanding demand for their products, leading them all to increase their demand for input at the same time. Prices of raw materials sold in more or less highly competitive markets may be forced up, raising costs more generally in the industrial and manufacturing sector. If labour, too, is in short supply, firms may be induced to pay above existing negotiated rates to attract labour from each other, and labour organizations will seize the opportunity to bargain for higher rates that, if conceded, must be paid by firms equally, irrespective of their market demand. Thus, although prices may appear to be rising because costs of production are rising, at bottom lies excessive aggregate demand for output which is causing producers to compete for limited supplies of materials and labour.

However, while excessive demand in total has clearly played an important role in all countries in the postwar period, it would be a mistake to believe that postwar inflation can be explained solely in these terms. Excessive demand can obviously cause inflation but it is not a necessary condition of it, except in the rather formal and perhaps trivial sense that a particular combination of price level and aggregate output must necessarily be accompanied by a level of aggregate monetary demand that would have been in excess of aggregate supply at a lower price level. Other factors have played a part in the postwar inflationary process and their role has probably increased sharply in more recent years.

Producers in general may experience a rise in their costs of production not attributable to a prior general increase in overall demands for labour and primary materials. The most obvious cause would be a general rise in money wages in excess of the increase in labour productivity forced on producers by successful trade union pressure. Another possibility, particularly relevant for a country like the U.K. which imports most of its required raw materials and most of its primary foodstuffs from overseas, would be an autonomous rise in its import prices. As far as this possibility is concerned, it is possible, of course, that a particular country's demand in the world markets for some primary products is so large relative to the total that its own demand pushes up the price level of these products as a consequence; but there are few countries so big that an expansion of their overall domestic demand and product has a significant influence on the prices of the goods they import from abroad. In general, a rise in the world price level of raw materials is due to an expansion of world demand for them, emanating from a world-wide expansion of demand for final production; so that the inflationary pressures that result must still be attributed to world-wide excess demand. However, a rise in raw material prices produced in this way may well cause a rise in costs of production even in countries which may not be sharing in the world-wide expansion of final demand and output. These countries will be subject to cost inflationary pressures which, as far as they are concerned, cannot be said to arise from their own excessive demand pressures.

On the other hand, a country may see its own import prices quoted in domestic currency rise sharply, imposing cost-raising pressures on domestic producers, even when the world price level shows no such tendency. This would happen if the country lowers the exchange value of its own currency in terms of all or most other foreign currencies, so raising the domestic price level of its imports. If this currency devaluation had been forced on the country by the fact that its own balance of payments with the rest of the world had been in serious deficit, and if this deficit was primarily the consequence of domestic demand outstripping the country's capacity to produce, then once again the inflationary pressures that on the surface appear to have been imposed by a rise in costs are fundamentally due to excess demand. Only in the case when the balance of payments deficit was attributable to export prices being forced up to uncompetitive levels as a consequence of rising domestic costs of production which was taking place even when domestic demand was clearly not in excess of the country's own capacity to produce, could the further inflationary pressure imposed by devaluation be judged as cost rather then demand. At bottom would lie upward pressures on money wages and labour costs referred to earlier and which we now consider in more detail.

Wages, productivity and inflation

Money wages may rise in response to a general attempt by firms to increase their labour force, particularly when the level of employment is already high and unemployment is low; but this is not the only situation in which money wages may rise. The initiative may come from labour's side, in the form of aggressive or defensive wage demands by organized labour. Since such wage demands are increasingly regarded as the major cause of inflation in industrial countries at the present time, it is necessary to look closely at the motivation underlying them and the constraints against which they come.

At the simplest level, demands for higher money wages reflect workers' natural desire for higher real incomes and higher standards of living: even so, the question arises as to why workers do not prefer to obtain these in the form of lower prices rather than higher money incomes. A long history of inflation is not, of course, conducive to belief that higher real incomes would in fact emerge through lower prices and money wage restraint, and it is fairly clear that present demands for higher money wages and present inflation are by no means independent of its previous history. But there are other elements in the situation also.

In an economy in which the division of labour has been carried to considerable lengths, a worker's standard of living does not depend significantly on what happens to the price of the product he himself is helping to produce. Although a worker may be reasonably convinced that if his own money wage remains stable the price of the product he produces may fall in line with productivity growth, he may not be similarly convinced that money wages and prices will behave similarly elsewhere. If they do not, his standard of living will not benefit no matter what happens to his own productivity. Hence, it is safer for him to secure higher real income in the form of higher money wages, even if as a consequence the price of the product that he helps to produce does not fall or even rises. This quite rational attitude on the part of the individual worker is obviously strengthened by the existence of trade unions. The object of these is to improve the bargaining position of the workers as a whole against the employers in order to secure higher real wages and better conditions of employment; but trade unions can play little or no part in decisions relating to prices and must, therefore, seek to operate in the only field open to them, namely in money wage determination. Moreover, it is much easier for a trade union to demonstrate its success in raising the real wages of its members by pointing to higher money wages obtained than in claiming credit for the widespread reduction in prices necessary if higher real wages are to be obtained in this way.

The attitude of trade unions in this respect is reinforced by that of firms which for a variety of reasons, both good and bad, prefer to compete with each other by the use of advertising and other non-price measures than to run the risk of a price war. Unless significantly changed, the attitude of firms and unions in this respect is likely to ensure that some inflation will be a permanent feature of a modern industrial economy, for reasons that will emerge a little later in this chapter.

When formulating money wage demands, trade unions are motivated by a number of considerations. They may sometimes be acting in a defensive role, demanding higher money wages to compensate for higher prices. At other times their motives may be more aggressive, when they seek to obtain compensation for productivity increases or to share in profits that they regard as excessive. Some unions may seek to emulate the success of others by bargaining for wage increases comparable to those achieved in other industries, even when the industries and firms in which they themselves are operating do not show comparable productivity growth or profit positions. But, as powerful as trade unions have become, their operations are clearly subject to market and political constraints which bear on their ability to obtain wage increases.

Clearly, the existence of widespread excessive demand for goods and labour is conducive to trade union wage pressure since firms are then competing for labour which is in short supply. In such conditions, trade unions can hardly be held responsible for the inflation of money wages and prices that results; indeed, in such conditions unions could play a moderating role in the interests of restraining general inflation. But widespread excessive demand is not a necessary condition for successful trade union action on the wage front. High demand and high employment, which are not excessive in the sense that output is at a maximum or that no unemployment exists, are also a background against which unions can make aggressive wage demands; for in these conditions, profits tend to be high and the cost of strikes to employers in terms of lost orders and sales can be relied upon to deter them from outright opposition. But such conditions are also those in which firms can raise their prices with relative impunity in response to any rise in their labour costs, for wage demands are likely to be affecting all producers indiscriminately. Underlying the behaviour of both employers and trade unions may be confidence in the government's determination to maintain a high level of employment and demand, irrespective of what happens to prices, a matter to which we return in a later chapter.

If aggressive trade union action results in money wage rates paid by a particular firm rising in line with labour productivity in that firm, neither labour costs nor price should rise. If this condition applied to all firms, no firms would be experiencing rising labour costs, and absolute and relative prices would remain unchanged: in effect the average wage level would be rising in line with the average productivity level. But in a situation in which labour productivity is rising at widely different rates in different firms and industries, a wide dispersion of money wage increases would then take place, with some wage earners securing much larger increases than others. This is not likely to be acceptable to trade unions operating in industries where productivity is growing more slowly and they will attempt to obtain wage increases comparable to those being paid in the more technologically advanced and faster growing industries. Insofar as these trade unions are successful, the former group of industries will experience rising labour costs and will be forced to raise their prices if they are to maintain their rate of profit; a rise in the general price level will therefore result. Defensive wage demands may then follow as all trade unions aim at compensation for a rise in price, and the rise in the general price level will be accelerated.

It is in this context of wage transfer, or wage spillover, plus defensive wage demands, that organized labour activity is most likely to play its most important independent role in the general level of wage determination. The activity of trade unions is supported by the fact that in modern welfare states there is a general feeling, based on moral considerations, that workers should get wage increases in line with their own productivity increases and also that a wide disparity between money wages paid by industry should be avoided. Trade unions therefore find it relatively easy to base their wage bargaining on productivity growth in technologically advanced industries, and use their power backed by these moral considerations to raise wages substantially in excess of productivity in other industries, such as services, where productivity is growing much less fast.

Even if trade unions did not actively pursue a policy of equalizing wage rates, it could be argued that the operation of a competitive labour market would work to the same end. The rise in relative earnings in the fast productivity growth sector of the economy would attract labour from the slower productivity growth sectors, which would tend to cause earnings to fall back in the former sectors as well as cause their output to rise. Either because of a decline in marginal physical product, or because of a fall in the price, or both, the marginal value product of labour would then tend to fall in the fast productivity growth industries. For opposite reasons, it would tend to rise in the relatively slow productivity growth sector which would be tending to lose labour. As a result of these tendencies, money and real wages would tend to become equalized in all industries. In practice, however, it may not be possible for output to be expanded easily in the short run on the basis of existing plant and capacity: nor is the mobility of labour particularly high in the short run. The equalizing tendencies may therefore tend to take a long time to work out. Trade union action is likely to take place well before the market performs the same function.

Even if trade unions did not pursue the policy of forcing fast productivity growth industries to pay money wages equal to the increase in productivity they are enjoying, a rise in the average price level may still occur if those industries whose labour costs are falling would then refuse to lower prices, although other industries whose labour costs may be rising are forced to raise them. Indeed, if prices are inflexible in the downward direction, any change in the pattern of demand necessitating relative price changes must cause a rise in the general price level irrespective of what happens to money wages.[5]

The asymmetrical pricing behaviour of firms implied in the conjecture that firms raise prices when their costs rise but do not reduce them when their costs fall could be explained by the fact that although firms may not actively seek to maximize their short run profits by an appropriate pricing policy, a fall in costs may give them an opportunity to move to a closer profit-maximizing position without raising their price; or it may arise because firms may be operating in an oligopolistic market situation in which pricing arrangements are not firmly coordinated, so that the safest policy for any individual firm to pursue is that of not rocking the boat by taking the initiative on prices. But, whatever its cause, lack of price competition among firms contributes to an inflationary rise in the general price level, even apart from the aggressive behaviour of trade unions.

In so far as the rise in the average wage rate is broadly determined by productivity growth in the industries in which it is growing fastest, usually the technologically advanced ones, and in so far as changes in average productivity growth in the economy as a whole are determined largely by what happens to productivity in the technologically advanced industries, inflation is likely to be higher in countries in which, and in periods when, average productivity is growing fastest.[6] This 'productivity-gap' type inflation, as it has come to be called, is likely to be largely independent of the short run state of aggregate demand for goods and labour, provided this is high enough to prevent serious unemployment; but, of course, if a state of excessive demand for goods and services does exist, inflation is likely to take place at an even faster rate, since in these conditions wage rate increases may take place in excess of productivity growth in the technologically advanced industries as well.[7]

Aggregate monetary demand

A sustained rise in the general price level must be accompanied or preceded if not caused by a rise in aggregate monetary demand. This remains true even if the proximate cause of the rise in price level is aggressive trade union wage bargaining operating in a situation not characterized by excessive aggregate demand in relation to the capacity of the economy to produce; for, if monetary demand did not rise as fast as the price level rose, profits would be squeezed and output and employment would fall, thereby weakening the basis on which trade unions can obtain wage increases in excess of productivity growth. But in fact a general rise in money wages produced by aggressive trade union activity can itself lead to a rise in aggregate monetary demand which sustains the inflation.[8]

Unless immediately offset by a fall in employment, a general rise in money wage rates itself produces a rise in aggregate monetary demand for goods and services because wages are incomes as well as costs. In this sense, wage inflation is self-supporting from the demand side. But of course this conclusion has to be qualified in a number of very obvious but important respects. In the first place, although wage earners' consumption undoubtedly represents a large proportion of total consumption, the money incomes of wage earners are not the only source of consumption demand. Profit earners and rentiers in general also consume, and if their incomes are significantly reduced in the process of rising costs and prices, their real expenditure on consumer goods may fall. In the second place, the disposable money incomes of wage earners, from which consumption expenditure is made, do not necessarily rise in line with their earned incomes owing to tax payments. If the marginal rate tax on money wage incomes is greater than the average rate, disposable money income rises in less proportion than does wage income itself. And in the third place, consumption demand, although the largest element, is not the only component of aggregate monetary demand. We cannot, therefore, assume that total monetary demand rises in line with money wages and price, even when the level of employment is assumed to be constant.

In Keynesian terms, the major components of aggregate demand are private and public sector capital formation including additions to inventories, personal consumption expenditure, government current expenditure, on goods and services, and exports. Total supply of final goods and services is made up of gross domestic product plus imports. The underlying determinants of the major components of demand include many factors, such as the level of incomes at home and abroad, interest rates and the money supply, profit motivation and expectations of entrepreneurs, which bear on investment decisions, psychological propensities bearing on consumption decisions of households, the distribution of income, and the political and economic objectives of government. Expansions or contractions of any, or all, of the components of demand in real terms will affect prices, output, and employment; and, as we have seen, changes in the latter in turn affect monetary expenditure.

In formal terms, a state of excess demand exists when, at a given price level and output level, the sum of public and private capital formation, public and private consumption and exports exceed the sum of gross domestic product of the economy plus imports: or expressed differently, if the sum of private capital formation, government expenditure on goods and services, and exports, exceeds the sum of personal saving, taxation revenue and imports, all expressed in *ex ante* terms. If output can be expanded on the basis of existing capacity and labour force without a rise in price, we do not have an inflationary situation; but beyond a point this will prove impossible and the basis of an inflationary situation then exists. Autonomous expansions of aggregate monetary demand may occur because of an autonomous expansion of any or all of the components of the total, but in practice autonomous expansions of business spending or government spending are probably the most important initiating causes.

If an autonomous expansion of aggregate monetary demand causes prices and incomes to rise, further induced changes in monetary expenditure will follow. Money incomes in the form of profits and wage incomes will rise causing a further expansion of monetary demand for consumption goods and possibly capital goods as well; but in an economy where the marginal tax rate is greater than the average rate, disposable incomes rise in less proportion than earned incomes. In this case, unless consumers are willing to reduce the proportion of their marginal increment of income that is saved, monetary expenditure on consumption will rise in less proportion than incomes and probably prices as well, thereby restricting the growth of total monetary demand. This effect may be reinforced if the inflation is accompanied by a shift in the distribution of income in favour of profit earners and against wage earners, since this tends to lower the overall propensity to consume; but operating in the other direction, expectations of continuing and accelerating inflation may cause a decline in the community's willingness to save.

Private capital formation may be stimulated by a rise in the price level, if present and expected future profits are favourably affected; but this will not necessarily happen if wages and labour costs are playing the leading role in the inflation. Moreover, what happens to interest rates and the availability of finance is also crucial for investment decisions; and a rise in general price level may discourage investment on these grounds for reasons that we come to in a moment.

As far as government expenditure is concerned, it is reasonable to assume that this will largely be fixed in real terms so that monetary expenditure is likely to rise in line with the price level. On the other hand, a counter-inflationary force in the economy may be exerted through the foreign trade sector: rising money incomes and prices may induce more imports, while the higher price of exports may reduce foreign demand for them, causing a decline in real demand for domestic production. If, however, the exchange rate is depreciated in order to prevent the implied worsening in the balance of payments, the deflationary effect of a decline in real demand would be averted: moreover, a further cost inflationary force would be introduced into the economy in the form of a rise in the domestic price level of imports. Thus the existence of a foreign trade sector cannot be relied upon to bring inflation to an end via an influence on aggregate monetary expenditure.

Money stock consideration

So far we have ignored the influence of the stock of money. It is evident, however, that an expansion of aggregate monetary expenditure required to support a continuous rise in the average price level in turn requires an expansion of money stock, and/or a rise in its velocity of circulation[9]. In the short run, an expansion of output, incomes and prices can take place on the basis of a given money stock; but beyond a point further expansion comes up against barriers which may be monetary or technical. A technical barrier arises when all money, which includes currency and bank deposits, is fully and actively engaged as medium of exchange, no money being held in idle balances explicitly as a store of value. A further increase in the rate of spending is then prevented unless changes in the payments structure or in the timing of transactions allows a given stock of the medium of exchange to do more work. In a modern monetary economy a technical limit of this sort is probably a theoretical possibility only, both because of the very high proportion of total money stock represented by idle balances (implying substantial scope for the reinforcement of active balances) and because the monetary barrier is likely to become effective a long time before technical constraints on spending become apparent.

The monetary barrier takes two forms, one operating directly through interest rates and the credit market and the other through the value of net wealth and its composition. The activation of idle balances tends to cause a rise in interest rates as transactors, seeking to obtain them for active use, offer alternative financial assets in exchange; the more inelastic is the demand for idle balances, the more must interest rates rise to induce their conversion into active balances. A rise in interest rates may, however, affect a variety of spending decisions in respect of capital formation, including stock-building, and possibly personal consumption as well; and the more interest rate elastic are these types of spending to a rise in the interest rate level, the more quickly does inflation come up against this aspect of the money barrier. The growth of money incomes and prices can, therefore, be quickly checked if the demand for idle money balances is very inelastic while at the same time spending decisions are very interest elastic; but if the demand for idle balances is elastic and spending decisions are inelastic, inflation can go a long way on the basis of a given stock of money. In the short run, the existence of sophisticated non-bank financial intermediaries offering a wide range of close money substitutes tends to make the demand for idle money balances very elastic. Moreover, available empirical evidence suggests that a wide range of important spending decisions is not at any rate in the short run significantly sensitive to changes in interest rates even in a stable price environment; furthermore, even when prices are rising and are expected to continue to rise, a rise in money rates of interest may not be accompanied by a rise in the real rate so that their potential dampening effect on expenditure will be much diminished. These considerations suggest that the first element of the monetary barrier at any rate cannot be relied on to produce a quick check to a general rise in the price level.

The second element of the money barrier enters through the relationship between people's net wealth and its composition and their demand for goods and services; we can suppose that in determining what proportion of their current income they save, people take into account their net wealth and changes in it. As we have seen earlier, a rise in the price level and in the monetary value of total transactions increases the demand for active money balances at the expense of idle balances; at the same time, however, the real value of the total stock of money (nominal stock deflated by the price level) falls, reducing, other things being equal, the real value of total net wealth and altering its composition. Asset holders may be induced to restore their total net wealth by raising their current rate of saving from current income and to return its composition to what it was initially by increasing their demand for nominal money balances. This they can do by disposing of other financial assets, the price of which will therefore be forced down causing a further fall in the net wealth of asset holders and bringing into play the interest rate effect referred to earlier. This again may affect spending decisions.

The impact of these developments on expenditure, however, depends on the relative importance of money holdings in total net wealth and on what is happening to the price of other financial assets that are held, or could be held, in wealth portfolios. Thus, if real money balances are typically the most important component of total net wealth, a rise in the price level of goods can be expected to have a significant effect on net wealth and, in time, on spending. On the other hand, if the prices of some other components of net wealth, or of components that can be added to it, are rising faster than the price level of goods and services in general, the fall in net wealth may be limited, or even prevented, as holders are willing to substitute them for assets denominated in nominal monetary terms. In practice, an inflation will tend to induce wealth holders to sell assets denominated in fixed monetary units in exchange both for nominal money balances and for other assets — such as equities and real estate — whose price level may be expected to rise relatively to the general price level.[10] Rising equity prices may well prevent an early fall in the value of net wealth and thereby prevent any significant impact of inflation on spending decisions. In the long run, however, if the total stock of money is kept constant, the attempt to add to nominal money balances as prices and incomes rise will continually depress the real value of other assets denominated in nominal money units, implying that the price of equities and real estate must rise at an accelerating rate relatively to the price of goods and services in general if the value of net wealth is to be maintained.

Thus, in a financial system in which money holdings are not of overwhelming importance in total wealth holdings and in which there exists an extensive range of equities and a large stock of real property, this wealth element of the money barrier is unlikely quickly to check the rate of inflation; since the interest rate element in the money barrier is also not likely to act quickly, a constant stock of money is not likely to provide a significant check to inflation in the short run, and the velocity of circulation rises to accommodate. However, as the ratio of total money stock to money income falls, the interest rate elasticity of the demand for idle balances is also likely to fall; and as the rate of interest rises the interest rate elasticity of spending decisions is likely to rise as well; moreover, the likelihood of the value of net wealth falling increases. All these factors tend to increase the effectiveness of the money barrier as inflation proceeds, implying that if it is to continue the money stock must be eventually raised. In practice, however, for reasons of a political nature that will be discussed later, the money stock is not likely to be kept constant or even its rate of growth restrained sufficiently to check, and eventually prevent, inflation by itself.

The inflation process

We may usefully summarize the course of this chapter so far by describing briefly the nature of the typical inflationary process in a single economy. It may be triggered off by an autonomous rise in some or all components of aggregate effective demand — public and private consumption and investment, and foreign demand for exports — or it may start as a result of an autonomous aggressively motivated increase in money wages or by a boom in commodity prices abroad not induced by a prior increase in aggregate demand in the economy itself. If prices are to rise and continue to rise, this initiating force must set up repercussions involving widespread pricing and income decisions throughout the economy, including those implicitly or explicitly made by government in its fiscal and monetary operation.

In a modern industrialized economy, if the initiating cause is a rise in aggregate demand, prices will not tend to rise immediately; output will respond at first, employment may rise and profits will also tend to increase. After a point, however, costs begin to rise as well, perhaps because of a rise in the price of important raw materials which are purchased in competitive markets at home or abroad, but more probably because firms find themselves having to pay higher money wages in the form of higher overtime payments or in the form of payments over negotiated wage rates. Once an expansion of output cannot be achieved with rising profits because costs are rising too, entrepreneurs will begin to raise their prices, thereby further raising the cost of inputs to other firms and industries and the cost of living to consumers.

In the early stages, labour unions may be playing a fairly passive role with firms taking the lead in offering and paying higher money wages. Profits may be rising and labour share in total income falling. But as the price level and cost of living rise, unions begin to play a defensive role by negotiating for higher money wages in compensation: indeed, some wage contracts negotiated between employers and unions may contain cost of living clauses obliging the employer to pay higher rates automatically as prices rise. If the expansion of demand and output continue, and labour becomes generally scarce, or becomes scarce in important regions of the economy, or in relation to the demand for labour by important key industries, trade union reactions may become more aggressive as workers seek to get the best from their scarce supply position. Wage increases are demanded, more than can be justified on cost of living grounds. Unions organized in key industries whose output may be playing the leading role in the overall expansion of demand may set the pace; but workers in less dynamic or demand favoured industries will attempt, usually successfully, to follow suit on parity grounds if nothing else. Employers in key industries may not put up much of a fight against such aggressive wage demands, preferring and able to grant them because of an expansion of demand for their product which enables them to pass on higher costs in the form of higher prices; but concessions on their part make it difficult, if not impossible, for other firms and industries to hold out even when higher money wages, costs and prices for them may adversely affect output. Profits may be squeezed in these industries and the share of labour in total income may recover, even to a level higher than initially.

The spiral of rising prices and wages that begins to develop is supported by a parallel expansion of monetary expenditure on consumption as a result of a rise in general money incomes associated with the rise in wage rates and employment. Other types of expenditure will also be rising in monetary terms as business and government attempt to maintain the real value of their investment and other expenditure. However, after a point, the increase in monetary expenditure may begin to lag behind the spiral of money wages and prices, so that output and growth become checked, and output may even fall in absolute terms. One obvious component of aggregate expenditure, mainly exports, may fail to be maintained in real terms as foreign purchases switch their purchases to cheaper sources of supply, although if inflation is proceeding in most or all competitive countries at broadly similar rates, or if the exchange rate is allowed to depreciate, this may not happen. Personal consumption expenditure, in monetary terms, may begin to lag behind the rise in prices and incomes generally, partly because with a progressive tax system disposable money incomes (i.e. earned money incomes less tax) rise in less proportion than earned incomes; partly because increased monetary expenditure on consumption may come up against contractual saving even when expectations are discouraging saving in general; and partly because some poorer sectors of the community may find their real incomes becoming increasingly depressed, forcing them to reduce their real consumption. Government is usually in a better position to increase monetary expenditure in line with prices, although even so it can come up against a monetary barrier imposed by public opinion or by legislation. Private investment expenditure, in monetary terms, may keep pace with the price level for some time as businessmen are successful in maintaining their source of finance either from their own increased monetary profits or by activating their own or other people's or institutions' idle money balances; but eventually the cost of acquiring finance in this way becomes too high, making some investment now not worthwhile – for some entrepreneurs finance becomes literally unavailable.

Whether or not this situation develops, and how soon it develops, depends very much on what happens to the money supply as determined by government policy. If money supply is kept constant, inflation comes up against a monetary barrier, so that although prices may continue to rise for some time, output and employment will be falling simultaneously. After a time, the rise in unemployment may check wage demands and the rate of inflation will diminish. The crucial question which then faces the government is whether to allow the money stock to rise to prevent or limit unemployment or to keep firm control on it in the interest of bringing inflation to an end.

The process of inflation is the same when the initiating cause comprises autonomous and aggressive wage demands by trade unions in industry generally or in key parts of it. If such demands are to be successful the level of employment has to be high, though full employment in any absolute sense need not exist; and the state of present and expected future aggregate demand has to be such that entrepreneurs are confident that they can pass on wage increases in the form of price increases, while the cost of not conceding such demands in the form of strikes that are provoked is high. A variant of this type of inflation, in which an expansion of aggregate monetary demand does not play the initial causal role, occurs when a country with relatively large international trading propensities is faced with an autonomous rise in the prices of its imports. Once the domestic price level has been raised as a consequence, defensive and further aggressive money wage demands take place, leading to the familiar wage and price spiral.

Once an inflation is in being it becomes difficult to disentangle the interaction between aggressive, defensive and induced wage and price increases on the one hand, and monetary demand on the other. The initiating cause recedes into the background and becomes largely irrelevant to the current inflationary process. The extent and speed of the inflation, i.e. the rate at which prices rise per unit of time, depends on a number of institutional, political and psychological factors, such as the strength of aggressive and defensive wage and price changes, on the time interval between successive wage negotiations, or the time required for making price changes (in a modern mass-production economy prices cannot be changed all that frequently) and on price expectations. The latter are particularly important since they determine the size of wage demands made by unions, of price increases made by firms, of saving and consumption decisions by households and investment decisions by firms. Once elastic price expectations have set in, then inflation can become very fast and go very far, even on the basis of a given money supply.

If aggressive and defensively motivated price and wage increases are muted, the inflation may quickly bring itself to an end no matter what the size of the initiating cause or existing monetary situation: if they are strong, even a firm monetary barrier may not prevent prices from rising for a considerable period of time, even when output and employment are being seriously restrained or reduced.

This latter point bears strongly on the controversy concerning the role of cost and demand in the inflationary process. As we have seen earlier, in a typical inflationary situation both cost and demand are playing trans-mitting roles, and it is, therefore, not very fruitful to identify the inflation as being demand-pull or cost-push, since inflation cannot take place or continue unless both are reinforcing each other. If the distinction is useful at all, it lies in the implications for appropriate anti-inflationary policy. The question that policy is faced with is 'how to prevent inflation starting' or 'how to stop it once it exists'. If by simply operating on aggregate demand, for example by fiscal or monetary measures, the rise in prices can be brought to an end without causing a fall in output and unemployment[11] or, more dynamically, if by aggregate demand policy alone the government can regulate the economy so that demand, output and employment can rise over time with prices being stable — then inflation can be appropriately defined as 'demand-pull'. If, however, the attempt to obtain price stability by operating on demand alone results in output and employment growth being restricted or falling simply because the wage price spiral continues independently of the state of demand, then there may be point in describing inflation as 'cost-push', the implication being that policies operating directly on cost may be required to keep prices stable. This is not to argue that control over demand is not necessary: as we have seen earlier, even when on the surface inflation seems to be largely of a cost variety, excessive demand may have played, and continue to play, the central causal role, and, therefore, needs to be controlled. It is simply to suggest that in a modern industrial economy with strong labour organiz-ations and far from competitive markets in which its products are sold, demand policy alone may be insufficient.

The point also bears on the role of money. As argued earlier in this chapter, inflation cannot continue indefinitely without a rise in the quantity of money. It is also true that sustained expansions in the quantity of money relatively to the growth of output of goods and services have typically been accompanied by inflation. Nonetheless, it is misleading to draw the conclusion that inflation is, therefore, first and foremost a monetary phenomenon. It may be that in the past fortuitous gold discoveries, or improved technology in money creation which was used by unscrupulous government to finance expenditure so as to avoid taxation or parliamentary accountability, were the root causes of increase in the money supply and, therefore, of inflation. In more recent times, for the reasons described earlier, it is much more likely that money supply has been allowed to increase largely because governments were faced with the unpalatable alternative of seeing unemployment rise, and output fall. It is true that inflationary pressures have been validated, but faced with a trade-off between inflation on the one hand, and lower output and employment on the other — a trade-off produced by the factors determining wage and price decisions considered earlier — governments chose inflation. To say that inflation could not have taken place without the rise in money supply is one thing and, no doubt, true; to say that prices rose because the money supply increased is another thing which overlooks important elements in the situation.

Whether or not governments are faced with the dilemma of choosing between inflation on the one hand and unemployment on the other, and if so how·they should resolve it, are questions which have been hotly debated by economists and others in recent years. Indeed, the so called 'trade-off' between inflation and unemployment has been at the heart of the inflation controversy, and has divided monetarists and institutionalists, and confused politicians. In the last resort, the question whether governments are faced with a trade-off situation can only be answered empirically, and Chapter 7 of this book will be devoted to examining the evidence for the main industrial countries of the world. But there are theoretical considerations as well, which will be reviewed in the next chapter.

3
Inflation and Unemployment

Very broadly, the analytical-cum-descriptive account of the inflationary process set out in Chapter 2 may be summed up by saying that in a modern industrial economy producers tend, as far as their capacity allows them, to adjust their outputs to changing demand and to raise their prices when pressure from the side of costs tends to reduce their profits. Trade unions, on the other hand, press for substantial wage increases when they see high profits in industry, when other unions have successfully won large increases elsewhere, and when prices have been rising rapidly, or can be expected to do so, threatening their real wages. Producers will be more ready to concede to such union demands when profitability is abnormally high or, if it is not, when the market situation is conducive to the belief that higher money wages can be passed on in the form of higher prices. They will also more readily concede when losses due to strikes are likely to be high, that is, when the ratio of capital employed to normal output is high, and when the prospects for a continuing high level of production in the absence of strikes is good. These considerations suggest that a general rise in money wages and prices is more likely to occur in a situation in which aggregate demand for goods and output and employment are high and rising, than in a situation in which output and employment are relatively low and falling.

The view that full or high employment and price stability are not compatible with each other, at any rate if wage determination is left to the process of free collective bargaining, is not a new one. The famous Beveridge Report, *Full Employment in a Free Society*, published in the U.K. in 1944[1], explicitly noted the danger, as did the U.K. government 1944 White Paper on Employment Policy published at the end of the Second World War. In a very early and comprehensive study of postwar inflation which afflicted most countries in the late 1950s, Professor A.J. Brown discussed the problem at some length, and concluded that much more attention would have to be devoted to it.[2] However, the most famous attempt to quantify the relationship between the level of employment and the rate of inflation empirically was provided by A.W. Phillips in 1958, in an article which introduced the notion of the 'Phillips Curve', a concept which ever since has occupied a central place in the discussion and analysis of inflationary situations.[3]

In his original article Phillips plotted the rate of change of money wages against the percentage of the labour force unemployed in the U.K. for the years 1861 to 1913. The scatter diagram is reproduced below.

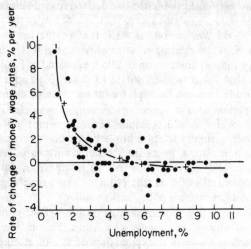

FIGURE 3.1.

The crosses shown in this figure give the average values of the rate of change of money wage rates and of the percentage unemployed in those years in which unemployment lay between 0 and 2, 2 and 3, 3 and 4, 4 and 5, 5 and 7, and 7 and 11 per cent respectively; and the curve connecting these crosses has come to be known as the Phillips Curve.

This curve indicates a negative relationship between the level of unemployment and the rate of change of money wages; but if the prices are related in some broad fashion to labour costs, then the transition from the rate of change in money wages to the rate of change of prices is obvious and direct: and unemployment and the rate of inflation are then also negatively related.

The evidence for the period 1861 to 1913 suggested to Phillips that in the U.K. wage stability was compatible with an unemployment level of about 5½ per cent; but given an annual rise in productivity of, say, two per cent which would allow for some rise in money wages without inflation, price stability would be compatible with an average level of unemployment of a little under 2½ per cent. At levels of unemployment below 2½ per cent, prices would tend to rise and at an increasing rate as unemployment fell. These results were qualified by the fact that at any given level of unemployment, prices and wages appeared to rise at a somewhat faster rate when unemployment was falling than when it was rising; moreover, it also appeared that a sharp rise in import prices, or an autonomous rise in domestic agricultural prices, could trigger off faster wage and price inflation than would be expected from the existing level of unemployment. But subject to these qualifications, Phillips appeared to have demonstrated successfully an empirical trade-off between unemployment and inflation. Significantly, too, the relationship which he had derived from an inspection of pre-First World War data also seemed to explain satisfactorily the inter-war and post Second World War periods as well; that is, the inter-war and post Second World War data relating to unemployment and the rate of change of money wage rates at any rate up to 1957, appeared to lie along the very same curve as that fitted to the 1861-1913 data.[4] This apparent stability of the relationship between unemployment and rate of change of money wages for a period of a hundred years or more was clearly an impressive piece of evidence which could have important implications for policy. Moreover, a similar relationship between unemployment and wage price inflation was found to exist in other countries as well. It is not surprising, therefore, that in a world suffering from the apparently intractable problem of inflation, the Phillips Curve attracted the attention of academics and government policy makers alike.

The Phillips Curve is an empirical relationship between unemployment and the rate of change of money wage rates. Phillips himself did not provide a complete theoretical explanation of it. An attempt to do this was later provided by Professor Lipsey,[5] who argued first, that in line with orthodox economic theory money wages would rise and fall with excess demand and excess supply of labour respectively, and second, that unemployment varied systematically and inversely with excess demand for labour. At first sight it might be expected that if excess demand for labour were zero, unemployment might also be zero, so that money wages would neither rise nor fall. Such a conclusion, however, would clearly not be in line with Phillips empirical findings that wage stability required a positive level of unemployment. However, Lipsey argued that the labour market is not frictionless. Apart from the fact that time is required for workers to move from one job to another, there is also no necessary coincidence between a particular job available and a particular worker looking for work. In other words, vacancies for labour can exist side by side with unemployment, and zero excess demand is compatible with unemployment. As excess demand for labour rises above zero, unemployment can be expected to fall, although at a diminishing rate; there may be some minimum level below which it cannot fall no matter what happens to vacancies and excess demand. This means that the relationship between unemployment and excess demand for labour is not linear when excess demand is positive. On the other hand, if excess supply of labour is positive its relationship with unemployment is more likely to be linear. Given, as Lipsey argued, that the rate of change of money wages is directly proportional to excess demand for labour, then the non-linear character of the Phillips Curve in the area of excess demand for labour at some positive level of unemployment automatically follows.

Lipsey also used his analysis to explain the anti-clockwise loops found by Phillips in his analysis of nineteenth-century wage and unemployment data, that is to say, the apparent tendency for wages to rise at a faster rate when unemployment was falling than when it was rising at any given level of unemployment. Phillips's own explanation seemed to rest on the argument that competitive bidding for labour was far keener when unemployment was falling than when it was rising: not only was there net hiring in the former case whereas there were net dismissals in the latter case, in addition a situation in which unemployment was falling created expectations of labour shortage in the minds of entrepreneurs, causing them to be anxious to hire labour before it was too late. Lipsey based his explanation, which although more sophisticated is not necessarily incompatible with that of Phillips, on the argument that the macro relationship between the rate of change of money wages and unemployment depends on the distribution of that unemployment between different sectors of the economy, and on the supposition that the upturn of an economic cycle tended to affect different labour markets at different times, while the downturn affected all markets more or less simultaneously.

If the macro relationship between the level of unemployment and the rate of change of money wages has the characteristics supposed by Lipsey — i.e. that the relationship is non-linear when excess demand is positive but linear when it is negative (so that wages tend to be rising faster in a market in which excess demand exists than they are falling in a market in which excess supply of a similar magnitude exists) — and if it is the same for all individual markets, it is evident that what is happening to the national index of money wages depends on how total unemployment — i.e. excess demand or supply of labour — is distributed between markets. A more equal distribution of unemployment (excess demand) among markets would tend, other things being equal, to be associated with a lower rate of increase of the national index of money wages than would a less equal distribution. It follows automatically that if Lipsey's supposition is correct — namely, that an increase in the demand for labour during a cyclical upswing tends to be less equally divided among markets than is a decline in demand for labour during a cyclical downswing which tends to affect all markets more or less simultaneously — about which there must be some doubt, it follows automatically that the index of money wages would tend to rise faster when unemployment was falling than when it was rising. The assumption of the same micro relationship between the rate of increase of money wages and the level of unemployment (i.e. an indicator for excess demand for labour) in all individual markets is of course crucial to this explanation.

Lipsey's explanation of the Phillips Curve gave rise to much subsequent micro analysis of the behaviour of labour markets, but it can fairly be said that this work has provided more of a refinement of the Lipsey-Phillips basic ideas than a departure from them.[6] The concept of excess demand in the labour market and the fact of the simultaneous existence of both unemployment and job vacancies in a typical labour market have come in for a great deal of scrutiny. The former is clearly due to frictions in the wage adjustment process and the latter to imperfections in the dissemination of information in the typical labour market. These factors prevent, or, at any rate, severely inhibit the adjustment of money wages to market clearing levels and the attainment of labour market equilibrium. On the one side of the market we have employers aiming to vary or maintain their work force; on the other side, we have workers, in employment as well as out of it, looking for jobs which will suit their talents and/or pay them more. Employers and workers are involved in search costs, both time and pecuniary, since the dissemination of information concerning workers and jobs available is not perfect. Lags in the adjustment of money wages to market demand conditions will exist since workers will not wish to accept lower money wages than they could conceivably get with the expenditure of more search time, while employers will seek to get more labour or retain what they have at the lowest wages they can get away with.

In any given unemployment and vacancy rate situation, the rate of change of money wages will depend on the behaviour of unemployed and employed workers in searching for jobs, and on employers' efforts to maintain their work forces. If unemployment is low and job vacancies abundant, workers are clearly in a more favourable position to get wage bargains satisfactory to them. The unemployed will find it easier to get new jobs at higher wages than they are at present receiving. The employer has to respond by offering higher money wages to retain existing employees and to attract new ones. But if unemployment is high and job vacancies scarce, the bargaining power lies with the employer. Workers will be more quickly paid off as soon as their services are not needed, and others may be retained at lower wages. Workers who become unemployed take longer to find new jobs, probably at lower wages than in their previous employment. It seems obvious that the upward pressure on money wages will be less in these circumstances than when unemployment is low and vacancies are plentiful. Conceivably if unemployment were very high and there were no trade unions, money wages might even fall.

If unemployment is actually falling and vacancies are rising, the upward pressure on money wages will probably be greater than if both are static. Employers advertise larger vacancies than usual and may well be faced with a rising supply curve of labour due to the scatter of unemployed workers each having different acceptance wages. Workers already employed may also have different transfer earnings. Thus a sudden rise in the demand for labour requiring a net increase in the level of employment and a net fall in the level of unemployment may induce or force employers to concede larger wage increases than they would normally have done in a static market situation. But as labour requirements are met and vacancies fall, the net hiring of workers begins to decline and the labour market reverts to a more normal static situation. Conversely, if labour demand falls off, implying an abnormally low level of vacancies and a net increase in the level of unemployment, employers may succeed in meeting their labour requirements with lower wage increases than would be normal in a static market; but again, as the labour force approaches requirements and unemployment and vacancies rise, the labour market returns to normal. Once a static labour market situation has been reverted to, wage increases revert to normal as determined by the static level of unemployment and advances. This explanation of the anti-clockwise loops found in the Phillips Curve data is an alternative one to that put forward by Lipsey but it is not, of course, inconsistent with it.

Since in a non-unionized labour market, it will be the employers who take the initiative in setting the money wage rate, it could be argued that the operative pressure on money wage rates will be the level of job vacancies rather than the level of unemployment. In fact vacancies and unemployment are likely to be rather closely related: as the number of job vacancies increases, the level of unemployment is likely to fall and vice versa. Empirical evidence suggests that the vacancy rate varies with the reciprocal of the unemployment rate, so that the curve relating vacancies to unemployment has the characteristic of a rectangular hyperbola.[7] Given such a relationship, it is immaterial whether we say that the rate of change of money wages is determined by the level of unemployment or by the level of job vacancies. In any case, if the rate of change of money wages is directly related to the level of vacancies while the latter is related to the reciprocal of the unemployment rate, it is clear that we are faced with a non linear relationship between the rate of change of money wages and the level of unemployment, which is the Phillips Curve.

Recent micro analysis of the labour market succeeds in explaining the non-linear relationship between the rate of change of money wages and the level of unemployment without invoking the power of trade unions and the influence of collective bargaining. Indeed, contrary to popular and governmental opinion on the matter, this analysis plays down the influence of trade unions on wage and price inflation generally. However, this may be due to the fact that the analysis has been very largely developed in the U.S., where trade unions have probably less influence on wage determination than is the case in the U.K. and other European countries in which trade union membership covers a much larger proportion of the total labour force.

On the face of it, there would seem no doubt that trade unions can and do have a strong influence on the outcome of wage bargaining. Collective bargaining would seem to have an inherent advantage over individual bargaining, and this is reinforced by the threat of collective strike action. But of course there are qualifications. Individuals can very often do better for themselves than unions can do for the collective membership, and the effectiveness of a threat to strike depends on the proportion of the labour force which is unionized and on its loyalty to the unions, as well as on the opportunity cost of a strike to employers and unions respectively.

The level of unemployment and the number of job vacancies is as important for the union as for the individual in governing the ability to secure larger money wages. We have given reasons why non-unionized labour is in a better position to maintain and raise money wages when unemployment is low and vacancies are numerous, as compared with the opposite situation. The same is surely true with unionized labour, if only because when unemployment is low the opportunity cost of strike action tends to be relatively small for unions but high for employers. It is costly for firms to have their production processes interrupted; moreover, rising costs are more easily passed on in the form of rising prices if aggregate demand is high than would be the case when unemployment is very low. Even so, the power of trade unions to obtain a union differential over and above the wage an individual might secure if not unionized could be less when unemployment is low than when it is high. When unemployment is low and vacancies are substantial, workers do not have to rely on unions to push up their money wages: the market situation may do this for them just as well. As a consequence, they have less motive to be loyal to union leadership and less incentive to support a strike which could be costly to them if the alternative was continual employment at high wages. The story may be different when unemployment is high, for now the power of the individual is much less while that of the unions remains strong owing to their ability to withdraw labour *en masse*.

If it is true that the power of the union to extract a differential over non-unionized wages is greater in high unemployment conditions than it is in lower unemployment conditions, this would seem to flatten the curve relating the rate of change of money wages to the level of unemployment — i.e. the Phillips Curve. It could mean that attempts to lower the rate of inflation by raising the level of unemployment would have less success when the mass of the labour force is unionized than when it is not, although at very low levels of unemployment the rate of inflation need not be significantly higher when unions exist than when they do not.

This view of the influence of trade unions on the rate of change of money wages and inflation clearly tends to minimize their role. Indeed, if no labour market imperfections of the sort we have been discussing existed — so that the rate of change of money wages did not depend on the unemployment and vacancy rates — the view would offer the unions no scope at all for influencing the rate of change of money wages. All that unions could do would be to produce a once-for-all differential in favour of unionized labour relative to non-unionized labour. However, this clearly understates the influence of trade unions. We have indicated in Chapter 2 the role they play in the 'wage-transfer' process which distributes the benefits of high productivity growth in some sectors of the economy across the economy as a whole at the cost of a rise in the general price level. If trade unions did not exist and industry operated in a more competitive environment than typifies most modern industrial economies, the spread of the benefit of uneven productivity growth would emerge in the shape of falling prices in some sectors of the economy which would offset rising prices elsewhere. Average money wages would rise less, and inflation would be less. It could be argued that the trade unions could not fundamentally alter this situation if governments refused to validate a rise in the general price level by increasing the quantity of money at a faster rate than total output is rising. But if organized labour prefers to take out the benefits of rising productivity in the form of rising money incomes than in the form of falling prices, and is prepared to enforce its preference by collective action, restriction of the money supply would tend to restrict output and employment at the same time; in other words, the government cannot escape the essentially political dilemma to which we have referred earlier.

Phillips Curve and classical wage theory

Lipsey's attempt to provide a theoretical explanation of the Phillips Curve and indeed the subsequent micro analysis of labour market equilibrium and disequilibrium we have been describing so far, are not completely satisfactory if judged by a need for the analysis to be consistent with established orthodox employment and wage theory. Classical wage theory teaches that real wages and employment are simultaneously determined by the demand and supply of labour, the former being governed by the relationship between the marginal product of labour and the level of employment, and the latter by the real disutility of working. Shifts in the demand and supply curves of labour can be expected to produce changes in the equilibrium real wage rate and the equilibrium level of unemployment, but given the existence of such an equilibrium, a unique relationship between on the one hand the levels of money wages and prices, and on the other, the level of employment, would be produced. Theoretically, of course, this relationship is compatible with a continuing rise in money wages and prices which leaves real wages unchanged, while employment remains at its equilibrium level, unaffected by the speed of the inflation. However, if we are primarily concerned, as we must be in studying inflation, with the disequilibrium dynamics of changing situations, rather than with the stability of markets, then it is clearly right to take money rather than real wages as the dependent variable. Moreover, in the real world although workers may be ultimately more concerned with their real wages than with their money wages, it is only the latter which they can directly influence or bargain over. Of course, what happens to prices enters the money wage bargaining process. In his demonstration of the empirical relationship between the level of unemployment and the rate of change of money wages, Phillips himself recognized that sharp rises in import prices or in domestic agricultural (food) prices would cause money wages in the U.K. to rise at a faster rate than could have been expected on the basis of existing unemployment and its direction of change; and although Lipsey's statistical findings were in some respects different from Phillips's, he agreed that price behaviour certainly entered into the determination of money wages. But neither Phillips nor Lipsey considered whether the attempt of workers to maintain or increase the level of their real wages affected the theoretical validity of the trade-off between money wage inflation and unemployment.

In principle, since money wage bargains are struck at discrete intervals, it is reasonable to believe that it is the expected rate of increase in the price level rather than its actual or past behaviour which will enter into the money wage bargaining process, although in practice, of course, price expectations will be based partly at least on recent past and current behaviour. But once it is admitted that workers are ultimately concerned with real wages and that price expectations enter into money wage determination, then it can be argued that there is no such thing as *the* Phillips Curve. On the contrary, there will be a different Phillips Curve for every expected rate of price inflation; in other words, a different rate of increase of money wages for any given level of unemployment and for any given rate of change of unemployment. A family of such curves is drawn in Figure 3.2., and they have the characteristic that each level of unemployment corresponds to a unique level of the real wage rate. But if it is also admitted that the real wage rate is determined by the demand and supply of labour, then, given the factors determining the demand and supply, and assuming no time lags in the adjustment of the real wage to excess demand or supply, a unique relationship between the rate of change of money wages and prices and the level of employment is established. Unemployment would of course exist but it would be at its 'natural' level i.e. a level determined by the structural characteristics and imperfections of labour and commodity markets.[8]

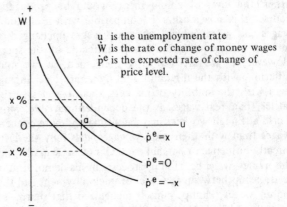

FIGURE 3.2.

How then can one explain Lipsey's original findings and subsequent evidence of a similar nature that unemployment and the rate of inflation have in fact been inversely related?[9] One explanation is that money wages respond only with a time lag to changes in excess demand for labour. Another is that inflation is not fully or accurately expected by the bargainers in the wage determination process; technically speaking, although people's expectations of future inflation are, for want of better information, based on past and current experience, the elasticity of such price expectations is less than unity, which is likely to be the case when rates of inflation are irregular. Both explanations are likely to contain some truth, so that we can say that the trade-off between inflation and unemployment arises from less than perfect expectations and from time lags in the adjustment process when demand and supply conditions are changing. But if this line of argument is accepted, then the Phillips Curve is essentially a short-run phenomenon.

With the passage of time the actual and the expected rate of inflation will come together and the slope of the Phillips Curve will become steeper. In a limiting case, assuming stable demand and supply conditions, it will eventually become a vertical straight line in the unemployment/money wage rate plane. The policy implications of this conclusion are of course substantial. It would mean that in the long run, governments are unable to choose between various combinations of unemployment and rates of inflation: on the contrary, in the long run, the natural rate of unemployment is determined by natural forces while the rate of inflation is determined by monetary policy. It would surely follow that since governments cannot buy more employment at the expense of faster inflation their principal aim should be to contain inflation. However, in practice, given some minimum threshold of inflation below which individuals do not adjust expectations rapidly to varying inflation rates, the short-run may be very long. If so, governments are hardly likely to agree that their employment and counter-inflationary policies can be dissociated. Some evidence on the point will be examined in Chapter 7, where it is shown that at any rate in the period 1954-68, a 'trade-off' between unemployment and inflation did exist in the major industrial countries.

A Keynesian view of the labour market

The theoretical conclusion that in the long run the Phillips Curve reduces to a vertical straight line is fundamentally based on the supposition that the classical model of the labour market is a true reflection of its actual behaviour in practice; that is, that allowing for time lags in adjustment the economy does have a tendency towards a full employment equilibrium. A level of real wages emerges at which the demand and supply of labour are equal to each other. But suppose this classical model is regarded as an unrealistic view of the workings of a modern industrial economy? Suppose, for instance, that entrepreneurs do not aim at profit maximization in any precise sense (which is an essential premise of the classical model); suppose also that workers are not able to adjust the amount of labour they offer until the real wage rate equals the marginal disutility of labour? In other words, suppose that output and employment are not determined simply by the operation of the labour market, and that there is not some unique equilibrium position to which the labour market tends? This would lead us to an explanation of the determination of unemployment and real money wages from the standpoint of the aggregate demand for goods, that is to say, from an essentially Keynesian viewpoint in which full employment is not automatically assumed.[10]

Within this alternative framework of thought, the aggregate demand for labour is derived from the aggregate demand for goods and not, in the short run at any rate, from a substitution of labour for other factor inputs at a given level of demand for output. Real wages will vary with the level of employment and the aggregate demand for goods, depending on the type of technology characteristic of the economy as a whole, on market structures and on the employment policies of firms. Real wages need not necessarily fall as employment rises; given increasing returns technology and/or oligopolistic market structures in key sectors of the economy, together with processes of production involving the use of substantial overhead labour — so that labour employment responds to changes in output with a significant time lag — output per man and real wages can rise with output and employment. Moreover, within this framework of thought money wages are assumed to be determined largely, but of course not wholly, independently of aggregate demand for commodities and labour; instead they are regarded as the outcome of bargaining in a labour market in which *bilateral monopoly* conditions tend to exist, i.e. strong trade unions and strong employer associations are assumed to exist. Although the normal economic forces of demand and supply provide constraints on the wage bargains arrived at, the actual level of money wage rates arising from the process of bargaining are not uniquely, nor even necessarily closely related to the level of employment, or to the level of aggregate demand for goods and labour.

In this connection, the factors governing the attitude of labour to money wage bargaining to which we have referred earlier are important. In the first place, while workers do have expectations, and indeed objectives, concerning their real incomes, and the rate at which they will rise over time, they cannot rely on achieving these through a falling price level. In the second place, they have sound reasons for putting up strong resistance to cuts in money wages even if they have (which given the oligopolistic nature of modern industry they do not), some assurance that prices will fall at the same time. These factors provide a rational basis for collective action via trade unions, the militancy of which is not simply governed by economic factors alone. As a consequence, autonomously and successfully exerted upward pressure on money wage rates may occur, which will, in the first instance, tend to raise aggregate demand for goods and therefore, in turn, output and employment. If adequate excess capacity in industry exists and output per man can rise, or at any rate not fall as employment rises, real wages can rise at the same time. But if the constellation of money wage increase, existing excess capacity and productivity growth is such that producers have to raise prices to maintain profitability, trade union expectations of real wage and income growth will be disappointed, and their upward pressure on money wage rates will be maintained or intensified. Inflation itself will then accelerate and the typical situation portrayed by the Phillips curve of falling unemployment and a rising rate of inflation will be produced. The closer the economy gets to full capacity working, the lower is the rate at which unemployment diminishes and the rate at which prices rise will be faster.

This account of an autonomously generated wage and price inflation assumes, as we have said, that no unique equilibrium relationship between employment and real wages exists. It also assumes that no monetary or fiscal restraint of the type described in Chapter 2 is operating. If such restraints are operating to hold back aggregate demand for goods, then the increase in money wage rates brought about by autonomously exerted trade union pressure will have less effect in lowering unemployment: indeed, in a limiting case governments can exert such countervailing fiscal and monetary policy that, far from falling as trade unions push up money wages, unemployment will rise.[11] Governments may adopt such a restrictive policy in the hope that the autonomous upward pressures on money wage rates will be weakened and inflation slowed down. In effect the government would be forcing the trade unions to choose between a higher rate of money wage increases and lower unemployment. But the policy may not succeed in restraining the rise in wages and prices: if the gap between actual real wages and real wages expected by the trade unions widens, due to the fact that as unemployment rises and output falls output per man also falls, trade unions may accelerate their wage demands, leaving it to the government itself to handle the problem of inflation and unemployment.

This view of how the modern industrial economy works, rather than the classical view described earlier in this chapter, is probably more in accord with the analytical cum descriptive account of the inflationary process we have presented in Chapter 2. Unlike the classical system of thought, it contains no implication that there is some natural rate of unemployment below which unemployment cannot be permanently forced if governments are willing to accept a high enough rate of inflation, although of course, there may be a structural minimum imposed by labour market friction. On the other hand, in common with underlying classical thought, this view of the *modus operandi* of the economy is consistent with a progressive acceleration in the rate of inflation at any given level of unemployment as inflationary expectations become incorporated into money wage bargaining. This development can be described in terms of an upward shift over time in the Phillips Curve, or alternatively in terms of the long run Phillips Curve being steeper than the short run one; but there does not seem much point in doing so. Moreover, the approach is not inconsistent with both the rate of inflation and the level of unemployment rising together, that is to say, an *upward sloping* Phillips Curve if, as suggested, the government is trying to contain inflation by employing restrictive monetary and fiscal policy which, although having success in holding down and reducing output and employment, fails to reduce the autonomous wage pressure being exerted by the collective action of trade unions. Unlike classical orthodoxy, therefore, the approach adopted here does not believe that restrictive monetary policy alone can, except perhaps in a time span long enough to make its use impractical, be relied upon to restrain and eventually eliminate inflation. When wages and prices are largely, and for all practical policy purposes, determined independently of aggregate demand for goods and labour, other methods of restraining inflation may have to be adopted. That there are reasons for believing that this has increasingly become the case in most developed countries in recent years will be shown in a later chapter.

In this chapter we have discussed some theoretical aspects of the trade-off between unemployment and inflation; and we end it by simply noting that although there is some relationship between unemployment and inflation (i.e. a trade-off) the relationship is by no means a simple one or necessarily one way. The actual empirical characteristics of the trade-off faced by major industrial countries in the post second war period will be the subject matter of Chapter 7.

Appendix

Further references on the trade-off between unemployment and inflation:

ASHENFELTER, O.C., JOHNSON, G.E. and PENCAVEL, J.H., 'Trade Unions and the Rate of Change of Money Wages in United States Manufacturing Industry', mimeo, 1970.

BOWEN, W.G., *The Wage-Price Issue: A Theoretical Analysis*, Princeton University Press, 1960.

CORRY, B. and LAIDLER, D. 'The Phillips Relation: a Theoretical Explanation', *Economica*, 1967, Vol. 34.

DICKS-MIREAUX, L.A., 'The interrelationship between cost and price changes, 1946-1959: a study of inflation in post-war Britain', Oxford Economic Papers, vol. 13, 1961, pp. 267-92.

DICKS-MIREAUX, L.A., and DOW, C.R., 'The Determinants of Wage Inflation: United Kingdom, 1946-1956', *Journal of the Royal Statistical Society*, series A, CXXII, 1959 pp. 145-74.

DOW, J.C.R., 'Analysis of the generation of price inflation', Oxford

Economic Papers, 1956, vol. 8, pp. 252-301.

DOW, J.C.R., and DICKS-MIREAUX, L.A., 'Excess demand for labour A study of conditions in Great Britain, 1946-56', Oxford Economic Papers, 1958, vol. 10, pp. 1-33.

DUNLOP, J.T., *Wage Determination under Trade Unions*, New York: Kelley, 2nd edition, 1950.

ECKSTEIN, O., and WILSON, T.A., 'The determination of money wages in American industry', *Quarterly Journal of Economics*, vol. 76, 1962, pp. 379-414.

FRIEDMAN, M. (1951), 'Some comments on the significance of labour unions for wage policy', in D. McCord Wright (ed.), *The Impact of the Union*, Harcourt, pp. 204-34.

FRIEDMAN, M., 'The Role of Monetary Policy', *American Economic Review*, 1968.

HANSEN, B. 'Excess Demand, Unemployment, Vacancies and Wages', *Quarterly Journal of Economics,* 1970.

HINES, A.G., 'Trade Unions and Wage Inflation in the United Kingdom 1893-1961, *Review of Economic Studies*, XXXI, 1964, pp. 221-52.

HOLMES, J.M. and SMYTH, D.J., 'The Relation between Unemployment and Excess Demand for Labour: an Examination of the Theory of the Phillips Curve', *Economica,* 1970, vol. 37.

HOLT, C.C., 'Job Search, Phillips' Wage Relation, and Union Influence: Theory and Evidence', in E.S. Phelps (ed.), *Microeconomic Foundations of Employment and Inflation Theory*, Norton, New York, 1970.

KLEIN, L.R. and BALL, R.J., 'Some Econometrics of the Determination of Absolute Prices and Wages', *Economic Journal*, LXIX, 1959, pp. 465-82.

KLEIN, L.R., BALL, R.J., HAZLEWOOD, A., and VANDOME, P., *An Econometric Model of the United Kingdom*, Blackwell, 1961.

KOYCK, L.M., *Distributed Lags and Investment Analysis*, North-Holland Publishing Co., 1954.

LIPSEY, R.G., 'The relation between unemployment and the rate of change of money wage rates in the United Kingdom, 1862-1957: A further analysis', *Economica* , 27. 1960, pp. 1-31.

LIPSEY, R.G. and PARKIN, J.M., 'Incomes Policy: A Reappraisal', *Economica*, 37, 1970, pp. 115-38.

LIPSEY, R.G., 'The Micro Theory of the Phillips Curve Reconsidered: A Reply to Holmes and Smyth', *Economica,* February 1974.

PARKIN, J.M. 'Incomes Policy: Some Further Results on the Determination of the Rate of Change of Money Wages', *Economica*, n.s., 37, 1970, pp. 368-401.

PHELPS BROWN, E.H. and HART, P.E., 'The share of wages in national income', *Economic Journal*, 62, no. 246, 1952, pp. 251-77.

PHELPS, E.S., 'Money-Wage Dynamics and Labour Market Equilibrium', *Journal of Political Economy*, LXXVI, 1968, pp. 678-711.

PHELPS, E.S., 'Phillips Curves, Expectations of Inflation and Optimal

Unemployment over Time', *Economica*, n.s., 34, 1967, pp. 254-81.

PHILLIPS, A.W., 'The relation between unemployment and the rate of change of money wage rates in the United Kingdom, 1861-1957', *Economica*, 25, 1958, pp. 283-99 (Reading 15).

ROTHSCHILD, K.W., 'The Phillips Curve and All That', *Scottish Journal of Political Economy*, November 1971.

SARGAN, J.D., 'Wages and Prices in the United Kingdom: A Study in Econometric Methodology', Colston Papers XVI, 1964, Butterworths Scientific Publications.

SOLOW, R.M., *Price Expectations and the Behaviour of the Price Level*, Manchester U.P., 1969.

SOLOW, R.M., 'Recent Controversies on the Theory of Inflation: An Eclectic View', in Stephen W. Rousseas (ed.), *Proceedings of a Symposium on Inflation: Its Causes, Consequences and Control*, Wilton, Conn.: The Calvin K. Kazanjian Economics Foundation Inc., 1969.

TOBIN, J., 'Inflation and Unemployment', *American Economic Review*, March 1972.

4
The International Transmission
of Inflation

Introduction

In Chapter 1 it was pointed out that in the post Second World War period inflation has been a world wide phenomenon: few countries, if any, have been exempt. It is clear from Table 1.1 of Chapter 1 that there has been a good deal of uniformity in terms of the average rate of inflation experienced by individual countries for the period as a whole and also considerable correspondence in the timing of the variation of actual inflation rates around the average. Until about 1968, and leaving aside the high inflation countries of Latin America (Argentina, Brazil, Chile, Colombia) and one or two countries such as Korea and Indonesia, inflation rates in most countries tended to fall within a range of two to six per cent per annum. There was a dramatic acceleration of inflation in the early 1970s and by 1973 many countries found that their inflation rates had more than doubled.

Most countries tended to experience their fastest rates of inflation roughly simultaneously. Thus inflation rates generally tended to be above the average in the period 1949-53, significantly below the average from 1954-65, and above average again in the latter part of the 1960s and early 1970s. This uniformity both in average rates of inflation and in timing suggests the operation of an international transmission process and also an international constraining mechanism: although the different factors discussed in Chapter 2 no doubt operated in different countries in different degrees and ways, nonetheless a mechanism existed which tended to keep inflation rates roughly in line.

It is, of course, to be expected that the existence of a world market for a substantial part of the output, particularly manufactured goods, of individual countries would operate to impose a high degree of uniformity in price behaviour generally. It is significant that export price levels of most countries have tended to keep more in line with each other than have price levels in general; moreover they have, until recent years, risen at a slower rate.[1] This latter point is particularly relevant to Japan, where domestic prices tended to rise at a much faster rate than in the other major developed countries, yet which remained very competitive in international trade. This overall uniformity is of course an important consequence of the operation of the postwar Bretton Woods international monetary system, which was based on the principle of 'par value' fixed exchange rates. This ensures conformity between the behaviour of prices measured in domestic currency or in foreign currency. Countries which did experience far higher domestic rates of inflation than the rest of the world are, of course, precisely those which frequently changed the par values of their currencies, in particular the high inflation Latin American countries referred to earlier. Frequent changes in exchange rates as well as resort to tariff protection against imports and subsidies to exports, clearly operate to break the regulative impact of international competition on national price levels. On the other hand, as will be explained later on in this chapter, the system of fixed exchange rates has probably contributed to force a higher rate of inflation on other countries whose domestic policies and labour situations might well have permitted less inflation.

We begin this chapter by describing the various ways in which inflationary impulses can be transmitted from one economy to another and throughout the international economy generally. Implicit in this discussion is the assumption of a fixed 'par value' exchange rate system; and following this discussion, we go on to examine more closely the apparent contribution of the Bretton Woods and reserve currency systems to the spread of inflation. We then briefly examine the implications of a more flexible or floating exchange rate system, and we finish the chapter with a reference to the possible role of multinational enterprise in the transmission and even generation of world inflation.

Elements in the international transmission of inflation

Demand and cost pressures on prices are transmitted throughout the international economy in a number of different ways. The most important element in this process is undoubtedly the operation of the foreign trade or international multiplier which transmits changes in aggregate demand from one country to another. This multiplier works through the fact that one country's imports are another country's exports. An expansion of aggregate demand in one country leads to an expansion of domestic production and incomes in that country, but also induces a rise in its imports. Other countries' exports therefore rise, setting up an expansionary multiplier force in these countries also. In turn their imports rise, and, as a result, the country in which the initiating boom in aggregate demand first took place may find its own exports rising as well. In other words, there occurs a sympathetic rise in aggregate demand throughout the international economy.

Obviously, if an expansion of demand in one country is to have a significant impact on aggregate demand internationally, that country must be a large and important country in world trade. It need not necessarily be a country with a high propensity to import, but it must be a country whose imports are a sizeable element in total world trade. This would obviously be true of the United States, but also, although less so, of the United Kingdom, Germany and Japan. The repercussion effects in the recipient countries may go well beyond the direct impact of rising exports on aggregate demand. Countries receiving these stimulating effects may well experience a rise in general economic and industrial confidence, leading to a rise in investment expenditure and capital formation at home. If this occurs in a number of countries simultaneously, a world boom is then in the offing.

The extent to which an expansion of home demand leaks into imports is determined by the country's structure of production and imports; but it is also related to how close the economy is working to full employment capacity output. If a country is operating at or near full employment, an expansion of demand is likely to cause a larger expansion of imports than if the country is operating with considerable surplus capacity in hand. This is not only because bottlenecks in production may occur, causing purchasers to look for foreign sources of supply, but it also may be due to the fact that domestic producers take the opportunity of raising their prices either to increase their profits or to meet a rise in their own cost of production. Imported goods, therefore, become cheaper than domestically produced ones, adding to the pressure to import generally. If all countries are operating near full employment, all will be trying to divert demand to each other's goods. Hence, in an international boom, demand pressures are being transmitted from one country to another, sustaining the inflationary demand pressures being experienced by each.

Quite apart from these aggregate demand pressures, price increases may be transmitted directly from one country to another. One country's exports are another country's imports. A rise in the general price level, including exports, of one country will, if the exchange rate between their currencies is kept constant, mean a rise in the import prices of another country, which may then feed through into a rise in the general price level of that country, even when domestic demand pressures are not inconsistent with domestic price stability. Similarly, a rise in world demand for a particular country's main export may push up its price. If the export good is consumed at home as well as exported abroad, the domestic price level of the exporting country rises, and repercussions on wage and other incomes may follow.

It is obvious that the more 'open' an economy is, that is, the larger its foreign trade sector is relative to its gross domestic product, the more likely and the more quickly is its domestic price level to be affected by such autonomously generated rises in its export and/or import price levels. Many less developed countries are particularly vulnerable to the direct inflationary impact of rising foreign trade prices. In the case of rising import prices they may find it less easy to substitute cheaper home-produced goods for more expensive foreign produced ones than do more developed countries, and therefore they cannot evade or limit a rise in the general price level. The same, of course, is true for many industrial countries which have to import a substantial proportion of their raw material and food supplies when the price level of these is rising on international commodity markets.

If a rise in a country's export prices is generated autonomously outside the country itself, the impact on its domestic price level may be transmitted in a number of different ways. As indicated above, exports may enter significantly into home consumption or investment, so that a direct and immediate rise in the domestic price level will occur. Rising export prices will also generally be accompanied by rising money incomes in the export sector so that multiplier-type spending effects on domestically produced goods and services will be generated. Whether such demand effects will have a significant impact on the domestic price level depends on the pattern of home demand and on supply conditions at home and abroad. Unless the rise in money incomes and demand is internationally widespread, however, these multiplier effects may not have a significant inflationary impact in the exporting country.

In the case of industrial countries, much of the increase in export income will be spent on manufactured goods and services. For reasons discussed in Chapter 2, the price level of manufactured goods is not particularly sensitive to demand pressures *per se*, particularly if manufacturers are not hard up against capacity. Prices will not be bid up unless manufacturers are experiencing significant increases in their costs at the same time. The supply of services also tends to be highly elastic and the price level more responsive to cost than to demand.

In the case of less developed countries a larger part of the increase in monetary demand stemming from the rise in export prices and incomes may be spent on food. The price level of home-produced food can be forced up sharply in the short run, causing generalized inflation in the afflicted country. If appropriate kinds and amounts of food can be imported from abroad, however, the inflation of food prices can be constrained. Similarly, since manufactured goods are largely imported, the price level of these may not be greatly affected by the export boom. Indeed, from this point of view the export boom is favourable to price stability since it adds to the country's capacity to import.

An important way, perhaps the significant way in practice, in which a rise in export prices can induce an acceleration of inflation in industrial countries — and perhaps in less developed countries as well if they possess strong trade union movements — is through the wage transfer mechanism described in Chapter 2. In this, the export sector of manufacturing countries can play a key role. There are two reasons for this. First, the export sector in these countries is typically the high productivity growth sector of these economies. Second, export pricing is subject to more competitive pressure than is pricing in other sectors of the economy.

The first of these reasons means that wage fixing in the export sector is likely to play a leading role in wage determination across the economy as a whole. Being typically high productivity growth industries, export industries can pay larger wage increases to their workers without having to raise their prices correspondingly; and they often have an incentive to do so, if only to ensure the avoidance of strikes and to maintain their ability to supply their customers abroad. The wage increases granted by the export sector then spread across the economy as a whole, as trade union. leaders seek to achieve wage comparability. Other industries, whose productivity is growing less fast than in the manufacturing export sector, are forced to raise their prices to cover their increased costs, so that inflation results.

On the other hand, there is a limit, imposed by competition from abroad, to the wage increases which export firms can afford to pay without making exports uncompetitive abroad or reducing their profitability. In other words, there is a limit to the ability of trade unions to force wage increases in export industries without causing a fall in export output and rising unemployment. But if export firms are enabled to raise their prices owing to a rise in the international price level of manufactured goods entering international trade, then the stage is set for a rise in wages paid by exporting firms. The wage transfer mechanism is then set in motion to produce a rise in wages, costs and prices generally.

A model in which the wage level in the economy as a whole is determined by productivity growth and price level increase in the export sector has been used successfully to explain postwar inflation in Sweden.[2] We shall make use of a similar model in Chapter 8 in an analysis of inflation in other OECD countries as well as Sweden. It is obvious however that such a model cannot provide a satisfactory explanation of a worldwide inflation that is afflicting most countries simultaneously. It may be that a rise in Swedish export prices precipitates inflation in Sweden throughout the wage transfer mechanism just described. But it leaves unexplained why Swedish export firms were able to raise their export prices in the first place. It could of course be that the particular type of export produced by Swedish firms was in short supply. But if the exports of all manufacturing countries were in short supply, or if the cost of producing manufactured goods entering into international markets was rising, this would clearly require an explanation which cannot be fully or solely explained by the model itself. Hence the model may be useful for analysing inflation in one country but not in all.

A situation in which all or most countries were experiencing simultaneously a rise in their export and import prices could be explained by a conjuncture of industrial booms in some or all of the main industrial countries. In these circumstances, the demand for primary products — the raw materials for manufacturing industry and the foodstuffs for the industrial countries' populations — may well come up against short term supply constraints, well before capacity levels of output are reached in the industrial countries themselves. To begin with, the rising cost of raw materials may be absorbed without causing a rise in unit costs of production since labour productivity throughout the manufacturing world may be rising quite sharply as output expands. But eventually unit costs of production will rise and producers will need to raise prices to ensure profitability. The pressure on costs will be accentuated if, as a result of rising food prices, wage increases have to be granted throughout industry generally. In short, cost-inflationary pressures are produced by rapidly expanding demand in industrial countries generally; these not only add to inflationary pressure in countries in which demand for domestic resources is excessive, but also afflict countries in which demand is not excessive and in which prices and wages would otherwise be stable.

Examination of the postwar period shows that countries did in fact tend to experience their highest inflation rates when there were world boom conditions, i.e. when all or most countries were experiencing demand pressures well above the average. There have been a number of such periods: that of the Korean war period covering the years 1949-53 is obviously an important case in point. As a result of the war a number of countries, in particular the United States and the United Kingdom, engaged in massive rearmament programmes, creating excess demand at home and a considerable demand for primary products and strategic materials in world markets. Fear of renewed and widespread international war caused all countries to stockpile and as a result primary product prices rose steeply. Demand and cost pressures were, therefore, experienced on a wide scale simultaneously and the price level in all countries rose steeply. Reference to the chart 5.1 Chapter 5 shows that there were other such periods, albeit on a smaller scale, when demand pressures tended to coincide in many countries with consequent effects on the rate of inflation. We can discern quite distinct periods when demand was above trend in all, or most, of the major countries simultaneously – for example, in the mid-1950s, mid-1960s and again in the late 1960s. These were all periods when countries experienced inflation rates well above the average for the period as a whole. A further exceptional commodity price boom, reminiscent of the Korean War boom, took place in 1972-3 and inflation rates throughout the world accelerated violently.[3]

On the other hand it is significant to note the long period, commencing around the mid-1950s and lasting until the beginning of the mid-1960s, when aggregate demand in both the United States and the United Kingdom appeared to be running well below trend. Inflation in these countries and in most other countries generally was well below trend. During this period some important European countries did experience significant domestic or local booms but these were not sufficient to push up primary product prices markedly and therefore did not produce a marked acceleration in the international rate of inflation. The ten years between the mid-1950s and the mid 1960s therefore constituted a long period of relative price stability. As can be seen, there were exceptions: France had quite high inflation rates in the late 1950s associated with its own domestic labour problems and with the consequential need to devalue the franc.

Japan also experienced sustained inflation of domestic prices throughout, exceeding that of most other industrial countries, although, as mentioned earlier, its export prices remained very stable. The importance of the United States in the world scene is well demonstrated in the latter half of the 1960s. Following the long period when demand was below trend, aggregate demand rose well above trend after 1964 and remained so until the end of 1969. In general, apart from a short period in 1966-68, the above trend demand pressure in the United States was accompanied by similar demand pressures in most of the other major countries, with the significant exception of the United Kingdom where in the latter few years of the period it was the government's deliberate policy to restrain demand in the interests of the balance of payments. Contemporaneously, inflation accelerated in the U.S. and the remainder of the world generally.

The general picture is, therefore, that the operation of the international foreign trade multiplier was an important element in the transmission of demand and cost pressures from one country to another and therefore in the international propagation of inflation.

The Bretton Woods international monetary system

However, the operation of the international multiplier in the postwar period was, as we have indicated earlier in the chapter, intimately related to the operation of the international monetary system. There were two facets to this. In the first place, the international spread of aggregate demand pressures was undoubtedly facilitated by the system of 'par value' fixed exchange rates which until mid-1972 underpinned the operation of international monetary system. If exchange rates are virtually fixed (the 'par value' system permits day-to-day fluctuations within very narrow margins) an expansion of domestic demand spills over into an increase in demand for imports, and produces, therefore, a deterioration in the balance of trade rather than a depreciation of the exchange rate. Conversely, countries whose exports have risen as a result of the expansion of demand abroad experience an improvement in their balances of trade rather than appreciation of their exchange rates. Foreign exchange reserves and domestic money supply tend to fall in the former group of countries and rise in the latter, as a result of which inflationary pressures may be moderated in the first group but exacerbated in the second.

These transmission effects would not take place if exchange rates were allowed to respond to pressures on the balance of payments. Countries experiencing an autonomous expansion of demand would tend to find their exchange rates depreciating, which would tend both to check the rise in imports and to simulate foreign demand for exports. The balance of payments could not worsen and domestic money could not leak out to other countries in the form of a loss of foreign exchange reserves. Of course, as a consequence of not being able to transmit some of its excessive demand abroad, and also because of a rise in import prices, the inflating country would find its domestic inflation much worse; but inflation would not be transmitted to other countries and would not then become world-wide.

It might be argued that even if exchange rates are rigid there is a limit to the extent to which inflationary pressures can be transmitted abroad. For example, as a consequence of a deterioration in its balance of payments, a country whose domestic demand had risen would find its domestic money supply falling: at some point this would provide a check to domestic demand and therefore to the rise in imports. Governments could, of course, offset the loss of domestic money by creating more, but doing so would cause the loss of foreign exchange reserves to persist. Countries with large reserves could permit this situation to continue for some time: eventually however loss of reserves would force a reversal of policy. Alternatively, the monetary authorities could rely on rising domestic interest rates to induce an inflow of international capital which would offset the loss of both domestic money and foreign exchange reserves arising from the balance of trade. If international capital flows are very sensitive to interest rate differentials and the government is prepared to use expansionary fiscal measures to offset the possible deflationary impact on aggregate demand of rising interest rates, inflationary pressures and their transmission abroad may continue for some time. Much would depend on the policy pursued by countries receiving the inflationary pressure from abroad. The dilemma facing them may be very acute. In a situation in which flows of international capital are very elastic in response to interest rate differentials, the application of monetary policy to check the spread of inflation domestically becomes virtually impossible. The inflow of money arising from their surpluses on trade account cannot easily be neutralised and any tendency for interest rates to rise, or credit to be squeezed domestically, rapidly induces more inflows. Interest rates may rise internationally without, at any rate in the short run, checking the spread of inflation significantly.

The check which loss of foreign exchange reserves can apply to demand expansion and inflationary pressure in particular countries would clearly not apply, or at any rate would apply much less severely, to countries whose currencies were in demand as a foreign exchange reserve asset and an international medium of exchange. This brings us to the second facet of the Bretton Woods international monetary system which facilitated the international transmission of inflation in the postwar period: the fact that the U.S. dollar was *de facto* at least the major reserve asset of the system.

In the case of a reserve currency country, a balance of payments deficit that may arise from an expansion of domestic demand results in an accumulation of currency liabilities in the hands of central banks abroad. While these foreign central banks are willing to hold these liabilities, no loss of its own reserve assets is incurred by the reserve currency country, and as a consequence it is not under the same pressure as other countries to restrict its domestic money supply and domestic demand pressure. It may continue, therefore, without serious check, to inject demand and inflationary pressures into the international economy as a whole. Thus, a reserve currency country whose imports also constitute a large proportion of total world trade, an association that almost by definition is bound to hold, occupies a key role in the operation of the international monetary and trading system and therefore in the international transmission of inflation.

The U.S. and the U.K. provide the two reserve currencies in the present system. However, the place of sterling in the system is much less important than that of the dollar, and the contribution of the U.K. to the international spread of demand and inflation was much less significant than that of the U.S. This is not simply because U.K. imports are a much smaller proportion of world trade than those of the U.S.: the main difference is that sterling played a much less fundamental role in the operation of the system than did the dollar. The U.S. dollar was the main 'intervention' currency in the system, i.e. it was the currency to which all other currencies, including sterling, were pegged, and in terms of which official dealings in exchange markets aimed at keeping exchange rates within the permitted margins from parity were conducted. Given also the massive position of the U.S. in world trade and finance it is not surprising that countries tended to accumulate by far the largest part of the increase in their reserves in the postwar period in terms of dollars. The role of sterling, on the other hand, was inherited from the dominant position of the currency in the nineteenth century and early part of this, and more immediately from the massive build up of sterling liabilities during the Second World War. In the postwar period itself, sterling liabilities held by other countries did rise and fall at various times, but taking the period as a whole they rose very little.

The reason for this is clear. The ability of the U.K. to induce other countries to hold sterling is limited by the potential threat of conversion into dollars, a threat which if there were an attempt to carry it out would enforce a devaluation of the pound against the dollar. Until mid-1972, when sterling was floated, this threat forced the U.K. government to pursue demand policies consistent with maintaining the parity between the pound and the dollar, policies which clearly were not always successful in terms of their immediate objective (i.e. prevention of sterling devaluation) and may indeed have been misplaced in terms of the economic performance and general well-being of the country. Hence the U.K. was not and is not in a position to inject demand pressures into the world economy on any large scale or for any long period. In theory, a similar restraint was exercised on the U.S.: although the U.S. dollar was the lynchpin of the network of exchange relationships existing in the system, the basis of it was gold since, in principle at least, the U.S. stood ready to buy and sell gold for its own currency at a fixed price. Gold was therefore the foreign exchange reserve asset of the U.S., the loss of which (if dollars are being exchanged for gold) should eventually have forced a restraint on U.S. domestic demand policies. In fact, throughout the 1960s, the U.S. became increasingly unwilling to exchange its dollar liabilities into gold, and it exerted diplomatic and other pressure on the central banks of other countries not to insist that it should do so.

The reason for this reluctance on the part of the U.S. to sell gold was the rapid decline of its monetary gold stock commencing in the late 1950s and continuing throughout the 1960s. As a result of almost continuous balance of payments deficits for a period of virtually two decades, its gold stock fell from a high of over $24 billion in 1949 to less than $12 billion by 1970. At the same time short term U.S. dollar liabilities held by foreign monetary authorities rose from about $3 billion to close on $16 billion. The build up of dollar liabilities in the early 1950s was generally welcomed by foreign central banks as was the redistribution of the world's gold stock, since practically all countries except the U.S. had come out of the war with vastly depleted reserves; the U.S. itself did not object to what was a moderate decline in her gold reserves from very high levels. Towards the end of the 1950s, however, there were clear signs that countries were no longer so willing to accumulate dollars at the same rate as earlier, and large scale conversions into gold took place. In the four years 1957 to 1961, U.S. gold reserves fell by $6 billion. Beginning in 1960, the U.S. government took a number of steps to improve its balance of payments: these are indeed reflected in Figure 5.2 (p.76) which shows that aggregate demand was kept well below trend in the early 1960s. As a result, the U.S. price level was kept relatively stable and the country's surplus of exports over imports rose substantially. But the balance of payments did not improve by anywhere near as much since private capital outflows also increased markedly. There was however a significant check to the rate of outflow of dollar liabilities and to the decline in gold reserves.

Restriction of aggregate demand in the U.S., although having success with the balance of payments, proved costly in terms of national product and employment. Policies were accordingly reversed in the mid 1960s and domestic objectives of full employment and growth were given priority. The balance of payments accordingly worsened in the latter half of the 1960s. There were again large conversions of dollars into gold in the middle of the 1960s which gave rise to intense private speculation as to the future dollar price of gold. This was eventually met in March 1968 by an agreement among seven of the major industrial countries not to supply gold to private markets in order to stabilise its price at or near the official parity: instead the unofficial gold price was to be left to find its own level. There was also agreement that countries would not convert surplus dollars into gold, a course of action designed to take off pressure from the sadly depleted gold reserves of the U.S. Meantime, intense discussions took place concerning the creation of a new international reserve asset, which finally culminated in an agreement to create a Special Drawing Right facility at the I.M.F.[4]

However, the creation of SDRs did not save the international monetary system. The U.S. balance of payments worsened markedly in 1970 and even more so in 1971; in the first half of this latter year the balance of payments recorded a massive deficit of over $12 billion. Some of the deficit was due to monetary outflows from the U.S. in response to interest rate differentials which favoured Europe, but a substantial part was due to speculation against the dollar which had as its basis an increasing realisation on the part of the international community that the rate of exchange between the dollar and other currencies was no longer compatible with full employment policies being pursued in the U.S.[5] In August 1971 the U.S. government eventually reacted aggressively by suspending the convertibility of the dollar into gold or other basic reserve assets (SDRs). The Bretton Woods system was thereby brought formally to an end. In addition the U.S. imposed a temporary ten per cent surcharge on most dutiable imports; foreign aid appropriations were also cut. Other measures were taken to favour exports and import substitution.

The object of the U.S. government was to force a revaluation of the currencies of its major trade competitors -- particularly Japan — and this was achieved as a result of agreement reached in an international conference (the Smithsonian Conference) in Washington in December 1971. The changes were not sufficient to convince speculators and further devaluations of the U.S. dollar took place. A major reform of the international monetary system was clearly required and is currently the subject of international discussion. An essential feature of any new system that emerges must certainly be provision for the flexibility of the rate of exchange of the U.S. dollar against other currencies on a par with the freedom of exchange rate flexibility enjoyed by the rest of the world.

Reserve currencies and inflation

European countries, particularly those that have run persistent balance of payments surpluses, blame the reserve currency system for much of their postwar inflation, which, as they see it, was 'exported' from the U.S. and forced on them. The Americans, on the other hand, tend to deny such a charge, pointing to their own relatively low domestic rate of inflation, at least until very recent years. The issue is certainly a complicated one.

On the U.S. side there are two important elements bearing on the situation. In the first place, the U.S. wished, as do other countries, to maintain a high level of employment and a satisfactory rate of economic growth; but again in common with other countries, and for the reasons explored in Chapter 2, the U.S. was and is faced with a trade-off problem between unemployment and inflation. In the second place, although the ratio of imports to GDP is very low by the standards of the European and most other countries as well, the U.S.'s income elasticity of demand for imports tends to be a good deal greater than unity. Thus an expansion of domestic demand aimed at reducing the level of unemployment to politically more acceptable levels tends to result in an immediate worsening in the U.S. balance of trade, partly as a result of exports becoming less competitive and partly because of the induced rise in imports. As noted earlier, other countries are therefore forced to absorb dollars in their reserves with consequent effects on their domestic money supply: this plus the direct effect of the rise in their exports increases the pressure of domestic demand. The deterioration in the U.S. balance of payments, in relation to the size of the country's GDP, appears a minor problem to the Americans: to the Europeans, however, it presents a nasty dilemma for domestic economic policy.

If at the existing rate of exchange the U.S. cannot attain a politically acceptable level of employment and a satisfactory rate of growth without incurring balance of payments deficits, this implies that it is suffering from 'fundamental disequilibrium' and an overvalued exchange rate. The dollar should be devalued against other currencies. But, given the intervention arrangements in the Bretton Woods system, the U.S. acting unilaterally could only raise the dollar price of gold: whether this resulted in a devaluation against other currencies depended on whether other countries were willing to see the par value of their own currencies raised in terms of the dollar. There were and are many supporters of a rise in the dollar price of gold, but most of these had in mind bringing about a rise in dollar value of international monetary reserves, thereby easing the international liquidity situation. Others opposed this step on the grounds firstly, that a substantial part of the benefit would accrue to gold producers, in particular South Africa and the U.S.S.R., since it would improve their commodity terms of trade, and secondly that there were superior methods, less costly in terms of real resources, of creating international liquidity, such as the eventually adopted SDR system. The U.S. itself has firmly opposed raising the price of gold since such action would clearly reward those countries which have been less cooperative in willingness to hold dollars and which have taken the lead in converting them into gold.

The onus of dealing with the U.S.'s fundamental disequilibrium therefore seemed to fall on other countries, particularly the balance of payments surplus countries. They had the choice of either allowing their internal price level to rise in line with, or even relatively to that of the U.S. — in this sense they would 'import' inflation from the U.S. — or of appreciating their exchange rates against the dollar. Although an appreciation of the exchange rate would seem to be a beneficial measure for a balance of payments surplus country to take, since it would improve the country's international terms of trade and therefore, cet. par. raise real income, there is often as much reluctance in a surplus country to take this step as there is in a deficit country to devalue. The measure is bound to be opposed by exporters whose competitive position or profit margins would be worsened,[6] as well as by others whose incomes are closely related to the exchange rate. Moreover, the government of the surplus country may accept the need for an appreciation of its currency against one particular currency, say the dollar, but not against third currencies. The difficulty is then to get action on the part of a number of countries to appreciate their currencies simultaneously against the deficit country's currency – a none too easy task, particularly when the balance of payments position of some of these countries may not be all that satisfactory or when their employment and growth situations are giving cause for concern. The problem in the later years of the postwar period was further complicated, at least for Europeans, by the establishment of the E.E.C. The effective implementation of the Common Agricultural Policy is facilitated by stable exchange rates between member countries; moreover in line with its long term objective of a full monetary union, the E.E.C. put pressure on its member countries, in particular Germany, not to alter exchange rates unilaterally. On the other hand there was a reluctance by other member countries, in particular in France, to agree to a general revaluation of all E.E.C. currencies together *vis-à-vis* the dollar. The result was, therefore, that Germany, a major surplus country, was forced to accept both the dollars being pumped out by the U.S. and a higher rate of inflation than German citizens normally like to tolerate.

The postwar period demonstrated that in the case of a fundamental disequilibrium a change in relative exchange rates cannot for long be denied. Once it becomes evident that nothing else can or is being done to correct the disequilibrium and that a country is being forced to augment its foreign exchange reserves and domestic money supply at a faster rate than its citizens are likely to put up with, then the certainty will grow that a change in the exchange rate must take place. There will then be a strong speculative demand for the currency of this country which can only be met at the existing exchange rate by a further rise in its reserves and domestic money supply. Inflation is then financed if not encouraged. Eventually the need to maintain domestic monetary stability becomes foremost and is given priority over other objectives, as important as these are, and the exchange rate is allowed to appreciate. Thus in May 1971, despite the strong opposition of France, and at a crucial stage of the move towards monetary union, Germany was forced to allow its currency to float upwards. A substantial revaluation of surplus country currencies was achieved in the Smithsonian agreement referred to earlier; but this turned out to be insufficient to satisfy speculators, and further revaluations of the mark and the yen took place in 1972 and 1973.

It is evident, therefore, that the operation of the international monetary system, based on par values and reserve currencies, has been an important element in the international transmission of inflation. Not only has it facilitated the transmission of short run demand pressures from one country to another via the foreign trade multiplier, it has ensured that in the longer run the price levels of most countries have kept broadly in line, despite the fact that the autonomous cost-raising pressures described in Chapter 2 have operated in different countries in different degrees. But while it has clearly forced some countries to accept more inflation than they might otherwise have been able to get by with, it has also tended to keep inflation down in other countries, at the expense possibly of lower rates of growth and higher unemployment. This is certainly true of countries whose currencies are not used as foreign reserves (except those who have been willing to make use of repeated devaluations) but it is also true of the U.K. and even of the U.S. For although the U.S. has been in the privileged position of being able to force other countries to accept some of the consequences of its domestic policies and of the fundamental imbalance of its balance of payments simply by offering other countries a choice between holding dollars, forcing the U.S. to go off gold or revaluing, nonetheless it has not been immune from pressure of a non economic nature, for example, political pressure exerted in the OECD and IMF, which has forced it to conduct its economic policies with some regard to other countries. Thus, although some countries have undoubtedly suffered a higher rate of inflation than they would probably have put up with in the absence of the system, it is not clear that the rate of inflation in the world as a whole was execerbated by the system.

Floating exchange rates

A floating exchange rate system would prevent the transmission of inflationary pressures from one country to another; but it does not follow that there would be less inflation in the world as a whole.

Countries suffering from domestically generated inflationary pressure, whether of the demand or cost type discussed in Chapter 1, could not export some of it to other countries, as happens in a fixed exchange rate system. The spilling over of excessive demand into other countries would be prevented by a depreciation of the exchange rate. This would tend to drive up the domestic currency price of imports and prevent the rise in the domestic currency price of exports from making them less competitive abroad. The inflationary economy could not increase its real domestic absorption at the expense of countries overseas.[7] Moreover, since foreign exchange reserves would remain constant, money supply would not tend to fall as it would if exchange rates were fixed. Inflation in the depreciating country would, of course, tend to be worse than if the exchange rate had been kept stable, partly because there is no leakage of demand abroad and also because the depreciation of the rate would raise the domestic currency price of imports and costs of production generally. An interaction between the domestic price level and the exchange rate could develop, adding fuel to the fire. But the process would not be unconstrained since, although the nominal quantity of money would not be reduced, the real quantity would fall as prices rose. Even so, because time lags between changes in the real money stock and the consequent restriction on aggregate demand and economic activity tend to be long in financially well developed economies,[8] the acceleration of inflation is likely to go some considerable way before checks become operative.

In theory, we would expect a floating exchange rate system to operate in the opposite direction in countries suffering from a deficiency of domestic demand in relation to resources. These are likely to find their deflationary problems exacerbated. Their exports may be prevented from increasing and their imports from declining by an appreciation of their exchange rate. Import prices in domestic currency will fall, lowering costs of production. Exporters will also be under pressure to lower their prices and reduce their costs. The money supply, of course, will not be affected since the exchange rate will adjust to prevent any loss in foreign exchange reserves. Even so, a fall in domestic currency price level generally might be expected. However, the system probably does not work in the symmetrical fashion suggested by this description.

Prices in industrial countries are a good deal more inflexible in the downward direction than they are in the upward direction. This is not to deny that prices will fall when there is a substantial deficiency of demand and a situation of falling costs; but there is likely to be considerable time lag before they do. This time lag is longer than that involved in the upward adjustment of prices to excessive demand, particularly when the latter is accompanied by rising costs of production, as it usually is. If the country whose exchange rate is appreciating is suffering from some inflation itself, it could expect to see its rate of inflation moderated; but if at the time when its exchange rate began to appreciate, it was enjoying a period of absolute price stability, an actual fall in its price level is not likely quickly or easily to take place. It follows from these considerations that if the rates of exchange between the currencies of various countries, all of which are enjoying relative price stability, are somehow caused to change, price inflation could be triggered off in some of them but not price deflation in others. The same cause operating in a fixed exchange rate system would produce changes in the balances of payments of these countries, rather than in their exchange rates; and prices may be very little affected. Hence we cannot conclude on *a priori* grounds that a more flexible exchange rate system will be less conducive to world inflation than is a fixed exchange rate system. If the historical evidence of the most recent period (1972-73) is anything to go by, unstable rates of exchange seem to have contributed to an acceleration of world inflation; but the evidence requires more scrutiny before this conclusion can be drawn.[9]

Perhaps the important question is not simply whether the world inflation rate is likely to be higher under a floating exchange rate system than under a fixed exchange rate system, since this depends on the policies governments pursue, but whether the former system worsens the inflation-unemployment trade-off dilemma facing governments (assuming one to exist), as compared with the latter system. If it does, and if governments are determined to maintain not more than a given level of unemployment, then, of course, world inflation will be accelerated by a move towards a more flexible system.

The theoretical and practical reasons for believing that a trade-off between unemployment and inflation might exist, at least in the short run, were examined in the previous chapter. It could be argued that the factors underlying the trade-off are quite independent of what is happening to the exchange rate. If all countries had settled at points on their respective Phillips Curves such that their domestic rates of inflation, including inflation of export prices, were roughly equal, exchange rates could remain stable. If one country had settled at a point on its trade-off curve at which its rate of inflation was greater than other countries, its exchange rate would be depreciating. However, the rate at which its exchange rate was depreciating would be determined by the difference between its inflation rate and the inflation abroad. It could not be said that its inflation rate was higher at the given level of unemployment *because* its exchange rate was depreciating. This is not to deny of course that, if a country expands its economy in order to move from one level of unemployment to a lower level of unemployment, the inflation rate may accelerate partly as a consequence of the depreciation of the exchange rate. But once the target level of unemployment has been achieved, whether or not the exchange rate continues to depreciate depends on the rate of inflation in this country relative to that in others. Of course, a country can try to check the interaction between the behaviour of the domestic price level and its exchange rate by supporting the latter. But clearly this policy cannot be sustained indefinitely without other measures being taken to reduce the level of demand and employment in the economy or to reduce the domestic trade-off coefficient; otherwise the trade balance would worsen, which would reduce reserves and the government's ability to support the rate. Hence we can see no reason why the trade-off between inflation and unemployment should be worse in a floating exchange rate system than in a fixed parity one.

As indicated earlier, the instability of exchange rates which followed the breakdown of the Bretton Woods system at the end of 1971 has been associated with a sharp rise in world inflation. There has been a tendency to attribute this acceleration to the instability of exchange rates. Since the events of the period are important in themselves and since also a number of other factors, apart from exchange rate changes, were operating at the same time, more detailed examination of the period will be left until Chapter 10. We shall finish this chapter by referring to the growing importance of another international phenomenon which has probably contributed to the international transmission of inflation in recent years — perhaps even to its acceleration: the multinational corporation.

The multinational corporation

The multinational enterprise is a recent phenomenon achieving economic and political significance only with the rapid increase in direct foreign investment in the late 1950s and 1960s, and arising as a result of changes in corporate structure and policy which are still going on.[10] Its origins are economic and lie in the direct foreign investment of the past century. It has, of course, no standing in international law — in the legal sense there is no such thing as a multinational corporation — and its legal basis is spread among the countries in which it has productive facilities. Nevertheless, the operations of governments have been instrumental in promoting it and making it feasible.

Direct foreign investment is stimulated by a number of economic forces. The establishment of productive facilities abroad follows the development of foreign markets through exporting from domestic sources of supply; it occurs when there are clear benefits in terms of lower costs to be obtained from producing abroad, in the form of lower manufacturing (not necessarily or perhaps generally labour costs) and transport costs, and in less damage to products; when the growing sophistication of products requires closer contact with consumers and customers in general; when capital can be obtained more easily abroad; and when government restraints on trade, such as tariffs and trading regulations, increase the difficulty of exporting. Not all firms and industries engage in foreign investment and there appears to be no firm rule. Typically, however, the firms and industries which do so have access to considerable capital and management potential and are involved in the application of new technology. They tend to be oligopolistic on their market structure, and to be growth rather than profit maximising oriented. They have substantial financial resources with which to meet initial promotion costs; they find it easier once they have reached a certain size in their domestic market, to enter or expand their market share abroad rather than at home, and their new technology, research and development expertise give them an advantage over domestic producers in the economy in which they invest. In the recent past the bulk of foreign investment has been done by U.S. firms and largely in Europe, although increasingly there has been some counterflow.

While government restraints on trade stimulated foreign direct investment, later removal of such barriers encouraged the appearance of the multinational corporation. Barriers to trade and economic nationalism, having encouraged the establishment of affiliates and branches abroad, operate to keep them apart and prevent specialism; but with a change in policy, the later removal of such hindrances to international trade permits the affiliates to begin to specialize and integrate their activities among themselves and with their parent. The multinational corporation is then born.

The essence of such a company is that it treats the various national markets as though they were one. It tends to have a single management centre and policy decisions are thus centralized. Its aim becomes the integration of the operations of its affiliates and the removal of competition between them: instead they become dependent on each other through vertical integration. Central decision making relates to location of production, product mix for each affiliate, expansion or contraction of investment and output, inter-company and external sales and purchases, finances, and research and development. Price policy is coordinated, and uniform prices may be established in separate markets: essentially, however, the principle and practice of oligopolistic pricing is applied on a worldwide basis rather than simply domestically. The enterprise makes use of a worldwide marketing service and a coordinated market strategy.

Given the nature and characteristics of multinational corporations as briefly outlined above, how can their operations contribute to the spreading and exacerbation of inflation? It is important to emphasize two facts. In the first place, multinational corporations are generally oligopolistic in character, capital intensive and advanced technology based. In the second place, U.S.-owned and controlled corporations tend to dominate.

Because of their oligopolistic nature, multinational corporations are likely to be wage and price leaders. Because they are capital intensive and are users of advanced technology, their capital costs are high relative to their labour costs, and their labour productivity is high relative to other sectors of the economy. They are therefore amenable to trade union pressure for higher money wages, partly because the impact on their average costs of production is attenuated by the high incidence of their capital costs and partly because strikes which cause capacity to remain unused for any length of time are costly in terms of profits. Also their power to control a substantial part of the market through advertising and other non-price competitive methods enables them to exert an important price-determining function.

An oligopoly operating in a single economy is however not without some restraint. Although it may not fear domestic competition it cannot ignore foreign competition and imports; nor can it ignore its competitive position in export markets abroad. Foreign competition will therefore tend to stiffen resistance of such firms against wage demands which would force them to raise prices to uncompetitive levels as far as their operations are concerned, although the wage increases they do in fact concede may still make inflation inevitable in the economy as a whole as a result of spillover effects analysed earlier. If a domestic oligopoly becomes an integral part of an international oligopoly as a result of a merger or closer economic ties with a parent and other affiliates abroad, part of this restraint is then removed. For example, Ford U.K. may be in effective competition with Ford Germany, each company acting quite independently, and each attempting to maximize its position in the world market as a whole. Suppose now they become more integrated and subject to central decision making from the U.S. There may now be some market sharing or product specialization which effectively reduces competition between them. They may also decide on a common labour relations policy, aimed at avoiding strikes and lost production and, therefore, be willing to grant substantial wage increases in both centres of production even if the result is a rise in costs that has to be covered by a rise in price. It is true, of course, that even though Ford U.K. and Ford Germany are no longer in effective competition with each other, General Motors operating in both countries may still be. Even so, the number of competitors has been reduced, and experience has demonstrated that the fewer the producers operating in any given market, the less they compete on price and the more they compete in other ways, which may in fact be costly and involve higher prices than would otherwise be the case.

The growth of the multinational corporation would therefore seem to have reduced the element of price competition in product markets and to have increased the bargaining power of trade unions in substantial sectors of industry. This brings us to the second factor, namely, the effect of wages. It is important to note that the great majority of multinational companies are U.S.-owned and based: in the words of Behrman 'these enterprises reflect the extension into the international realm of the business methods large U.S. corporations have developed for the continental market and the U.S'.[11] Equally likely, they may also have injected U.S. wage standards and wage bargaining practices into the world economy as a whole. Affiliates have probably been able to pay U.S. or near U.S. wages without serious effects on their costs and profits, largely because U.S. capital intensive technology has been injected as well; but the spillover effects on other sectors of the European economy into which U.S. technology has not been imported and which have not achieved comparable productivity growth have been serious and have probably exacerbated inflation generally.[12]

The influence of multinational corporations on the behaviour of wage and price levels generally will probably not stop here. It can be anticipated that the multinational corporation will be followed by the appearance of the multinational or international trade union: indeed the antecedents are already apparent. Trade unions everywhere are becoming aware of the bargaining power available to the multinational firm and gearing themselves to it. So far, trade unions in the host countries in which multinational operate have largely concerned themselves with obtaining parity of earnings between multinational firms and domestic firms operating in the same country; but it will surely not be long before parity of earnings between subsidiaries of international enterprises operating in different countries will become a major objective.[13] Given that one of the major impacts of the multinational enterprise is to standardize technologies and production functions in use, at least in developed industrial countries, the companies themselves are not likely to oppose this development.

The long term aim of international trade unionism seems likely to be to compel all subsidiaries of an enterprise to pay the same money wage rate (after conversion into a common currency unit at current exchange rates) to all workers of comparable skill, grading and performance, irrespective of country of employment. The wage rate paid by the best practice country is likely to be the standard. Some evidence for this can be seen in a resolution passed at a recent conference of the World Automobile Council (in the setting up of which the United Automobile Workers' Union of the U.S. took a leading part), the substance of which was that all workers employed by a given multinational automobile firm should have parity of *real* wages.

The parity that would be achieved by a policy of demanding equal money wages converted at current exchange rates into the currencies of the countries in which the subsidiaries are located would of course be parity of 'own product' wages rather than 'real' wages since the latter depends on the prices of a wide range of goods entering into workers' consumption, including many, perhaps a majority of, non-traded goods, the composition and relative price of which would differ from country to country. Moreover, it is obvious that there are formidable difficulties in the way of full internationalization of trade unionism: unions are far from achieving parity of 'own product' wages in the countries in which the multinational firm operates. Once it does happen, however, the consequences will be considerable. In all probability, fewer and fewer countries will remain 'feasible' currency areas and many governments will find increasing difficulty in employing exchange rate policy to maintain full employment and balance of payments equilibrium.[14]

5
The Anatomy of Inflation in the Developed Industrial Countries of the O.E.C.D.

In this chapter we describe as briefly as we can the anatomical features of post-Second World War inflation in the developed industrial countries of the West i.e. those countries, with one or two exceptions, that comprise the Organization for Economic Co-operation and Development (the O.E.C.D.). We leave until later chapters any attempt to analyse the causes of this inflation.

Inspection of all the various statistical series we present indicates very clearly that towards the end of the 1960s a marked acceleration occurred in the rate of inflation in virtually every country we are concerned with. During the 1950s and most of the 1960s, the countries of the O.E.C.D. experienced persistent but moderate inflation. After 1968,[1] the typical inflation rate accelerated, and by 1973 prices were rising at three or four times the rate experienced in the preceeding decade and a half. Some evidence suggests that the nature of inflation changed radically after about 1968; for example, the relation between unemployment levels and the rate of inflation showed a substantial change. For this reason, the period 1968-1973 warrants separate description and analysis which we attempt to provide in Chapter 10. In this chapter and the three that follow, we concentrate largely on the period 1954 to 1968.

The behaviour of prices

After the short but very severe inflation associated with the Korean War and its immediate aftermath in 1950-53, the rate of inflation as measured by the GDP deflator in the countries of the O.E.C.D. averaged about 3¼ per cent per annum in the next 15 years. As can be seen from Table 5.1. some countries fared better than others. The average rate of inflation in the U.S., Canada, Germany and Belgium was significantly lower than the O.E.C.D. average, while at the other end of the scale France and Denmark experienced inflation at a rate approaching five per cent per annum. All countries of course experienced yearly variations in the rate of inflation around their own average for the period as a whole. The very inflationary years 1957-9 in France for example, clearly pulled up the average for that country very considerably: leaving aside these years France was no more inflationary than most other O.E.C.D. countries. In all countries there appears to be a tendency for the rate of inflation to increase over time, but this did not become significant until after 1968. In the next five years the

O.E.C.D. inflation rate averaged over six per cent per annum, nearly twice what it had been earlier, and by the end of 1973, the rate had increased to nearly nine per cent per annum.

FIGURE 5.1.

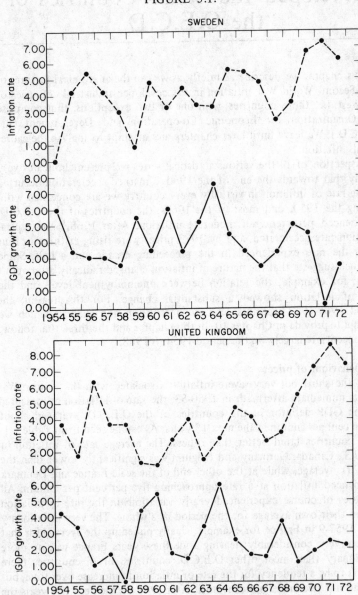

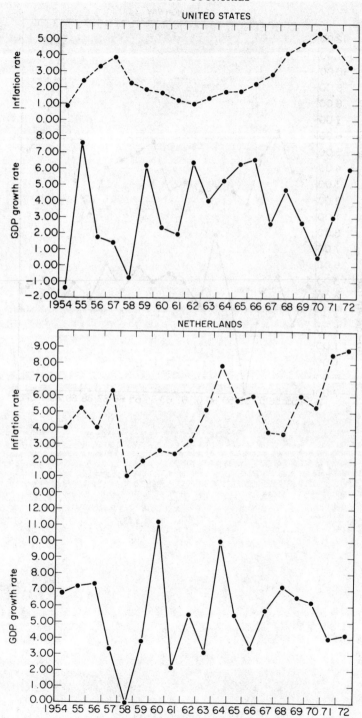

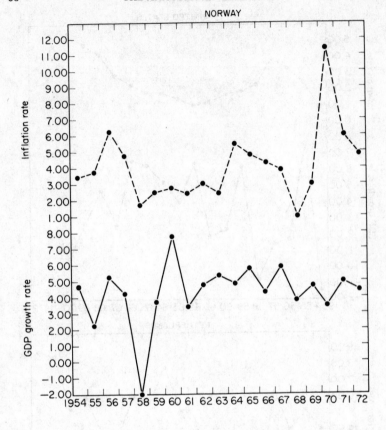

JAPAN

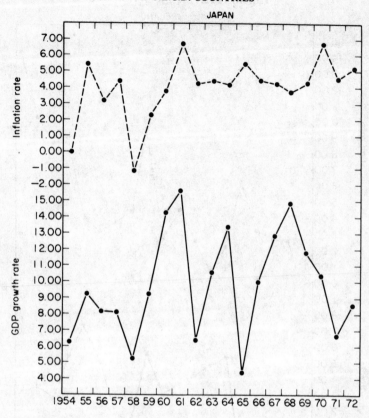

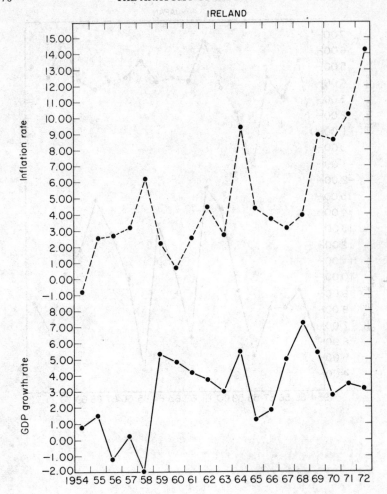

IRELAND

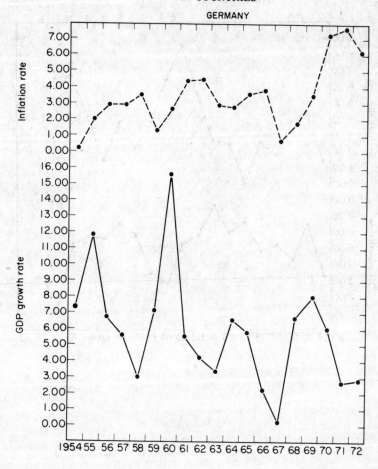

GERMANY

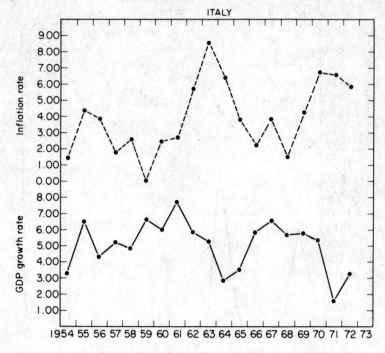

ITALY

CANADA

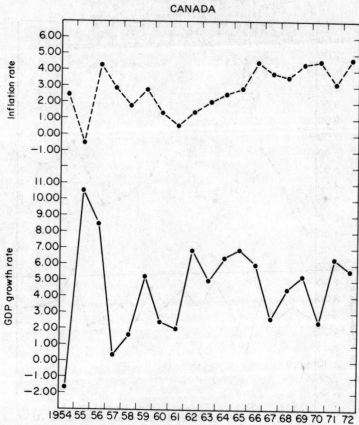

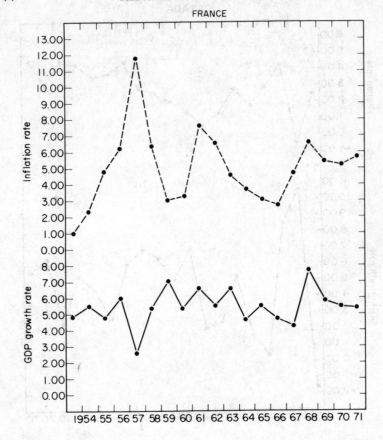

FRANCE

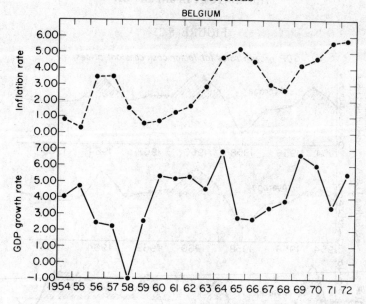

BELGIUM

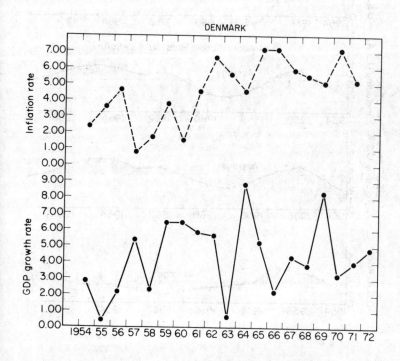

DENMARK

FIGURE 5.2.

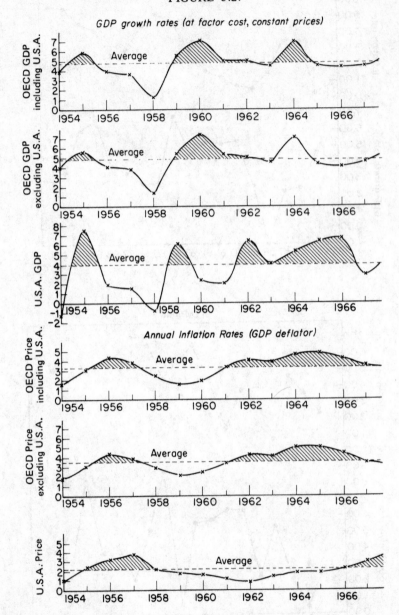

GDP growth rates (at factor cost, constant prices)

In the case of most countries the annual variations in the inflation rate
were related to annual variations in the pressure of demand as indicated by
variations in the GDP growth rate, but as Figure 5.1 (Annual GDP growth
rates compared with annual inflation rates) shows, the association in the
case of any one country was loose rather than close. More significant is
the fact that countries tended to experience faster inflation rates at the
same time. Austria, Belgium, France, Germany, U.K., U.S., Sweden, all
experienced above average (1954-1968) inflation rates in 1956-57, and
most of these, plus Italy and Japan, were again above average in 1962-67.
Many countries had inflation rates below average in 1958-61.

However, annual variations in the overall O.E.C.D. inflation rate were
not always correlated with annual variations in the overall O.E.C.D.
growth rate. For instance, Figure 5.2 shows that although the O.E.C.D.
growth rate was above its 1954-68 average in the years 1959-61, the
O.E.C.D. growth rate was significantly below its longer term average,
except for 1964. It is perhaps significant to note that the behaviour of the
O.E.C.D. inflation rate appears to be more closely geared to the behaviour
of the U.S. growth rate than to the overall O.E.C.D. growth rate, although
this does not appear to be due to the weight of the U.S. price level in the
O.E.C.D. average. In the years 1956-61 the U.S. growth rate was relatively
depressed (apart from the short lived boom of 1959), while many other
O.E.C.D. countries were enjoying a substantial boom in their growth rates,
particularly in 1959-61. However, the O.E.C.D. price level, including or
excluding the U.S., rose at a slower rate than the average for the period as
a whole. On the other hand, when U.S. growth rates were well above
average during 1962 and, again in 1964-66, the O.E.C.D. inflation rate was
also well above its longer term average even though the rate of inflation in
the U.S. remained relatively low. This fact gives some credibility to th
staunchly held European view that for much of the decade of the 1960s,
the U.S. successfully exported its inflationary pressure to Europe. Although
the U.S. was the least inflationary country in the industrial world in the
1950s and 1960s, part of this stability — in the mid-1960s at least — may
have been purchased at the expense of the rest of the world. During these
years the U.S. significantly raised its growth rate; at the same time its
balance of payments deteriorated sharply. The rest of the world was
therefore forced to accumulate dollars at a high rate, a process which, as
we now know, eventually led to the collapse of the Bretton Woods international monetary system. To what extent this breakdown might have
ushered in and contributed to a period of even faster world inflation
remains to be examined.

In Table 5.1 the rate of inflation is measured by the GDP deflator which
provides the best indicator of the inflationary forces operating generally
in the economy. However, as is to be expected, other prices paralleled the
behaviour of the GDP deflator.

Table 5.1. O.E.C.D. ANNUAL INFLATION RATES (G.D.P. DEFLATOR)

	54	55	56	57	58	59	60	61	62	63	64	65	66	67	68	69	70	71	72	Annual average 1954-68	Annual average 1969-72
Belgium	0.9	0.4	3.5	3.5	1.5	0.6	0.7	1.2	1.7	2.9	4.8	5.1	4.5	3.0	2.7	4.3	4.7	5.7	5.9	2.5	5.1
Canada	2.5	-0.5	4.3	2.9	1.8	2.8	1.3	0.6	1.3	2.0	2.5	2.9	4.5	3.8	3.6	4.5	3.7	3.3	4.4	2.4	4.1
Denmark	2.4	3.7	4.8	0.9	1.8	3.9	1.6	4.7	6.8	5.7	4.7	7.3	7.3	6.0	5.7	5.1	8.1	6.0	8.8	4.5	7.0
France	1.0	2.3	4.9	6.1	11.8	6.4	3.0	3.3	7.7	6.6	4.7	3.8	3.0	2.7	4.8	6.6	5.5	5.2	5.7	4.8	5.7
Germany	0.1	2.0	2.9	2.9	3.6	1.3	2.6	4.3	4.4	2.9	2.7	3.6	3.8	0.6	1.7	3.5	7.1	7.7	6.1	2.6	6.0
Italy	1.5	4.4	3.9	1.8	2.6	0.0	2.5	2.7	5.8	8.6	6.3	3.9	2.1	2.8	1.5	4.3	7.4	7.6	5.7	3.4	5.8
Ireland	-0.9	2.7	2.8	3.2	6.3	2.1	0.7	2.6	4.6	2.7	9.5	4.4	3.8	2.8	4.0	8.1	9.6	10.3	14.3	3.4	10.7
Japan	0.0	5.5	3.1	4.5	-1.1	2.3	3.8	6.8	4.2	4.4	4.1	5.5	4.5	4.2	3.1	3.1	6.7	4.4	4.9	3.7	5.2
Netherlands	4.0	5.2	4.0	5.4	2.0	2.0	2.7	2.5	3.2	5.2	7.9	5.8	6.0	3.8	3.7	6.2	5.4	8.1	9.3	4.2	7.2
Norway	3.5	4.9	6.3	-0.8	1.7	2.6	2.7	2.4	3.0	2.5	5.4	4.8	4.3	4.4	2.5	3.0	-	6.0	4.3	3.5	3.9
Sweden	0.0	4.3	1.3	4.3	7.1	0.4	4.7	3.0	4.6	3.5	3.4	5.7	5.5	4.9	2.6	3.4	7.1	7.3	6.2	3.8	6.0
U.K.	3.8	1.9	6.4	3.8	3.8	1.3	1.1	2.9	4.0	1.6	2.9	4.8	4.1	2.7	3.2	5.6	7.3	8.8	7.8	3.2	7.3
U.S.	1.9	1.3	3.3	3.9	2.2	1.9	1.7	1.2	1.0	1.4	1.8	1.8	2.3	2.9	4.1	4.7	4.7	4.7	3.3	2.2	4.3
Average	1.6	3.0	4.3	3.8	2.4	2.1	2.4	3.1	4.0	3.8	4.6	4.7	4.2	3.4	3.1	4.7	6.4	6.4	6.5	3.3	5.9

NOTE: 1954-68 GDP at factor cost; 1969-72 GDP at market prices.

Source: Yearbook of National Account Statistics

Table 5.2 O.E.C.D. ANNUAL G.D.P. GROWTH RATE

(1954-68: factor cost*; 1969-72: market prices)

	54	55	56	57	58	59	60	61	62	63	64	65	66	67	68	69	70	71	72	Average 1954-68	Average 1969-72
Belgium	(4.0)	(4.8)	2.5	2.2	-1.0	2.6	5.3	5.1	5.2	4.6	6.9	2.8	2.7	3.3	3.8	6.6	6.0	3.4	5.5	3.6	5.4
Canada	-1.6	10.5	8.5	0.4	1.7	5.2	2.4	2.0	6.9	5.0	6.4	6.9	6.0	2.7	4.5	5.2	2.5	6.3	5.7	4.5	4.4
Denmark	2.9	0.4	2.1	5.4	2.2	6.5	6.5	5.9	5.7	0.7	8.9	5.2	2.2	4.2	3.9	8.3	3.1	4.0	4.9	4.1	4.8
France	4.9	5.5	4.9	6.0	2.6	5.3	7.0	5.4	6.7	5.7	6.6	4.7	5.5	4.7	4.2	7.7	5.9	5.5	5.4	5.3	6.1
Germany	7.4	11.9	6.8	5.6	3.0	7.1	15.6	5.6	4.2	3.4	6.7	5.8	2.2	0.2	6.8	8.0	6.0	2.7	2.9	6.1	4.9
Italy	3.3	6.6	4.3	5.1	4.9	6.6	6.0	7.8	5.9	5.2	2.9	3.5	5.8	6.5	5.7	5.8	5.3	1.6	3.2	6.1	4.0
Ireland	(0.9)	(2.5)	(-1.2)	(0.3)	(-2.0)	5.3	4.9	4.1	3.7	3.0	5.5	1.1	1.9	5.0	7.2	5.4	2.9	3.5	3.2	2.8	3.7
Japan	6.3	9.2	8.1	8.1	5.3	9.3	14.2	15.7	6.4	10.6	13.4	4.4	10.0	12.9	14.9	11.9	10.4	6.7	8.6	10.3	9.4
Netherlands	6.9	7.1	4.4	3.4	0.0	3.9	11.1	2.2	5.5	3.1	10.0	5.5	3.5	5.8	7.1	6.6	6.2	4.0	4.2	5.3	5.2
Norway	4.8	2.3	5.3	4.2	-2.0	3.8	7.8	3.5	4.9	5.4	4.9	5.8	4.4	5.9	3.7	4.7	3.6	5.0	4.3	4.3	4.4
Sweden	6.0	3.4	3.0	3.0	2.6	5.6	3.5	6.0	3.5	5.1	7.6	4.4	3.4	2.5	3.3	5.0	4.5	0.0	2.5	4.2	3.0
U.K.	4.1	3.4	1.0	1.8	0.0	4.5	5.4	1.8	1.4	3.3	6.0	2.6	1.7	1.6	3.8	1.1	1.9	2.5	2.2	3.1	1.9
U.S.	-1.4	7.6	1.8	1.5	-0.8	6.2	2.4	2.0	6.4	4.0	5.3	6.3	6.6	2.7	4.8	2.7	0.5	3.0	6.0	3.9	3.0
Average (inc. U.S.)	3.95	5.78	3.96	3.62	1.27	5.53	7.08	5.16	5.11	4.55	7.01	4.54	4.30	4.46	5.67	6.0	4.5	3.7	4.5	4.80	4.6
Average (excl. U.S.)	4.16	5.63	4.14	3.79	1.44	5.48	7.48	5.43	5.0	4.59	7.15	4.39	4.11	4.61	5.74	6.3	4.8	3.8	4.4	4.87	4.7

Source: National accounts of O.E.C.D. countries

* The numbers in parentheses (Belgium and Ireland) prior to 1969 are the annual

G.D.P. growth rates at constant market prices.

In most countries, consumer prices rose at a slightly slower rate than did the GDP deflator, mainly as a consequence of a slow decline in the price level of primary product imports entering the O.E.C.D. area (see Table 5.3.).

Table 5.3. O.E.C.D. PERCENTAGE CHANGES IN THE CONSUMER PRICE INDEX – 1954-1973

	54	55	56	57	58	59	60	61	62	63	64	65	66	67	68	69	70	71	72	73	Annual average 1954-68	Annual average 1969-73
Belgium	1.4	-0.6	2.9	3.1	1.4	1.1	0.3	0.9	1.5	2.1	4.2	4.0	4.2	4.2	2.9	3.7	4.0	4.4	5.4	6.9	2.2	4.9
Canada	0.6	0.2	1.4	3.3	2.6	1.1	1.3	0.9	1.2	1.7	1.7	2.6	3.7	3.5	4.1	4.5	3.4	2.8	4.8	7.6	2.0	4.6
Denmark	0.0	5.5	6.0	2.5	0.7	1.8	1.2	3.5	7.3	6.2	3.1	5.4	7.1	8.1	8.0	3.5	6.5	5.9	6.6	9.3	4.4	6.3
France	0.3	1.1	4.3	-0.7	15.2	5.7	4.1	2.4	5.2	4.9	3.1	2.7	2.6	2.8	4.6	6.1	5.9	5.6	5.8	7.3	3.9	6.1
Germany	0.2	1.7	2.5	2.3	2.3	1.0	1.3	2.4	3.0	2.8	2.4	3.1	3.7	1.7	1.5	2.7	3.8	5.1	6.9	8.7	2.1	5.4
Ireland	0.0	2.6	4.3	4.1	4.5	-2.0	3.1	2.7	4.3	2.4	6.7	5.0	3.0	3.1	4.8	7.4	8.3	8.9	8.7	11.4	3.2	8.9
Italy	2.9	2.3	3.4	1.2	2.9	2.0	0.1	2.1	4.6	7.0	5.9	4.4	2.4	3.6	1.4	2.7	4.9	4.8	5.7	10.8	3.1	5.6
Japan	5.4	1.3	0.7	3.2	0.9	1.5	3.4	5.3	6.9	7.9	4.1	7.2	4.8	4.1	5.5	5.7	7.2	6.3	4.8	11.7	4.1	7.1
Netherlands	4.0	1.9	2.0	6.5	1.7	3.0	0.0	1.6	1.8	3.7	5.5	4.0	7.0	3.4	3.8	7.4	3.6	7.5	7.5	7.8	3.3	6.7
Norway	4.4	0.9	3.7	2.7	5.0	1.0	0.0	2.5	5.3	2.5	5.7	4.3	3.3	4.4	3.5	3.1	10.6	6.3	7.2	7.5	3.3	7.7
Sweden	1.4	2.7	3.9	5.1	4.8	0.0	4.6	2.2	4.3	3.0	3.0	5.8	6.4	4.3	1.7	2.4	7.1	7.4	6.2	7.1	3.5	6.0
U.K.	2.1	4.2	5.4	3.7	3.0	0.0	2.0	3.4	4.3	1.9	3.3	4.7	4.0	2.5	4.7	5.4	6.4	9.5	7.1	9.2	3.3	7.3
U.S.	0.5	0.3	1.6	3.4	2.8	1.0	2.0	1.1	1.1	1.2	1.3	1.6	3.1	2.8	4.1	5.4	5.9	4.5	3.3	6.2	1.9	5.1

Source: International Financial Statistics, I.M.F.

Table 5.4. O.E.C.D. Consumer Prices by Standard Groups
Average annual rates of change, 1960-1969.

Eight industrial countries.

Country	Food	Other goods	Rent	Other services	Total
		Price rise			
United States	2.6	1.7	1.6	3.6	2.4
Canada	2.6	1.4	3.4	4.2	2.7
Japan	6.2	3.1	8.2	7.2	5.5
United Kingdom	3.8	3.2	5.1	5.1	4.0
France	3.9	2.6	8.9	5.9	3.9
Germany	2.0	1.6	6.4	4.0	2.6
Italy	3.4	2.8	6.3	6.1	3.8
Netherlands	4.2	3.1	4.9	5.4	4.2
		Weighting pattern in 1963			
United States	22	42	6	31	
Canada	34	34	18	14	
Japan	43	34	4	19	
United Kingdom	43	37	12	8	100
France	45	40	5	10	
Germany*	36	35	11	17	
Italy**	46	32	5	17	
Netherlands	37	32	9	22	
		Contribution to total price rise			
United States	23	29	4	44	
Canada	34	19	24	23	
Japan	49	19	7	25	
United Kingdom	42	31	16	11	100
France	46	27	12	15	
Germany	27	21	26	26	
Italy	41	23	9	27	
Netherlands	37	24	11	28	

* 1968 weights
** 1967 weights

Note: 'Food' includes alcoholic beverages, tobacco and meals taken in restaurants.

'Other goods' include fuel, heat, light and water.

'Rent' includes home repairs and maintenance.

Major exceptions are: the United States, where drink and tobacco is included in 'Other goods'; Canada, where house repair materials are included in 'Other goods'; France, where tobacco is included in 'Other goods'; Italy, where restaurant meals are included in 'Other services'. Source: *Main Economic Indicators* – O.E.C.D.

Source: Report of the General Secretary of the O.E.C.D. on 'The present problem of inflation', December 1970.

The consumer price index reflects the price behaviour of a wide variety of products. It is not to be expected that prices of all products or services would rise at the same rate. Table 5.4 gives the average annual rates of change of consumer prices by standard groups in the period 1960-69 for a number of the major industrial countries. We see that in most of these countries food prices rose at about the same rate as the total consumer price index. Manufactured goods prices (i.e. the major component of the 'Other Goods' group) rose at a slower rate and Rents and Service prices rose at a faster rate. The faster rise in 'Services' prices is to be expected given both the importance of labour in their production and the relatively slow growth of labour productivity as compared with manufacturing production. After 1969, however, when the inflation rate in O.E.C.D. countries rose, the behaviour of food prices became a more important elements in the overall inflation rate.

The contribution of the rise in price of particular groups of products to the total price rise depends on the weight of those groups in consumers' expenditure. In this respect there is clearly a marked difference between the U.S. and most other countries. In the U.S. the share of food in total expenditure is much lower than elsewhere, while the share of services is much higher. Hence the rise in 'service' prices contributed almost a half of the total rise in the price level while food prices, although they rose at a somewhat faster rate than the total price index, contributed less than a quarter. In other countries, apart from Germany, food prices contributed to between one third and one half of the rise in the total index, while the contribution of service prices was about a quarter or less. In the U.K., the large contribution of manufactured goods prices to the rise in the total price index is not typical and is therefore noteworthy. It probably reflects the slower growth of productivity in U.K. manufacturing industry as compared with most other industrial countries. Despite the relatively slow growth of labour productivity in services, the contribution of the services group to the overall rate of inflation in the U.K. was small, owing to the surprisingly small weight of services expenditure in total expenditure.

We may also examine inflation in terms of the behaviour of sector of production prices. This is done in Table 5.5 for a number of countries for which data are available. It will be seen that in all the countries listed, agricultural and industrial sector prices rose at a much slower rate than the GDP deflator, while the price level of the building and service sectors (both labour intensive sectors of the economy) rose at a much faster rate. The contribution of the service sector to the overall rise in the GDP deflator is very noticeable. Indeed, building and service sector prices contributed about three quarters of the rise in the GDP deflator, the contribution of agriculture being insignificant in the majority of cases.

Table 5.5. O.E.C.D. PRICE RISE BY SECTORS
(1958-68 at annual rates − 6 countries)

| | Agriculture | Industry* | | Building | Services | GDP |
		Total	Manufacturing			
		Price rise**				
United States	0.9	0.9	1.1	5.2	2.6	2.1
United Kingdom	−0.3	2.2	2.1	3.5	4.5	2.8
France†	2.6	2.4	2.5	4.8	5.1	3.9
Germany	0.1	1.7	1.8	4.4	4.2	2.8
Italy	1.9	1.8	1.8	6.1	5.1	3.7
Netherlands	1.7	2.6***	−	−	4.9	3.7
		Weight in GDP				
United States	4.6	32.4	27.3	4.6	58.1	
United Kingdom††	4.3	41.0	34.8	5.9	47.2	
France	9.2	40.1	36.4	8.0	42.7	100
Germany	6.5	47.0	41.2	6.3	40.0	
Italy	18.5	28.6	26.3	7.3	45.6	
Netherlands	11.2	41.3***	n.a.	n.a.	47.5	
		Contribution to total price rise				
United States	1.8	13.2	14.0	13.4	75.0	
United Kingdom††	−0.4	31.4	25.2	7.6	81.9	
France†	6.0	23.9	22.6	10.3	59.5	100
Germany	0.2	27.4	25.4	10.7	65.0	
Italy	8.6	12.3	10.9	13.5	67.3	
Netherlands	4.7	27.2***	−	−	68.0	

* Mining, manufacturing and public utilities
** Change of implicit price deflator of the value-added of each sector.
† 1959-1968
*** Including construction.
†† The weights and the contributions do not add up to 100 due to adjustment for stock appreciation.

Source: National Accounts of OECD countries.

Source: Report of the General Secretary of the O.E.C.D. on 'The present problem of inflation, December 1970.

Foreign trade prices

In all countries *export prices* measured in national currencies rose much more slowly than the GDP deflator and consumer prices in general, at any rate up to 1968. Indeed in some countries, namely Belgium, Italy and Japan, export prices were lower in 1968 than in 1953 (see Table 5.6). On average, the rise of export prices in O.E.C.D. countries generally was less than one per cent per annum. France topped the list for the fastest inflation rate at over 2.5 per cent per annum, but most of the increase occurred during the years 1956-60, that is, before and after the franc devaluation in 1958. Export prices also rose faster in the U.K. than in most other O.E.C.D. countries, particularly after 1962, foretelling sterling devaluation in 1967. U.S. export prices also began to rise quite sharply in the

Table 5.6. O.E.C.D. Export Prices (National Currencies)

	54	55	56	57	58	59	60	61	62	63	64	65	66	67	68	69	70	71	72	73
Belgium	100	103	110	113	105	101	103	102	101	101	103	103	106	105	104	110	115	111	113	122
Canada	100	102	106	106	105	107	107	108	111	112	113	115	121	123	127	130	133	133	137	157
Denmark	100	101	105	101	99	101	100	98	100	102	105	106	110	108	110	115	122	125	131	148
France	100	101	105	113	123	134	140	139	139	141	146	149	153	151	150	161	178	188	190	210
Germany	100	100	103	105	105	102	103	104	106	106	106	108	109	108	106	108	110	111	113	115
Ireland	100	103	98	100	102	106	104	103	104	106	112	113	115	115	124	132	141	152	173	n.a.
Italy	100	97	95	98	94	86	90	87	88	89	91	90	88	88	87	91	94	100	101	115
Japan	100	94	97	98	96	95	97	95	93	92	91	90	90	93	93	97	102	103	101	109
Netherlands	100	102	104	107	103	103	102	101	100	102	104	106	106	105	104	106	110	112	113	121
Norway	100	105	109	112	106	104	104	103	102	101	104	108	109	108	105	107	116	121	120	132
Sweden	100	103	105	105	104	101	104	105	104	105	108	112	113	114	114	118	128	135	136	149
United Kingdom	100	102	106	111	110	109	111	112	112	115	117	120	124	126	136	141	152	163	175	196
United States	100	101	104	108	107	107	108	111	109	109	110	113	117	120	121	125	132	136	141	164

Source: International Financial Statistics, I.M.F.

second half of the 1960s relative to what was happening in its major
competitors, Germany and Japan, a development which not unexpectedly
culminated in the substantial devaluation of the dollar against the
currencies of these countries in December 1971.

The very marked difference between the behaviour of the GDP
deflator − i.e. a measure of the general inflation rate − and the behaviour
of export prices is brought out very clearly in Figure 5.3. The experience
of Japan and Italy, where export prices actually fell despite domestic
inflation exceeding the O.E.C.D. average, is especially noticeable; and that
of Germany and the Netherlands is not much less so. In the U.K. and the
U.S. however, domestic prices and export prices tended to rise together,
especially after the first few years of the 1960s.

FIGURE 5.3.

O.E.C.D. Export prices and the GDP deflator 1953-68
GDP deflator ——— Export Prices ———

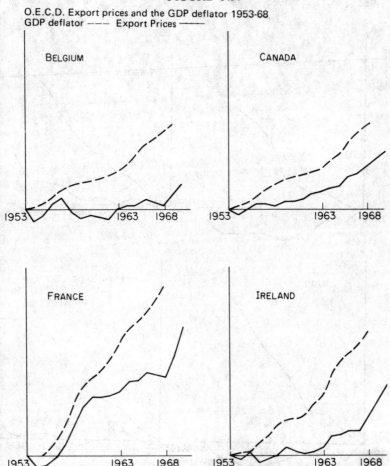

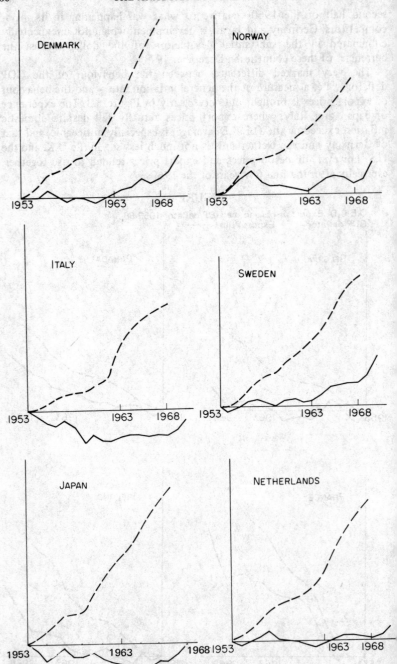

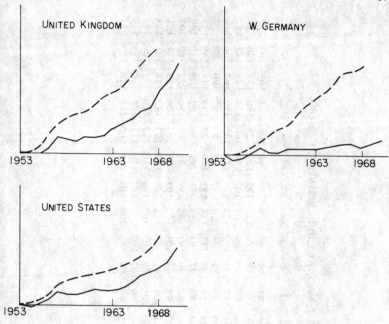

Perhaps the most interesting feature of these charts is the sharp rise in export prices in virtually all countries after 1968. Indeed, export prices began to rise at a faster rate than did domestic prices, in marked contrast to what happened in the preceding decade. However, we shall return to a discussion of this in Chapter 10.

Import prices measured in domestic currency of the major industrial countries also remained remarkably stable throughout the years 1954-68 (see Table 5.7). In some countries (Belgium, Germany, Italy, Japan, Netherlands) import prices were in fact lower in 1968 than they were in 1954. The countries whose import prices had risen most (namely France, Canada, Ireland and the U.K.) were precisely those whose exchange rates had been devalued at one time or another during the period. In general, all industrial countries benefitted from the long decline in primary product prices which had begun in the mid 1950s.[2] After 1968 import prices began to rise sharply, in line with the rise in export prices of the industrial countries.

Table 5.7. O.E.C.D. IMPORT PRICES (NATIONAL CURRENCIES) (1954 = 100)

	54	55	56	57	58	59	60	61	62	63	64	65	66	67	68	69	70	71	72	73
Belgium	100	100	103	106	99	97	97	99	97	99	99	99	99	97	98	101	104	105	104	113
Canada	100	100	103	106	106	105	106	108	113	118	119	120	121	122	124	128	130	132	136	151
Denmark	100	101	105	104	99	95	97	97	96	98	99	100	101	101	104	108	114	123	123	137
France	100	99	103	113	119	128	133	131	131	132	134	137	138	139	134	143	159	165	166	179
Germany	100	103	104	105	97	93	96	93	90	90	91	94	94	93	90	93	91	90	88	92
Ireland	100	103	105	111	106	104	106	107	107	108	109	111	111	111	120	125	134	142	149	177
Italy	100	101	104	110	97	90	89	88	88	90	92	91	92	94	95	96	99	108	110	140
Japan	100	101	102	107	94	89	87	89	87	88	90	91	92	92	91	91	96	97	89	101
Netherlands	100	101	104	109	103	100	101	98	97	98	101	101	102	101	98	101	108	112	111	121
Norway	100	102	106	112	129	105	104	104	103	104	105	105	106	105	103	105	113	118	121	128
Sweden	100	105	111	112	108	99	99	99	110	101	105	106	109	109	110	112	120	127	129	146
United Kingdom	100	103	105	107	99	98	99	96	95	99	103	103	105	105	116	121	126	130	138	177
United States	100	99	101	102	97	96	97	95	93	94	97	98	100	101	102	105	113	118	127	151

Source: International Financial Statistics, I.M.F.

Table 5.8. O.E.C.D. TERMS OF TRADE* (1954 = 100)

	54	55	56	57	58	59	60	61	62	63	64	65	66	67	68	69	70	71	72	73
Belgium	100	103	106	106	106	104	106	103	104	104	104	104	107	108	106	108	109	106	109	108
Canada	100	101	103	100	99	102	101	100	99	95	95	96	100	101	101	101	101	100	99	104
Denmark	100	100	100	94	100	107	103	101	104	104	106	106	109	107	107	107	102	102	106	108
France	100	102	102	100	103	104	106	106	106	107	109	107	109	109	113	112	112	115	115	117
Germany	100	98	99	100	108	110	107	114	118	117	117	116	115	115	117	115	120	124	128	125
Ireland	100	100	94	91	96	102	98	97	97	98	104	104	104	104	97	105	104	106	116	n.a.
Italy	100	96	91	89	97	96	101	99	100	98	99	98	96	97	96	98	98	95	94	82
Japan	100	95	97	93	97	96	98	104	104	102	98	97	95	98	99	98	105	104	110	108
Netherlands	100	101	100	98	100	104	110	104	103	104	104	105	104	104	116	104	105	102	102	100
Norway	100	106	109	105	99	101	101	103	101	100	100	105	106	106	105	105	106	106	102	103
Sweden	100	98	96	97	102	101	105	106	104	103	103	106	103	104	103	105	106	105	107	102
United Kingdom	100	99	101	104	111	111	112	116	118	116	115	117	119	120	117	116	119	125	126	111
United States	100	102	103	106	110	111	111	116	118	116	114	116	117	119	119	120	118	116	111	109

* Export prices divided by Import prices.
Source: International Financial Statistics, I.M.F.

All industrial countries, with the exception of Italy and Japan, experienced some improvement in their net barter terms of trade, that is, in the ratio of their export prices to their import prices, between the mid 1950s and the latter part of the 1960s (Table 5.8). The improvement was in general small, and achieved namely at the expense of primary producing countries. It is significant that, with the exception of Germany, those countries whose terms of trade improved most, namely the U.K. and the U.S., were precisely those countries which had experienced most difficulty with their balance of payments. Owing to relatively slow productivity growth in their export industries and/or a generally faster rate of overall inflation, their export prices became less and less competitive relative to those of their major competitors. Devaluation of their currencies eventually became necessary to reverse the trend. In the case of the U.S. it seems to have done so: by 1972, the terms of trade were some eight per cent worse than they were in 1968/9, and the U.S.'s current balance of payments was showing substantial recovery. The U.K's terms of trade also worsened somewhat after the devaluation of 1967, but it is significant and perhaps ominous that owing to a high rate of domestic inflation the U.K's terms of trade were better in 1972 than they had been in 1967. The sharp deterioration in the U.K.'s balance of payments in 1972/3, following an equally sharp improvement in 1970/1, was not therefore to be unexpected, and suggests that by 1972 sterling had returned to its earlier overvalued position. A further substantial devaluation of sterling in 1973 was inevitable.[3]

It will be noted that Germany's terms of trade improved by almost as much as those of the U.K. and the U.S., yet Germany's balance of payments remained strong, indeed became stronger, during the 1960s. Unlike the U.K. and the U.S. however, the improvement in Germany's terms of trade was due to a strong fall in its import prices rather than to a rise in its export prices. Germany's balance of payments clearly benefitted both from a fall in import prices, due partly to the strength of Germany's currency, and from the stability of its export prices vis-à-vis those of the U.K. and the U.S.

Wages and productivity

Turning now to the behaviour of maney wages and labour productivity, we find somewhat greater diversity among the industrial countries than was the case with prices. Whereas rates of inflation generally fell within a range of about two per cent at the low end and five per cent at the top end, we see from Table 5.9. that during the years 1954-68 country variations in the rate of increase of money wages lay between about three per cent and nine per cent per annum. Wage increases in the countries of the European Economic Community were generally greater than in the U.K. and the U.S. The average annual increase for the O.E.C.D. area generally was about 6.6 per cent. After 1968, money wages began to rise more quickly

Table 5.9. O.E.C.D. MONEY WAGES (1954 = 100)

	54	55	56	57	58	59	60	61	62	63	64	65	66	67	68	69	70	71	72	73
Belgium	100	103	111	121	127	129	134	138	150	163	180	197	217	233	245	264	235	331	378	438
Canada	100	103	108	117	117	122	126	129	132	137	143	150	158	169	181	196	212	230	249	271
Denmark	100	105	113	119	124	134	142	161	177	192	210	233	261	284	319	331	394	453	507	585
France	100	108	120	130	144	155	166	181	187	215	230	245	258	275	307	331	372	417	467	—
Germany	100	108	118	128	137	145	158	174	195	208	226	248	264	272	285	310	356	395	431	476
Ireland	100	106	112	115	122	127	135	145	160	168	188	194	213	228	250	281	323	375	432	522
Italy	100	104	114	114	119	121	125	130	140	155	177	193	198	208	214	228	268	298	322	386
Japan	100	104	110	115	116	121	128	139	153	168	187	205	223	250	284	319	371	425	492	584
Netherlands	100	105	108	120	126	129	140	149	163	175	203	224	247	263	282	310	343	383	431	489
Norway	100	106	114	121	127	138	144	155	169	178	188	206	227	239	256	281	315	352	386	427
Sweden	100	107	115	122	129	135	143	156	166	181	195	202	230	252	268	290	328	353	404	436
United Kingdom	100	107	115	121	125	129	132	137	142	147	154	160	181	187	201	216	243	270	303	344
United States	100	105	110	116	119	124	127	131	134	139	143	148	154	160	170	181	190	202	215	229

Source: International Financial Statistics, I.M.F.

and by 1973 increases of over ten per cent per annum or more were common among O.E.C.D. countries.

There is of course some presumption that faster rising money wages will go hand in hand with faster rates of inflation either as cause, effect or both. If we rank countries in order of their average annual rates of inflation over the period 1954-68 and also rank them in order of the average annual rates of wage increase, as is done in Table 5.10., the rankings clearly do not correspond exactly. Nonetheless they do correspond to a significant extent, particularly at top and bottom ends of the scale. France, for instance, is top of the league in inflation rates and second in the money wage league. Denmark is second in the former league and top in the latter league. The Netherlands and Japan are near the top of both leagues. At the other end, the U.S. and Canada are conspicuously bottom in both leagues and the U.K. and Belgium near bottom. In general, it appears to be true that countries with above average inflation rates also experienced above average money wage inflation. A conspicuous exception to this general-ization is Germany which experienced a well below average price inflation rate but was third in the league of wage inflation.

The effect of rising money wages on prices is of course offset by rising labour productivity. Table 5.11. provides an index of a broad measure of labour productivity (net manufacturing production per employed person) for each of the industrial countries. The table reveals a significant disparity between productivity growth in the various countries both before and after 1968. At one end of the scale we have Japan with a labour productivity increase of nearly ten per cent per annum; at the other end we have the U.K. and the U.S. with around three per cent annual rates of increase. The average annual increase for the O.E.C.D. group of countries as a whole was about 4.8 per cent during 1954-68, compared with an average annual increase in the money wage level and in the general price level (GDP deflator) of about 6.6 per cent and 3.3 per cent respectively. After 1968 the rate of increased productivity slowed down a little, although as indicated earlier, wage inflation sharply accelerated.

The ranking of productivity increase in the period 1954-68, as shown in Table 5.10., clearly does not correspond closely with the ranking of money wage increase. But comparing the three rankings there is some evidence that above average rates of inflation, money wage increase and productivity increase go together, and conversely. France, Netherlands, Sweden, Japan are high in all rankings; the U.K., Canada and the U.S. are near the bottom. Evidently, despite low growth of labour productivity, inflation in the U.S. and the U.K., at any rate up to 1968, was held down by very moderate wage inflation compared with the other major industrial countries. Germany provides an interesting case. General opinion to the contrary, Germany's very good inflation record in the 1950s and 1960s was apparently not due to moderate wage inflation as compared with other countries (Germany lies third in the ranking of wage increases), nor due to conspicuously fast productivity growth (Germany was sixth in the ranking). The strong fall in its import prices and improvement in its terms of trade may have contributed more than has been generally realized to its relatively low inflation rate. Belgium stands out as the 'average' country. Wage inflation was a little below average; productivity increase was a little above average; import prices fell slightly and the terms of trade improved moderately. The inflation rate, perhaps not unexpectedly, was somewhat below average.

Table 5.10. O.E.C.D. INFLATION, MONEY WAGES, PRODUCTIVITY AND MONEY SUPPLY 1954-68

(annual percentage increase)

Inflation rate (GDP deflator)		Money wages		Productivity		Money supply	
	%		%		%		%
France	4.8	Denmark	8.7	Japan	9.8	Japan	15.5
Denmark	4.5	France	8.3	Italy	7.2	Italy	12.3
Netherlands	4.1	Germany	7.8	France	6.0	France	10.5
Japan	3.7	Japan	7.8	Netherlands	5.3	Denmark	9.7
Sweden	3.7	Netherlands	7.7	Sweden	5.0	Germany	9.0
Norway	3.5	Sweden	7.2	Belgium	4.8	Canada	7.3
Italy	3.4	Norway	7.0	Germany	4.5	Netherlands	6.2
Ireland	3.4	Ireland	6.8	Norway	4.1	Ireland	6.2
U.K.	3.2	Belgium	6.5	Canada	3.8	Norway	5.7
Germany	2.6	Italy	5.6	U.S.	3.5	Belgium	5.2
Belgium	2.5	U.K.	5.1	Denmark	3.0	Sweden	4.2
Canada	2.4	Canada	4.5	Ireland	3.0	U.K.	3.3
U.S.	2.2	U.S.	3.3	U.K.	3.0	U.S.	3.2

Country rankings under each variable

	Inflation rate (GDP deflator)	Money wages	Productivity	Money supply
Belgium	11	9	6	10
Canada	12	12	9	6
Denmark	2	1	11	4
France	1	2	3	3
Germany	10	3	7	5
Ireland	7	8	12	8
Italy	7	10	2	2
Japan	4	4	1	1
Netherlands	3	5	4	7
Norway	6	7	8	9
Sweden	5	6	5	11
U.K.	9	11	13	12
U.S.	13	13	10	13

Table 5.11. O.E.C.D. PRODUCTIVITY IN MANUFACTURING
(Net manufacturing production per employed person) (1954 = 100)

	54	55	56	57	58	59	60	61	62	63	64	65	66	67	68	69	70	71	72
Belgium	100	109	114	112	111	120	126	130	138	145	155	162	171	178	191	206	210	213	217
Canada	100	107	111	110	113	119	124	126	133	139	146	152	154	157	168	172	176	188	196
Denmark	100	104	106	110	113	113	112	114	119	119	132	136	142	145	157	161	163	173	188
France	100	109	121	126	133	140	152	159	167	172	183	188	202	212	228	248	266	279	305
Germany	100	104	108	109	111	118	125	129	133	139	150	156	158	165	185	197	204	208	221
Ireland	100	101	102	102	106	110	117	122	124	128	137	142	145	154	160	167	171	179	186
Italy	100	110	113	119	129	140	156	167	185	192	194	210	231	248	267	278	282	288	283
Japan	100	106	117	125	117	148	169	185	190	208	233	242	273	319	365	419	477	508	510
Netherlands	100	103	106	108	112	120	132	133	138	145	159	165	174	186	206	223	239	251	275
Norway	100	106	110	114	117	121	128	131	135	141	151	156	163	169	175	185	186	n.a.	n.a.
Sweden	100	104	107	112	116	120	123	128	135	145	154	164	171	184	200	212	220	230	238
United Kingdom	100	104	104	104	106	112	117	116	117	123	132	136	137	141	151	154	157	162	169
United States	100	110	110	111	111	119	120	123	132	137	144	152	153	152	160	163	162	167	178

Source: Yearbook of Labour Statistics   O.E.C.D. Monthly Bulletin of Statistics

Table 5.12. O.E.C.D. MONEY SUPPLY (1954 = 100)

	54	55	56	57	58	59	60	61	62	63	64	65	66	67	68	69	70	71	72	73
Belgium	100	105	108	108	114	118	120	129	139	152	163	174	185	191	205	210	228	253	289	313
Canada	100	107	105	110	124	120	126	142	146	157	171	196	210	242	275	262	295	376	436	497
Denmark	100	103	108	112	128	141	145	161	176	200	220	243	281	306	357	401	397	426	327	372
France	100	113	124	135	144	160	181	209	247	283	306	334	357	374	404	398	442	491	566	617
Germany	100	110	118	133	150	168	179	205	219	235	255	274	279	307	333	353	387	437	498	502
Ireland	100	102	102	110	108	112	133	144	158	176	188	196	207	224	232	254	269	283	324	373
Italy	100	111	121	128	141	161	181	209	298	282	304	350	399	461	517	560	768	911	1136	1329
Japan	100	116	135	140	158	184	220	261	306	389	439	519	582	684	753	908	1061	1376	1715	2006
Netherlands	100	109	105	103	115	120	128	138	148	162	175	194	206	218	232	263	294	338	398	398
Norway	100	103	106	105	108	113	120	125	135	142	151	156	176	188	217	235	265	295	343	405
Sweden	100	101	108	111	113	131	134	147	157	169	183	195	171	185	192	176	192	210	225	246
United Kingdom	100	100	102	100	100	108	110	114	119	120	124	129	129	139	144	145	158	166	230	242
United States	100	102	103	103	107	107	107	111	113	117	123	128	131	141	153	159	165	175	195	209

Source: International Financial Statistics

After 1968, the disparity between productivity growth and money wage increases widened generally, but some countries suffered much more than others. In the O.E.C.D. area as a whole, the rate of increase of money wages rose from an average annual figure of 6.6 per cent over the period 1954-68 to ten per cent in 1968-73. The rate of increase in productivity may have fallen slightly. In the U.K. money wages rose twice as fast in 1968-73 than in 1954-68, while annual productivity growth fell by 20 per cent. In the U.S., also, the rate at which money wages rose increased much more than did the O.E.C.D. average; at the same time, productivity growth fell. Similar, although less extreme, experiences were recorded by Japan, Canada, Belgium and Italy: the fall in the latter country's productivity growth was very marked and more extreme even than the acceleration in money wage increase. The acceleration of money wage inflation was much less marked in France and Germany than in other major industrial countries; moreover, in these countries the rate of productivity increase either did not fall or it rose. Clearly, these different developments among O.E.C.D. countries bear on their different experiences with respect to inflation after 1968, the examination of which we return to in Chapter 10.

Money supply and interest rates

Money supply grew at widely different rates in the O.E.C.D. countries. Taking the area as a whole, the rate of increase in the years 1954-68 averaged about 7.5 per cent per annum, but it was twice as fast as this in Japan and less than half as fast in the U.K. and the U.S. (see Table 5.12.). Superficially there is not much support in the figures for any naive version of the Quantity Theory of money: relative inflation rates among the various countries do not correspond at all closely with relative rates of increase in money supply. If the countries are ranked in order of inflation rates and rates of increase of money supply, as is done in Table 5.10., there is no exact correspondence. Three countries (Denmark, France and Japan) were high in both rankings and three others, (Belgium, U.K. and U.S.) low in both rankings, but most other countries were high in one and low in the other.

We would not necessarily expect to associate higher rates of money increase with higher rates of price inflation. In relating the increase in the money supply to the rate of inflation we have to take account of the rate of growth of real output and the velocity of circulation of money. In Table 5.13. we subtract from the average annual rate of increase in money supply the average annual rate of increase of GDP. This gives us an indication of what we might expect for the rate of inflation on the assumption that the velocity of circulation of money itself remained constant.

It is evident that the *difference* between the rate of increase of the money supply and the rate of increase of real GDP brings us closer to the rate of inflation than does the rate of increase of the money supply itself: even so, the ranking of countries in order of the size of this difference does not

Table 5.13. O.E.C.D. MONEY SUPPLY, GDP GROWTH AND INFLATION (1954-68)

	(1) Rate of Increase of money supply per cent p.a.	(2) Rate of Increase of GDP (constant prices). per cent p.a.	(3) (1) − (2)	(4) Inflation Rate
Belgium	5.2	3.7	1.5	2.5
Canada	7.3	4.5	2.8	2.4
Denmark	9.7	4.2	5.5	4.5
France	10.5	5.3	5.2	4.8
Germany	9.0	6.2	2.8	2.6
Ireland	6.2	2.8	3.4	3.4
Italy	12.3	5.3	7.0	3.4
Japan	15.5	10.3	5.2	3.7
Netherlands	6.2	5.3	0.9	4.1
Norway	5.7	4.3	1.4	3.5
Sweden	4.2	4.2	0.0	3.7
U.K.	3.3	3.1	0.2	3.2
U.S.	3.1	4.0	−0.9	2.2

correspond to the ranking in order of rates of inflation. The velocity of circulation of money clearly did not remain constant in most of our countries over the period in question; nor did it change in the same way in each country. This is confirmed more directly in Table 5.14. which shows the behaviour of the income velocity of circulation of money in the main O.E.C.D. countries.

We can distinguish between three groups of countries: those in which the velocity of circulation of money remained broadly constant in the period up to 1968 − Canada, Denmark, France, Germany, Ireland; those in which it fell − Italy, Japan; and those in which it rose − Belgium, Netherlands, Norway, Sweden, U.K. and the U.S. The interesting thing to note from the tables is the apparent negative relationship between the rate of increase of money supply and the velocity of circulation of money: in countries where money supply increased fastest the velocity of circulation fell; in those in which the former rose less fast, the velocity of circulation rose. Rates of inflation of the different countries were however not greatly different. There is some presumption therefore that the factors underlying the monetary side of the 'equation of exchange' (MV = PO) adjusted to the factors underlying the price and output variables of the real side of the equation rather than the other way round.[4]

Table 5.14. O.E.C.D. INCOME VELOCITY OF MONEY

	54	55	56	57	58	59	60	61	62	63	64	65	66	67	68	69	70	71
Belgium	2.33	2.36	2.44	2.58	2.46	2.46	2.56	2.53	2.53	2.49	2.60	2.64	2.67	2.77	2.74	2.96	3.04	3.03
Canada	5.11	5.23	5.97	5.99	5.48	6.01	5.94	5.46	5.73	5.99	6.00	5.79	6.03	5.62	5.41	6.25	5.93	5.07
Denmark	3.95	3.99	4.09	4.17	3.82	3.83	4.04	4.03	4.15	3.89	4.05	4.06	3.89	3.92	3.67	3.72	4.16	5.07
France	3.03	2.88	2.90	2.98	3.28	3.28	3.18	2.99	2.83	2.77	2.84	2.78	2.81	2.89	2.94	3.48	3.50	3.47
Germany	5.99	6.21	6.46	6.29	5.93	5.73	6.47	6.25	6.34	6.31	6.23	6.37	6.63	6.08	6.11	6.45	6.66	6.54
Ireland	3.27	3.37	3.43	3.31	3.45	3.56	3.17	3.16	3.10	2.89	3.18	3.27	3.27	3.29	3.48	3.74	3.93	4.25
Italy	3.30	3.33	3.35	3.42	3.32	3.09	2.98	2.85	2.70	2.72	2.76	2.55	2.43	2.32	2.23	2.11	1.85	1.68
Japan	3.87	3.69	3.58	3.92	3.62	3.49	3.74	3.90	3.71	3.18	3.32	3.10	3.13	3.23	3.42	3.30	3.33	2.86
Netherlands	3.02	3.10	3.50	3.88	3.50	3.58	3.74	3.67	3.68	3.65	3.97	4.00	4.09	4.22	4.14	4.37	4.38	4.28
Norway	3.48	3.62	3.96	4.23	4.10	4.18	4.21	4.38	4.38	4.49	4.67	4.80	4.86	4.98	4.61	4.61	4.72	4.75
Sweden	6.08	6.51	6.70	7.07	7.28	7.12	6.81	6.87	6.85	6.79	7.00	7.38	7.41	7.38	8.25	9.31	9.53	9.39
U.K.	2.92	3.18	3.42	3.68	3.74	3.63	3.85	4.03	4.03	4.14	4.36	4.51	4.82	4.72	4.88	5.20	5.21	5.00
U.S.	2.69	2.87	2.99	3.18	3.08	3.32	3.47	3.47	3.65	3.67	3.81	3.92	4.23	4.16	4.17	4.33	4.37	4.42

Source: International Financial Statistics, I.M.F.

Table 5.15. O.E.C.D. QUASI-MONEY SUPPLY (1954 = 100)

	54	55	56	57	58	59	60	61	62	63	64	65	66	67	68	69	70	71	72	73
Belgium	100	111	109	114	129	154	181	222	240	275	301	351	406	499	571	704	759	894	1080	1328
Canada	100	108	115	117	131	132	138	146	152	162	171	186	196	225	261	288	319	341	382	489
Denmark	100	104	111	118	132	148	162	175	190	212	234	252	284	311	347	376	410	448	508	589
France	100	118	138	224	241	318	529	688	818	859	1012	1188	2165	3370	4182	5258	6559	8600	10665	13118
Germany	100	114	134	166	196	236	271	302	344	397	460	537	627	725	880	1002	1122	1305	1513	1755
Ireland	100	101	102	105	109	113	119	127	136	136	145	154	172	199	242	273	310	338	369	435
Italy	100	118	139	162	195	226	264	310	364	413	455	526	609	685	768	821	796	893	1055	1370
Japan	100	121	151	188	231	285	351	436	525	608	708	823	800	815	943	1106	1293	1561	1947	2278
Netherlands	100	134	144	155	179	210	256	282	317	357	400	445	488	573	645	733	779	877	909	1202
Norway	100	107	116	119	130	138	148	157	167	180	196	218	238	264	293	327	380	431	477	531
Sweden	100	104	111	121	134	149	154	161	177	191	207	214	229	263	322	338	347	387	444	519
United Kingdom	100	93	97	110	115	117	124	130	135	135	147	168	183	211	235	250	274	304	440	654
United States	100	103	108	120	134	140	148	168	199	228	256	297	320	368	412	390	470	564	650	754

Source: International Financial Statistics, I.M.F.

Table 5.16 . O.E.C.D. INCOME VELOCITY OF MONEY AND QUASI-MONEY

	54	55	56	57	58	59	60	61	62	63	64	65	66	67	68	69	70	71
Belgium	2.07	2.08	2.16	2.28	2.15	2.11	2.15	2.08	2.07	2.02	2.10	2.10	2.09	2.08	2.02	2.08	2.14	2.09
Canada	2.48	2.52	2.77	2.81	2.51	2.77	2.74	2.61	2.72	2.86	2.91	2.88	3.03	2.83	2.70	2.88	2.77	2.59
Denmark	2.02	2.03	2.06	2.08	1.92	1.92	1.96	1.98	2.05	1.94	2.01	2.05	1.98	1.99	1.91	1.97	2.09	n.a.
France	2.94	2.79	2.80	2.82	3.06	3.01	2.85	2.65	2.49	2.45	2.47	2.39	2.35	2.25	2.21	2.44	2.37	2.22
Germany	3.34	3.32	3.28	3.03	2.80	2.60	2.82	2.76	2.69	2.56	2.47	2.40	2.29	2.02	1.90	1.90	1.94	1.86
Ireland	1.48	1.55	1.57	1.55	1.58	1.63	1.56	1.56	1.55	1.55	1.68	1.70	1.66	1.62	1.60	1.66	1.70	1.78
Italy	2.18	2.14	2.08	2.05	1.92	1.77	1.69	1.62	1.54	1.55	1.56	1.44	1.36	1.31	1.26	1.24	1.21	1.12
Japan	1.71	1.59	1.48	1.46	1.27	1.18	1.50	1.56	1.45	1.31	1.34	1.26	1.24	1.27	1.32	1.30	1.31	1.17
Netherlands	2.53	2.59	2.88	3.07	2.73	2.67	2.69	2.67	2.63	2.61	2.80	2.82	2.86	2.78	2.66	2.71	2.83	2.81
Norway	1.59	1.61	1.72	1.75	1.69	1.70	1.70	1.75	1.77	1.79	1.84	1.85	1.86	1.86	1.77	1.73	1.74	1.73
Sweden	2.47	2.63	2.73	2.73	2.61	2.46	2.58	2.70	2.66	2.64	2.72	2.88	2.91	2.79	2.72	2.89	3.08	2.99
U.K.	1.95	2.16	2.30	2.36	2.37	2.37	2.46	2.54	2.55	2.65	2.74	2.74	2.82	2.68	2.69	2.79	2.80	2.73
U.S.	2.01	2.14	2.21	2.28	2.16	2.30	2.34	2.27	2.26	2.20	2.20	2.17	2.28	2.17	2.15	2.33	2.19	2.08

Source: International Financial Statistics, I.M.F.

This conclusion is not greatly qualified if we observe the behaviour of the income velocity of circulation of money including *quasi-money* (Tables 5.15 and 5.16). In nearly all countries quasi-money supply grew at a faster rate (in some countries at a much faster rate) than money supply more narrowly defined, and in all countries apart from Canada and Ireland the ratio of quasi-money supply to current price GDP rose over the period. The income velocity of money plus quasi-money tended to rise in the U.K., Ireland and Belgium, and fall in France, Germany and Japan. In other countries it remained broadly unchanged. As with the income velocity of money itself, there seems to be no connection with relative rates of inflation.

Interest rates

In all countries interest rates rose fairly steadily from the early 1960s onwards (see Table 5.17. and Figure 5.4.). We would of course expect interest rates to rise in countries where money supply growth was being restrained and in which near-money assets were being substituted for monetary ones, i.e. in which the velocity of circulation of money was rising. The Scandinavian countries, Belgium, the U.K. and the U.S. are cases in point. But the coincidence of fast money supply growth, falling velocity of circulation and rising interest rates in Italy and Japan is less easily explained.

In nearly all countries we are examining the rate of increase of money supply and quasi-money supply increased sharply after 1968; at the same time, with the exception of Italy and Japan where it continued to fall, the velocity of circulation of money narrowly defined also rose. Real GDP growth rates, averaged over the period 1968-1973, probably rose a little, but in nowhere near the same proportion as the acceleration in the rate of increase of money supply. Monetarists, at any rate, will not be surprised that rates of inflation generally also accelerated. We return to this topic in Chapter 10.

Table 5.17. O.E.C.D. INTER

	1958	1959	1960	1961	1962	1963	196
BELGIUM							
Exchange rate per US $	49.84	49.94	49.70	49.78	49.75	49.83	49.6
Call money rate	1.41	1.47	2.79	2.56	2.13	2.28	3.3
Government bond yield	5.55	4.99	5.48	5.90	5.24	4.98	5.5
CANADA							
Exchange rate per US $	0.9641	0.9528	0.9962	1.0431	1.0778	1.0809	1.0
Treasury bill rate	2.29	4.81	3.32	2.82	4.00	3.57	3.7
Government bond yield	4.22	5.14	5.26	5.08	5.09	5.07	5.1
DENMARK							
Exchange rate per US $	6.906	6.908	6.906	6.886	6.902	6.911	6.
Discount rate	4.50	5.00	5.50	6.50	6.50	5.50	6.
Government bond yield	5.24	5.32	5.76	6.02	6.32	6.44	6.
FRANCE							
Exchange rate per US $	4.906	4.909	4.903	4.900	4.900	4.902	4.
Call money rate	6.49	4.07	4.08	3.65	3.61	3.98	4.
Government bond yield	5.68	5.27	5.15	5.07	5.02	4.97	5.
GERMANY							
Exchange rate per US $	4.178	4.170	4.171	3.996	3.998	3.975	3.
Call money rate	3.08	2.69	4.55	2.94	2.66	2.97	3.
Public authority bond yield	6.6	5.8	6.4	5.9	5.9	6.0	6.
IRELAND							
Exchange rate per US $	2.8031	2.8006	2.8044	2.8088	2.8031	2.7975	2.
Discount rate	4.25	4.25	4.62	5.56	3.86	3.98	6.
Government bond yield	5.61	5.10	5.45	6.04	6.06	5.48	5.
ITALY							
Exchange rate per US $	624.00	620.60	620.60	620.60	620.60	622.38	624
Discount rate	3.50	3.50	3.50	3.50	3.50	3.50	3
Government bond yield	6.16	5.43	5.24	5.18	5.26	5.43	6

ES AND EXCHANGE RATES

	1966	1967	1968	1969	1970	1971	1972	1973
4	50.05	49.63	50.14	49.67	49.68	44.76	44.06	38.73
4	3.88	3.19	2.84	5.40	6.25	3.70	2.51	4.04
)	6.62	6.70	6.54	7.20	7.81	7.35	7.04	7.35
750	1.0838	1.0809	1.0728	1.0731	1.0103	1.0022	0.9956	0.9997
7	4.99	4.64	6.27	7.19	5.99	3.56	3.56	5.15
2	5.69	5.94	6.75	7.58	7.91	6.95	7.23	7.53
)1	6.916	7.462	7.501	7.492	7.489	7.062	6.847	5.983
)	6.50	7.50	6.00	9.00	9.00	7.50	7.00	7.75
7	7.86	8.17	8.43	9.34	10.57	10.67	10.37	11.24
)2	4.952	4.908	4.948	5.558	5.520	5.224	5.125	4.401
3	4.79	4.77	6.21	8.97	8.67	5.84	4.95	8.09
2	5.40	5.66	5.86	7.64	8.06	7.74	7.35	8.00
)6	3.977	3.999	4.000	3.690	3.648	3.268	3.202	2.596
2	5.34	3.35	2.58	4.81	8.67	6.06	4.30	10.18
	8.1	7.0	6.5	6.8	8.3	8.0	7.9	9.2
)31	2.7900	2.4063	2.3844	2.4007	2.3938	2.5522	2.3455	2.449
3	6.87	7.78	7.17	8.25	7.31	4.81	8.00	10.00
3	6.96	6.99	7.36	8.84	9.56	9.71	9.64	11.08
)	624.45	623.86	623.50	625.50	623.00	594.00	582.50	584.64
)	3.50	3.50	3.50	3.75	5.50	4.50	4.00	5.25
3	6.54	6.61	6.70	6.85	9.01	8.34	7.47	7.40

Table

	1958	1959	1960	1961	1962	1963	1
JAPAN							
Exchange rate per US $	359.7	359.2	358.3	361.8	358.2	362.0	358
Call money rate							
Discount rate	7.30	7.30	6.94	7.30	6.57	5.84	6
NETHERLANDS							
Exchange rate per US $	3.775	3.770	3.770	3.600	3.600	3.600	3
Treasury bill rate	3.01	1.85	2.14	1.12	1.84	1.94	3
Government bond yield	4.32	4.12	4.20	3.91	4.21	4.22	4
NORWAY							
Exchange rate per US $	7.15	7.16	7.15	7.14	7.15	7.16	7
Discount rate	3.50	3.50	3.50	3.50	3.50	3.50	3
Government bond yield	4.77	4.62	4.58	4.64	4.66	4.64	4
SWEDEN							
Exchange rate per US $	5.180	5.185	5.180	5.185	5.188	5.200	5
Discount rate	4.50	4.50	5.00	5.00	4.00	4.00	5
Government bond yield	4.33	4.28	4.56	4.55	4.40	4.45	4
UNITED KINGDOM							
Exchange rate per US $	2.8031	2.8006	2.8044	2.8088	2.8031	2.7975	2
Treasury bills	4.56	3.37	4.88	5.13	4.18	3.66	4
Government bond yield	4.98	4.82	5.43	6.22	6.00	5.59	6
UNITED STATES							
Treasury bills	1.84	3.42	2.94	2.38	2.78	3.16	3
Government bond yield	3.43	4.07	4.02	3.90	3.93	4.00	4

t.

5	1966	1967	1968	1969	1970	1971	1972	1973
	362.5	361.9	357.7	357.8	357.6	314.8	302.2	269.2
8	5.84	6.39	7.88	7.70	8.29	6.42	4.72	6.40
11	3.614	3.596	3.606	3.624	3.597	3.254	3.226	2.730
7	4.74	4.57	4.46	5.55	5.97	4.34	2.16	3.54
1	6.24	6.00	6.22	7.04	7.76	7.05	6.67	7.13
5	7.16	7.15	7.15	7.15	7.14	6.71	6.65	5.61
0	3.50	3.50	3.50	4.50	4.50	4.50	4.50	4.50
5	5.00	5.00	4.94	5.12	6.29	6.40	6.26	6.17
80	5.180	5.165	5.180	5.170	5.170	4.865	4.748	4.351
0	6.00	6.00	5.00	7.00	7.00	5.00	5.00	5.00
1	6.57	6.06	6.31	6.98	7.39	7.23	7.29	7.38
19	2.7900	2.4069	2.3844	2.4006	2.3938	2.5522	2.3481	2.4491
	6.10	5.82	7.09	7.64	7.01	5.57	5.54	9.33
2	6.94	6.80	7.55	9.04	9.22	8.90	8.91	10.71
	4.88	4.33	5.35	6.69	6.44	4.34	4.07	6.88
	4.66	4.85	5.26	6.12	6.58	5.74	5.63	6.30

FIGURE 5.4.

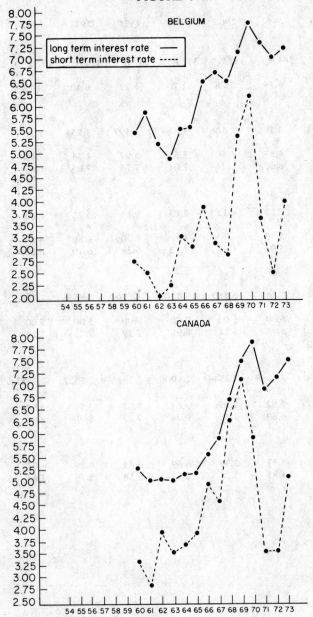

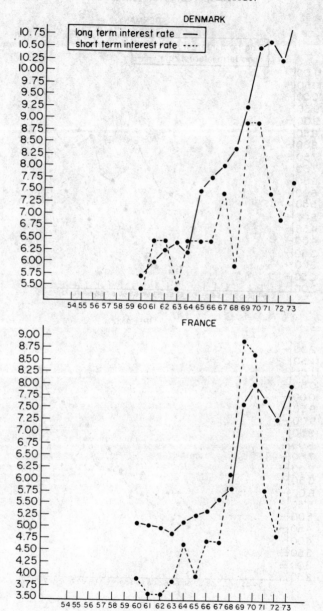

GERMANY

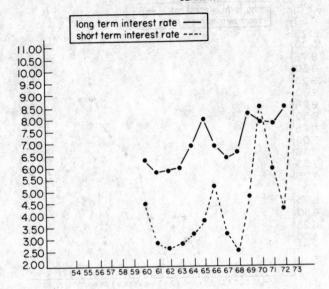

IRELAND

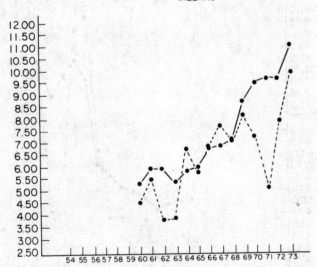

nflation Fig 5-4

ITALY

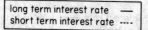

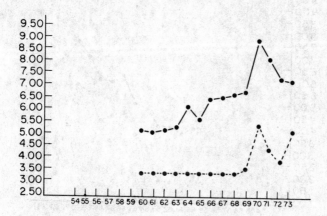

JAPAN

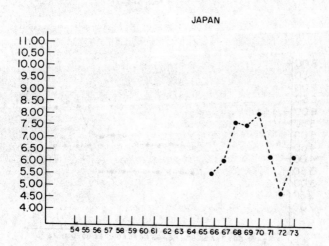

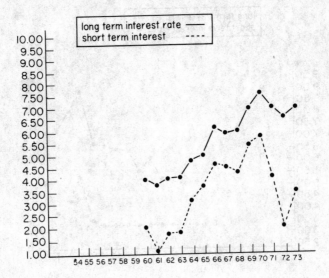

NETHERLANDS

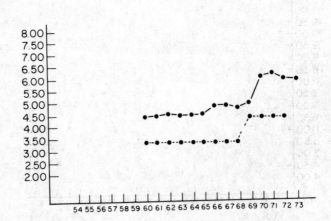

NORWAY

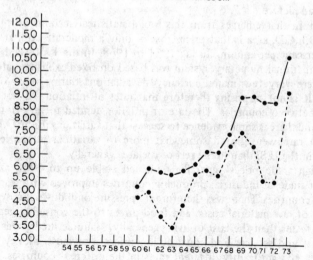

SWEDEN

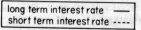

long term interest rate ——
short term interest rate ----

UNITED KINGDOM

UNITED STATES

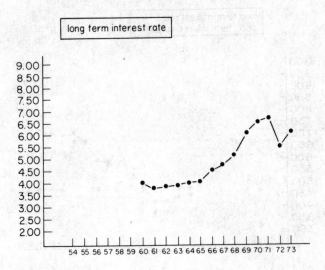

The broad picture

The picture that emerges from this broad statistical account of inflation in the O.E.C.D. area is that prices rose at only a moderate rate, at about three per cent per annum, during 1954 to 1968. In the 1950s and 1960s the international monetary system was based on fixed exchange rates and there were very few major currency devaluations during most of that period. It is not surprising therefore that rates of inflation did not differ greatly between countries. The rate of inflation tended to vary from year to year and there is some evidence to suggest that variations in the O.E.C.D. inflation rate were geared somewhat more to variations in the level of activity in the U.S. than in the rest of the area generally.

Foreign trade prices generally remained stable up to 1968 and the terms of trade of industrial producing countries improved with respect to primary countries. There was therefore no pressure on industrial costs from the side of raw material costs, and food prices to the consumer generally rose no faster than the cost of living generally. Manufactured goods prices rose least and services and construction prices rose most. Money wages increased at significantly different rates in the different countries, but in general they rose faster in countries where labour productivity rose faster. Finally there were also wide differences in the rate of increase of money supply, but here again output tended to rise faster in those countries where money supply rose faster, although in some of them the velocity of circulation tended to fall. Interest rates rose fairly steadily throughout the period, reaching levels around six or seven per cent in countries whose inflation were around or above the O.E.C.D. average and five or six per cent for those with lower rates of inflation. This suggests that the real rate of interest was of the order of three per cent or so.

After 1968, the picture changed drastically. Inflation began to accelerate; foreign trade prices began to rise as fast, if not faster than, domestic prices, and food prices to the consumer rose faster than most others. The rate of increase of money wages rose sharply, although the rate of increase of productivity showed little change as compared with the earlier period. Money supply also began to rise at a much faster rate. The background to the post-1968 period is examined in Chapter 10.

6
The Contribution of Government to Inflation in the O.E.C.D Countries

General considerations

A widespread view, which is perhaps held more strongly by non-economists than by economists, holds that government spending and government policies generally have been the mainspring behind the almost continuous rise in prices which has taken place since the end of World War Two. This view takes many forms. Leaving aside the rather naive version that, irrespective of the way in which it is financed, a pound spent by government is more inflationary than a pound spent by a private citizen, the view is supported in a number of different ways. There is the simple monetary argument, namely that the government has deliberately created, or allowed to be created, money at too fast a rate in relation to the underlying forces determining the real growth of the economy and the private sector's demand for money consistent with that growth. Some comment on this view has been given at the beginning of Chapter 2 and reference has been made in Chapter 5 to the actual growth of money supply in O.E.C.D. countries in the period 1954-68. Secondly, there is the view that government spending has contributed in a fundamental fashion to chronic postwar excess demand. Thirdly, there is the view that accepts the argument that if government expenditure is financed by an appropriate level of taxation no net demand on the community's resources will be exerted, but maintains that the high level of taxation which is required to neutralise government spending is itself inflationary, since by deterring effort and incentive it significantly reduces available output. Finally, there is the view which stresses the importance of government full employment objectives and policies *per se*.

These arguments, of course, are not unconnected. The creation of money for instance is one method by which government spending can be, and is, financed; but it is generally true of the governments of the advanced industrial countries that when taking decisions about the appropriate level of the money stock, they are less concerned with the choice between financing expenditure by money creation and financing it with taxation than with the appropriate level of interest rates and liquidity in the economy which they regard as necessary to maintain full employment and growth. Whatever might be true over the period as a whole, it is evident that governments have attempted to manipulate spending and taxation in a counter-cyclical way to absorb an excess or substitute for a deficiency

Table 6.1. Private Gross Fixed Asset Formation* as a Percentage of GDP at Factor Cost

	1954	1955	1956	1957	1958	1959	1960	1961	1962	1963	1964	1965	1966	1967	1968	1969	1970	1971	1972
Belgium																			
Canada	21.15	21.16	24.80	25.76	23.74	22.09	20.68	19.04	18.38	18.54	20.66	22.03	22.94	21.70	20.06	20.32	19.91	20.49	20.33
Denmark	17.01	15.60	14.67	15.56	15.79	17.67	18.24	19.08	19.37	18.64	20.70	20.02	20.00	20.14	18.83	19.62	19.67	18.84	—
France	16.83	17.87	18.22	19.70	19.55	21.27	21.00	22.24	22.66	24.31	24.88	25.32	25.23	24.67	25.66	25.89	25.86	26.02	
Germany	21.49	13.16	23.02	21.83	22.01	23.16	23.81	25.27	25.58	24.31	25.63	25.32	22.26	21.94	23.39	25.04	25.70	25.41	
Italy	18.65	19.34	19.82	20.98	19.68	20.09	21.37	22.43	23.09	23.56	21.17	18.30	17.74	18.94	19.39	20.48	21.03	19.60	18.50
Netherlands	19.84	21.37	20.92	20.34	17.72	18.46	18.88	22.52	21.96	20.93	22.68	22.50	23.72	23.71	24.01	21.67	23.28	23.25	21.88
Norway	29.96	30.01	27.21	28.34	31.81	28.81	27.67	29.25	28.41	26.42	27.05	27.61	29.10	25.23	22.38	25.75	29.34	30.84	
U.K.	10.68	11.65	12.59	13.12	13.40	13.67	14.37	15.57	14.92	14.47	15.67	15.86	15.59	15.67	15.72	15.80	15.79	15.61	15.67
U.S.	16.45	17.09	16.61	15.95	15.39	15.77	15.31	14.58	14.98	14.92	15.20	15.66	15.38	15.20	14.79	14.97	15.34	14.56	15.11

*Including nationalized industries.

of private sector demand. How far their efforts to stabilise the economy have been successful is a matter of dispute.[1]

The view that postwar full employment has been specifically due to Keynesian-type full employment policies actively pursued by governments has been recently challenged by Professor R. Mathews, at any rate as far as the U.K. is concerned.[2] In his view, there are two main reasons which explain the transition from the widespread unemployment situation of the 1930s to the full employment position characteristic of the 1950s and 1960s. The first is a significant trend rise in the scarcity of labour relatively to capital which, among other things, reflects the end of the long term shift of labour from agriculture to industry: this obviously cannot be attributed to Keynesian-type full employment policies. The second is a major rise in the level of aggregate demand relative to aggregate supply which is due not in any direct fashion to fiscal policies but to a substantial recovery of private investment expenditure. In the U.K. private gross investment expenditure averaged less than ten per cent of G.D.P. in the 1930s but over 14 per cent in the 1950s and nearer 16 per cent in the 1960s; similar high levels of investment expenditure can be found in other O.E.C.D. countries as well. (Table 6.1.) Professor Mathews does not deny that government spending has in fact been much higher in the postwar period than in the 1930s but he points out that taxation has also been much higher. Even allowing for a 'balanced budget' multiplier effect,[3] the net fiscal demand effect, in his view, contributed very little to the higher postwar level of aggregate demand. However it is possible that Professor Mathews may have underestimated the direct expansionary impact of fiscal policy: some evidence for believing this will be presented later on in this chapter. Moreover, he may also be giving insufficient weight to indirect effects, such as those operating through the distribution of income and the existence of the welfare state which may have had an important effect on the propensity to save.

As far as private investment expenditure is concerned, Professor Mathews believes there were powerful autonomous forces inducing this at the end of the war. The real capital stock of the U.K. economy and of European economies in general was then very low, partly as a result of the war itself during which only essential replacement investment was carried out, and partly because in the U.K. at any rate, there had been no significant domestic investment boom in the half century preceding 1945. Moreover, in all countries there was a massive pent-up demand for consumer durables and housing which provided the basis for a high rate of investment in productive facilities. The marginal efficiency of investment could, therefore, be expected to be high. Professor Mathews agrees that government policy contributed something to this. For much of the postwar period, in other countries as well as the U.K., nominal money interest rates were kept low and real rates even lower: moreover many governments, including that of the U.K., encouraged private sector investment by direct financial incentives in the shape of investment grants and allowances and favourable treatment of depreciation for tax purposes. This was certainly the case in the late 1950s and the 1960s when, after the immediate post-war pent-up demand had exhausted itself, governments generally began to pursue policies for faster growth. In general, however, it is probably true to say that for much of the postwar period governments were as much, if not more, concerned to restrain aggregate demand as to increase it, in the interests of balances of payments and/or of restraining inflation.

This does not deny that government policies had an important indirect effect on aggregate demand. It would seem reasonable to believe that the sustained rate of investment in the postwar period was underpinned by a climate of expectations of continued growth and full employment that had been established in the minds of entrepreneurs early on in the postwar period as a result of well publicised political commitments to such policies: moreover, investment and growth tend to induce more investment still. The firm commitment of governments to maintain full employment was an important element in the establishment and maintenance of these expectations: it was buttressed by an obvious unwillingness of governments to push demand restraint policies, often made necessary by precarious balance of payments difficulties or inflation, so far that full employment was threatened. Thus, it is understandable that there was widespread belief and confidence among entrepreneurs, at least until the late 1960s, that governments would not permit unemployment to rise more than margin-ally. Macroeconomic policy did not succeed in preventing fluctuations in rates of growth: indeed it may have contributed to short run instability; but booms started from already high employment and demand levels, and periods of slower growth ended well before unemployment became at all significant — at least in inter-war terms.

The fact that apart from relatively small fluctuations in rates of growth, aggregate demand was stabilized at a high absolute level, either directly or indirectly by deliberate government short-term economic policy, has undoubtedly been a significant factor underlying the sustained postwar inflation as well. Since downswings in activity were never allowed to proceed to the point where unemployment and deficiency of demand became more than marginally significant, there was never any sustained downward pressure on prices: recession never reached the point where prices had to give. Indeed, they tended to rise even when the rate of growth of output was falling, although usually at a slower rate than when the rate of growth of aggregate output was above trend. Thus postwar inflation had a persistent and long-run character.

While this demand element was a significant factor underlying postwar inflation, the major inflationary impact of government operations and full employment policies has probably been exerted through costs. This effect has taken two forms, as described in Chapter 2. In the first place, a govern-ment commitment to full employment, if firmly believed in by both unions and entrepreneurs and if accompanied by policies designed to stimulate growth, obviously creates an environment favourable to wage demands and wage concessions. It is not surprising, therefore, that, even when excess demand pressures have been temporarily absent, money wages and prices have shown a long term tendency to rise. Certainly there have been variations in the rate at which money wages and prices have risen during the postwar period and these have been related, at least until very recently, to variations in the state of demand for labour;[4] but while full or near full employment has existed there has been a persistent autonomous upward pressure on wages which has acted broadly independently of demand.

The second manner in which labour costs and, therefore, prices have been affected by government operation is through so called 'productivity inflation'.[5] Because of the nature of its product and techniques of production the government sector tends to be labour intensive and subject to rather slow productivity growth as compared with industries in the private sector. Thus the relative expansion of the government sector in terms of labour employed, which has been a feature of the postwar period in many countries, tends to hold back the growth of average productivity in the economy as a whole as compared with the growth of productivity in the more highly technological industries and sectors of the economy. In part, the inflationary effect of this trend is disguised since the output of the sector on the whole is not sold in the market place, but financed by general tax revenue. However, insofar as indirect taxation is resorted to, the price level is raised so that inflation results as a direct consequence of rising labour costs in the government sector.

Government policies may have contributed to postwar inflation in yet other ways which are difficult to quantify. It is often argued that the creation of the welfare state in all the developed countries of the West, and policies aimed at a more equal distribution of income and wealth, have significantly lowered the propensity to save. This, in conjunction with the higher level of private investment expenditure of the postwar era probably goes a substantial way to explaining the high level of aggregate demand as compared with the interwar years. However, the direct impact of government expenditure itself cannot be ignored, and in the remainder of this chapter some attempt will be made to assess the *net* impact on aggregate demand of government expenditure and taxation in the O.E.C.D. countries for which the necessary data exists.

The macroeconomic effects of government expenditure and taxation

That there has been a massive rise in the scale of government expenditure and taxation in the developed countries of the Western world in the postwar era can hardly be denied. It has been estimated[6] that in the interwar years government expenditure on goods and services averaged about 10 to 14 per cent of gross national product: in the postwar period, after allowing

Table 6.2. O.E.C.D. GENERAL GOVERNMENT REVENUE AND EXPENDITURE (PERCENTAGE OF GDP AT MARKET PRICES)

(Annual average)

	1950-68	1950-53	1954-59	1960-65	1966-68	1969-72
BELGIUM[3,5]						
Tax revenue	26.8[1]	23.0	23.8	27.6	32.5	34.6
Expenditure	27.3	25.4	24.9	27.8	31.5	33.1
CANADA[4]						
Tax revenue	24.0	23.4	23.4	25.6	29.4	31.3
Expenditure	28.3	24.0	26.9	30.5	32.4	35.8
DENMARK[3]						
Tax revenue	25.9	21.4	24.3	27.0	32.6	38.9[7]
Expenditure	26.2	21.4	24.5	27.6	33.5	38.9
FRANCE						
Tax revenue	34.0	31.2	33.2	35.3	36.8	36.9
Expenditure	34.7	33.3	34.4	34.6	37.3	36.5
GERMANY						
Tax revenue	33.5	31.9	32.7	34.7	34.9	36.0
Expenditure	32.9	30.3	30.4	34.8	37.8	37.4
IRELAND						
Tax revenue	—	—	—	23.9	27.9	31.0
Expenditure	—	—	—	30.7	34.0	38.1
ITALY						
Tax revenue	26.0	20.7	25.0	27.9	29.8	30.2
Expenditure	30.5	26.3	29.4	31.4	35.2	37.6
JAPAN[3,5]						
Tax revenue	18.7[2]	20.2	18.2	18.8	18.7	20.0
Expenditure	—	—	—	19.0	19.9	19.0[6]
NETHERLANDS[4]						
Tax revenue	31.6	30.8	29.1	32.0	37.0	40.9
Expenditure	35.8	29.2	34.2	38.0	43.8	45.5
NORWAY						
Tax revenue	32.2	29.0	30.6	33.5	36.9	43.3
Expenditure	31.8	26.5	29.7	33.8	37.6	42.1
SWEDEN[3,5]						
Tax revenue	31.2	24.3	28.2	34.0	40.6	41.7
Expenditure	28.5	23.7	27.1	29.8	35.1	44.0
UNITED KINGDOM[4]						
Tax revenue	30.1	32.3	28.5	28.8	33.0	35.9
Expenditure	33.5	34.3	31.5	33.3	37.1	40.1
UNITED STATES[3,4]						
Tax revenue	26.6	25.2	25.5	27.6	28.9	30.2
Expenditure	27.5	25.0	26.7	28.4	30.7	33.0

Notes   *Definitions*   (a) General government includes central and local government.

                              (b) Tax revenue is the summation of direct taxes on households and corporations, contributions to social security, and indirect taxes.

                              (c) Expenditure is the summation of current expenditure on goods and services and transfers (including interest on national debt and subsidies, but not net transfers to the rest of the world), gross fixed asset formation, and net capital transfers to private sector.

              Other   1. 1953-68
                                2. 1952-68
                                3. Excludes net capital transfers to private sector
                                4. Includes increase in stocks
                                5. Excludes gross fixed asset formation
                                6. 1969-70
                                7. 1969-71

Source: **O.E.C.D.**, *National Accounts of O.E.C.D. Countries,* 1950-68, 1960-71 and 1961-72.

for the rundown of military expenditure from its postwar high, such expenditure was typically 15 to 22 per cent of GNP, an increase of something like 50 per cent. Transfer payments were also considerably higher as was government tax revenue, which varied between 20 and 35 per cent of GNP as compared with 12 to 21 per cent in the inter war period (see Tables 6.2. and 6.3.) In two countries, the U.S. and the U.K., in which expenditure on goods and services amounted to over 20 per cent and tax revenue 30 per cent or more of GNP, the higher level of defence expenditure was an important factor: but in all countries there was a major expansion of social and welfare expenditure in the fields of education, health and public services in general. This reflected the increasing responsibility of all governments in these areas.

It is well recognised in macroeconomic theory that government expenditure has an expansionary influence on economic activity. Direct payment to civil servants and purchase of goods and services from private firms raise money income of households, leading to further expenditure on consumption goods and services in the well-known multiplier fashion. Transfer payments of a social welfare nature, or interest on national debt, also raise disposable (after tax) incomes of households, increasing the demand for consumption goods and producing multiplier effects on income, although again for well-known reasons the multiplier effect of an increase in transfer payments tends to be smaller than that of an increase in expenditure on goods and services, including payments to civil servants. Taxation, on the other hand, by reducing disposable incomes of households and the retained profits of firms tends to reduce expenditure on goods and services and produces downward multiplier effects on the economy. Moreover, in addition to these downward multiplier effects the manner in which a government budget deficit or surplus (i.e. total expenditure less total tax revenue) is financed is also important, since this has an important influence on interest rates and the money supply which in turn bear' on private spending and saving decisions. In general, faced with a given budget deficit to be financed, the government must choose between allowing interest rates to rise sufficiently to induce the non-bank private sector to take up new government debt, or allowing the money supply to rise instead. The latter course of action probably adds to the expansionary influence of the deficit, while the former may lessen it if private sector expenditure is at all sensitive to interest rates.

It might be thought that if the government balances its budget, i.e. keeps tax revenue in line with expenditure, the net impact on economic activity would be zero, but this is not necessarily or even generally so. In its simplest form the balanced budget multiplier theorem holds that the income multiplier associated with an equal increase in expenditure and taxation is equal to unity, i.e. national income rises by an amount equal to the rise in government expenditure. This implies that the level of expenditure and taxation, as well as the balance between them, is important. The theorem, however, depends on some rather artificial assumptions, in particular that the propensity to consume is the same for taxpayers, income earners in general and recipients of government transfer payments, so that distribution effects can be ignored; and it is based on the fact that whereas an increase in government expenditure on goods and services initially (that is before the multiplier effects) raises national income by an amount equal to itself, an increase in taxation tends to have a smaller initial downward effect on aggregate demand and income owing to the fact that taxpayers would normally tend to reduce their saving as well as their consumption expenditure.

More realistically, the multiplier effect of a balanced increase in expenditure and taxation could be greater or less than unity, depending on the division of total expenditure between expenditure on goods and services and expenditure on transfers, and on the respective propensities to consume of the community as a whole, of income taxpayers and of transfer payment recipients respectively. With a progressive tax system, for instance, the propensity of taxpayers to consume might well be lower on average than the propensity of the community as a whole to consume, while the propensity of the beneficiaries of transfer payments to consume may be higher than that of the community as a whole although still less than unity. Moreover, it is necessary to distinguish between the effects of direct and indirect taxation. As indicated earlier, direct taxation reduces the disposable incomes of households and probably the retained profits of firms: consumption expenditure and possibly investment expenditure will therefore be affected, but so too will saving. The main effect of indirect taxation is, however, not to reduce monetary expenditure on consumption and investment goods, but to siphon off part of that expenditure to government revenue, so that producers do not receive all that consumers spend. For a given level of total final expenditure on goods and services, the money value and the real value of gross national product measured at factor cost is reduced. In this sense an increase in indirect taxes involves a deflationary impact on aggregate demand and on GDP at factor cost equal to itself. Of course, to the extent that producers pass indirect taxes forward to consumers, prices will rise: this, in fact, provides the basis on which real consumption may fall. Consumers could respond by raising their average propensity to consume so as to maintain real consumption despite the rise in price: alternatively, they may be induced to substitute saving for consumption. It remains true, however, that given the propensity to consume, a pound's worth of indirect taxation is more deflationary in the sense of reducing aggregate demand for output than is a pound's worth of direct taxation.[7]

Taking all these things into account, therefore, the size of the multiplier depends on the relative shares of expenditure on goods and services and of transfers in the increase in total government expenditure; on the distribution of the increase in total tax revenue between direct and indirect taxes; and on the progressiveness of the income tax system. Given an appropriate distribution of tax revenue between direct and indirect taxes, a rise in government expenditure which is accompanied by an even larger rise in tax revenue so as to produce a larger surplus or smaller deficit in the total account may still therefore have a net expansionary impact on aggregate demand and income.

Even with these complications the balanced (and *a fortiori* the unbalanced) budget multiplier analysis still ignores possible monetary and balance of payments effects of increases in government expenditure and taxation. As far as the former are concerned, a rise in money national income, induced, say, by a change in expenditure, increases the transactions demand for money, so that if the money stock is constant, interest rates will tend to rise. Investment expenditure may therefore be reduced and the propensity to save of the community may also be raised, thus causing income to rise less than would otherwise be the case. However, if flows of international capital are very sensitive to interest rate differentials, a rise in interest rates in the economy in which government expenditure is rising may be prevented or greatly attenuated; the monetary effect can then be ignored. On the other hand, the rise in income will certainly induce a rise in imports which by itself would reduce the size of the multiplier. Against this, however, activity in other countries would be stimulated by the rise in the first country's imports, as a result of which the first country's exports would also rise, offsetting in part its import leakage. It is clear, in other words, that the impact of government expenditure and taxation can only be analysed adequately in terms of a rather detailed model of an open economy.[8]

In the absence of such complex models, the net impact of government expenditure and taxation on the economy can only be assessed very approximately. To do so does not mean that we have to return to the very simplest budget multiplier models: it does mean that we have to ignore the monetary effects and some of the balance of payments effects.[9]

The concept of the multiplier is normally applied to *changes* in government expenditure and taxation. However, by stretching the underlying reasoning somewhat, the factors determining the net expansionary or deflationary impact on the economy of total government expenditure and tax revenue taken together can be indicated, and the net effect measured at least approximately. The following model will be used.

Let
Y = Gross domestic product at factor cost
I = Private capital formation
C = Private consumption
E = Exports
M = Imports
G = Total Government expenditure
T = Total Government Tax Revenue
R = Retained Business Profits (Saving)
g = share of expenditure on goods and services in G
t = share of transfer payments in G
u' = share of direct taxation in T
u'' = share of indirect taxation in T
c = marginal (=average) propensity to consume of the economy as a whole
c'' = marginal (=average) propensity to consume of income taxpayers (normally $c'' < c$)
c' = marginal (=average) propensity to consume of the recipients of government transfer payments (normally $c' > c$)
m = marginal (=average) propensity to import
r = marginal (=average) ratio of retained business profits to GDP at factor cost.

Then:

(i) $Y = I + E + G_g + C - Tu''$

(ii) $C = A + Yc - rYc - Tu'c'' + Gtc'$

(iii) $Y = I + E + Gg + A + Yc - rYc - Tu'c'' + Gtc' - mY - Tu''$

$$= \frac{I + E + Gg + A - Tu'c'' + Gtc' - Tu''}{1 - c(1 - r) + m}$$

Now let N_p and N_t be the *net* primary and *net* total impact respectively of government expenditure and taxation on national income.
Then:

(iv) .a. $N_p = G(g + tc') - T(u'c'' + u'')$

and

(iv) .b. $N_T = \dfrac{G(g + tc') - T(u'c'' + u'')}{1 - c(1 - r) + m}$

If $\bar{\alpha}$ is the *required* ratio of T to G such as to produce a zero (neutral) net impact of government expenditure and taxation on the economy, then

(v) $(g + tc') = \bar{\alpha}(u'c'' + u'')$

and $\bar{\alpha} = \dfrac{g + tc'}{u'c'' + u''}$

$\bar{\alpha}$ can clearly be equal to or greater or less than unity. It will tend towards being greater than unity the larger are g and u' and the smaller is c''. It will tend towards being unity or less the larger are t and u'' and the smaller is c'. In other words, the more government expenditure is directed towards goods and services and the less towards transfer payments, and the more government relies on a progressive income tax system to finance its expenditure, the larger must the budget surplus be to obtain a neutral (zero net) impact on economic activity.

In the remainder of this chapter we shall attempt to estimate $\bar{\alpha}$ (i.e. the *required* ratio of government tax revenue to government expenditure for obtaining a neutral impact on national income) for each country for which data exists and to compare it with *actual* ratio of revenue to expenditure for that country. The purpose will be to assess and compare the impact of government activity in O.E.C.D. countries in the postwar period, and to look for some connection with relative rates of inflation.

Estimation of net impact of government expenditure and taxation

The calculation of $\bar{\alpha}$ for each country is based on the ratio of government expenditure (g), on the ratios of direct and indirect tax revenue to total tax revenue (u', u''), and on the propensities to consume of various income earners (c, c', c''). Table 6.3 shows the structure of expenditure and taxation of the O.E.C.D. countries in the postwar period. It will be seen that the former shows quite marked differences between countries. In most countries, expenditure on goods and services averaged between one half and two thirds of total expenditure. It was particularly high in the U.S. at three-quarters, and relatively low at below a half in France and Belgium. In Italy the proportion fell from well above 50 per cent at the beginning of the period to well below 50 per cent at the end, but in all other countries despite year-to-year fluctuations there was little change in the period as a whole. *Current* expenditure generally composed four-fifths or more of total expenditure and *capital* expenditure one-fifth or less. There was, however, a significant rising trend in capital expenditure in many countries, representing the rising contribution of government to many forms of social capital (housing, roads), and also increased intervention in normally private sector productive activities.

The structure of taxation also showed significant differences. At one end of the scale the U.S. raised 60 per cent of its total tax revenue in the form of direct taxation and 40 per cent by indirect taxes: at the other

O.E.C.D. COUNTRIES: STRUCTURE OF GENERAL (CENTRAL PLUS LOCAL)
GOVERNMENT EXPENDITURE AND TAXATION

g = ratio of expenditure on goods and services to total expenditure
u = ratio of direct tax revenue to total tax revenue

		1950	1951	1952	1953	1954	1955	1956	1957	1958	1959	1960	1961	1962	1963	1964	1965	1966	1967	1968	Average 1950-68
Belgium	g	—	—	—	—	—	—	—	—	—	—	—	0.49	0.49	0.50	0.51	0.52	0.49	0.49	0.48	0.50
	u	—	—	—	—	—	0.37	0.38	0.37	0.36	0.38	0.37	0.38	0.37	0.38	0.37	0.38	0.40	0.40	0.41	0.38
Canada	g	0.60	0.66	0.68	0.63	0.66	0.67	0.68	0.64	0.63	0.61	0.60	0.60	0.59	0.59	0.59	0.60	0.61	0.59	0.57	0.63
	u	0.43	0.46	0.47	0.45	0.43	0.43	0.42	0.41	0.42	0.42	0.43	0.42	0.42	0.42	0.42	0.42	0.43	0.43	0.46	0.43
Denmark	g	0.61	0.61	0.62	0.62	0.65	0.64	0.66	0.64	0.64	0.65	0.65	0.64	0.66	0.66	0.66	0.65	0.65	0.64	0.64	0.64
	u	0.50	0.52	0.54	0.53	0.53	0.52	0.52	0.53	0.51	0.50	0.49	0.49	0.49	0.48	0.50	0.50	0.50	0.49	0.49	0.51
France	g	0.45	0.47	0.51	0.50	0.47	0.47	0.48	0.48	0.48	0.48	0.47	0.40	0.45	0.44	0.44	0.44	0.43	0.43	—	0.46
	u	0.24	0.22	0.21	0.22	0.22	0.21	0.24	0.25	0.26	0.28	0.27	0.26	0.26	0.27	0.28	0.27	0.27	0.29	—	0.25
Germany	g	0.53	0.56	0.56	0.55	0.54	0.55	0.54	0.50	0.49	0.52	0.53	0.53	0.54	0.55	0.55	0.54	0.53	0.52	—	0.54
	u	0.41	0.40	0.41	0.42	0.40	0.41	0.41	0.41	0.41	0.42	0.43	0.44	0.44	0.45	0.44	0.44	0.44	0.45	—	0.42
Ireland	g	—	—	—	—	—	0.54	0.55	0.56	0.54	0.54	0.52	0.54	0.54	0.55	0.55	0.54	0.52	0.50	—	0.54
	u	0.27	0.28	0.25	0.26	0.26	0.24	0.23	0.22	0.24	0.24	0.25	0.27	0.28	0.28	0.28	0.29	0.29	0.30	—	0.26
Italy	g	0.57	0.55	0.55	0.53	0.54	0.53	0.50	0.51	0.50	0.50	0.50	0.50	0.51	0.51	0.51	0.48	0.47	0.45	0.45	0.51
	u	0.33	0.34	0.35	0.35	0.35	0.34	0.35	0.37	0.37	0.36	0.36	0.38	0.38	0.40	0.40	0.40	0.40	0.41	—	0.37
Japan	g	—	—	—	—	—	—	—	—	—	0.75	0.75	0.76	0.76	0.75	0.75	0.73	0.71	0.70	—	0.74
	u	—	0.46	0.44	0.45	0.43	0.43	0.41	0.44	0.45	0.48	0.48	0.48	0.48	0.49	0.48	0.49	0.48	0.49	—	0.46
Netherlands	g	0.56	0.57	0.58	0.59	0.58	0.63	0.61	0.56	0.57	0.57	0.56	0.58	0.57	0.58	0.56	0.55	0.54	0.53	—	0.57
	u	0.40	0.40	0.46	0.42	0.37	0.37	0.41	0.45	0.46	0.46	0.46	0.45	0.45	0.45	0.46	0.46	0.46	0.44	—	0.44
United Kingdom	g	0.59	0.64	0.67	0.68	0.66	0.66	0.66	0.64	0.64	0.64	0.63	0.63	0.60	0.64	0.60	0.64	0.62	0.60	—	0.64
	u	0.47	0.46	0.49	0.47	0.47	0.46	0.47	0.48	0.47	0.45	0.46	0.46	0.48	0.45	0.45	0.45	0.46	0.45	—	0.46
United States	g	0.68	0.79	0.83	0.84	0.80	0.78	0.78	0.77	0.77	0.76	0.76	0.75	0.76	0.76	0.76	0.76	0.77	0.76	—	0.77
	u	0.59	0.64	0.63	0.63	0.61	0.61	0.60	0.59	0.59	0.59	0.58	0.58	0.57	0.59	0.59	0.59	0.60	0.60	—	0.60

Source: O.E.C.D., National Accounts of O.E.C.D. Countries, 1950-68; O.E.C.D., Economic Surveys of B.L.E.U. and Japan, 1970.

Notes: Dash (–) indicates non-availability of required data.

extreme, France raised 75 per cent of its revenue in indirect taxes and only 25 per cent directly. It is of interest to note that countries with a relatively low proportion (around 40 per cent or less) of their total expenditure falling on goods and services (Austria, Germany, Italy, France and Belgium) also tended to rely more heavily in indirect taxation. This fact clearly has significance for the net impact of government expenditure and taxation on economic activity, as indicated by the expression in equation (v) on page 124. In general, countries with relatively low values of g and u′ require a smaller ratio of tax revenue to expenditure to produce a neutral impact on the economy than do countries with relatively high values of these structural parameters.

The estimation of $\bar{\alpha}$ is made difficult by a lack of direct knowledge of the propensities to consume of transfer recipients and income taxpayers of the countries being considered. However, we can arrive at an approximate estimation of the values of $\bar{\alpha}$ by making use of the ratio of consumers' expenditure to disposable income which is available for most countries for most of the period being examined. (Table 6.4.) As is to be expected, this ratio shows year-to-year fluctuations and in some countries quite significant longer run changes from the beginning to the end of the period. The ratio is of course *ex post* and does not necessarily represent the *ex ante* value of the propensity to consume. However, since we are concerned with total government expenditure and taxation and not with changes in them, it is plausible to assume that marginal values approximate to average values of the propensities, and that, in respect of average values, *ex post* values are not widely different from *ex ante*.

As a first step therefore we have calculated for each country the annual values of $\bar{\alpha}$ making use of the values of g and u′(and therefore the implied values of t and u″) of Table 6.3. and putting both c′ and c″ equal to the actual (*ex post*) ratios of consumption expenditure to disposable income as set out in Table 6.4. The results are shown in Table 6.5.

The estimated $\bar{\alpha}$'s clearly show significant differences among countries. Towards the high end of the scale, we have the U.S., Switzerland and Sweden which, because of relatively high ratios of expenditure on goods and services in total expenditure and high ratios of direct taxes in total tax revenue, required a significant excess of revenue over expenditure to produce a neutral impact of government spending and taxing operations on the economy. Towards the other end of the scale there are France, Germany, Belgium, Italy and to a lesser extent the Netherlands (i.e. the E.E.C. countries), in which a neutral impact of government expenditure on the economy is consistent with a ratio of tax revenue to expenditure of less than unity, largely because of a greater reliance on indirect taxes and a smaller share of expenditure on goods and services in total expenditure. The U.K., Canada and Denmark fall somewhere in between. In general, leaving aside the very early 1950s, the respective time series for each country show little time trend and not much annual or short term

Table 6.4. O.E.C.D. COUNTRIES: RATIO OF CONSUMER EXPENDITURE TO DISPOSABLE INCOME

	1950	1951	1952	1953	1954	1955	1956	1957	1958	1959	1960	1961	1962	1963	1964	1965	1966	1967	1968
Belgium	–	–	0.91	0.91	0.90	0.91	0.90	0.91	0.88	0.90	0.89	0.88	0.88	0.89	0.87	0.85	0.85	0.85	0.85
Canada	0.94	0.90	0.91	0.91	0.94	0.94	0.92	0.93	0.92	0.93	0.92	0.93	0.90	0.90	0.92	0.90	0.90	0.89	0.90
Denmark	0.91	0.92	0.90	0.88	0.92	0.93	0.92	0.89	0.90	0.88	0.88	0.87	0.89	0.90	0.89	0.88	0.90	0.89	0.92
France	0.95	0.96	0.96	0.97	0.94	0.93	0.93	0.92	0.93	0.91	0.90	0.90	0.88	0.89	0.89	0.88	0.88	0.88	0.88
Germany	0.92	0.90	0.90	0.91	0.89	0.87	0.87	0.86	0.85	0.85	0.85	0.86	0.87	0.87	0.85	0.84	0.86	0.87	–
Italy	–	–	–	–	–	–	–	–	–	–	–	0.84	0.83	0.84	0.85	0.83	0.84	0.85	0.84
Ireland	0.94	0.94	0.91	0.90	0.92	0.94	0.93	0.91	0.96	0.92	0.93	0.91	0.91	0.92	0.89	0.90	0.90	0.88	–
Japan	–	–	0.89	0.91	0.89	0.86	0.85	0.83	0.84	0.82	0.81	0.80	0.80	0.81	0.82	0.81	0.81	0.79	0.79
Netherlands	1.04	1.01	0.98	0.94	0.91	0.86	0.89	0.88	0.86	0.87	0.85	0.86	0.87	0.87	0.84	0.84	0.85	0.85	0.84
United Kingdom	1.01	1.01	0.99	0.98	0.98	0.98	0.96	0.96	0.97	0.96	0.94	0.92	0.93	0.93	0.93	0.92	0.92	0.93	0.93
United States	0.93	0.92	0.92	0.92	0.93	0.94	0.93	0.93	0.93	0.94	0.95	0.94	0.94	0.95	0.94	0.94	0.93	0.92	0.93

Source: O.E.C.D. National Accounts of O.E.C.D. Countries 1950-68.

Table 6.5. O.E.C.D. Countries: Summary Table of Impact of General Government Activity on GDP

		1950	1951	1952	1953	1954	1955	1956	1957	1958	1959	1960	1961	1962	1963	1964	1965	1966	1967	1968
B	$\bar{\alpha}$											0.98	0.98	0.99	0.99	0.99	0.98	0.98	0.98	0.98
E	$\bar{\alpha}^*$											1.04	1.04	1.07	1.05	1.07	1.05	1.05	1.05	1.05
L	α											0.92	0.98	1.01	0.99	1.05	1.02	1.05	1.05	1.00
G	n_p^*											0.04	0.02	0.02	0.03	0.01	0.01	0.01	0.01	0.03
I	n_p											0.06	0.04	0.04	0.04	0.04	0.04	0.03	0.03	0.05
U	n_T											Average 0.03								
M	n_T^*											Average 0.07								
C	$\bar{\alpha}$	1.01	1.02	1.01	1.01	1.01	1.01	1.00	1.01	1.00	1.00	1.00	1.00	1.00	1.00	1.00	1.00	1.00	1.00	1.01
A	$\bar{\alpha}^*$	1.08	1.08	1.08	1.08	1.08	1.08	1.08	1.07	1.07	1.07	1.07	1.08	1.07	1.07	1.07	1.07	1.07	1.08	1.08
N	α	1.00	1.07	0.94	0.91	0.87	0.90	0.93	0.90	0.80	0.84	0.82	0.81	0.82	0.83	0.88	0.90	0.91	0.89	0.91
A	n_p^*	0.00	0.01	0.02	0.03	0.04	0.03	0.02	0.03	0.06	0.05	0.06	0.07	0.06	0.06	0.04	0.03	0.03	0.04	0.04
D	n_p	0.02	0.00	0.04	0.05	0.06	0.05	0.04	0.05	0.08	0.07	0.08	0.09	0.08	0.08	0.06	0.05	0.05	0.07	0.06
A	n_T^*											Average 0.11								
	n_T^*											Average 0.16								
D	$\bar{\alpha}$	1.00	1.01	1.01	1.01	1.01	1.01	1.02	1.02	1.01	1.02	1.02	1.01	1.01	1.01	1.01	1.02	1.02	1.01	1.01
E	$\bar{\alpha}^*$	1.09	1.09	1.10	1.10	1.10	1.09	1.09	1.10	1.09	1.09	1.09	1.09	1.09	1.09	1.09	1.09	1.09	1.09	1.09
N	α	1.03	0.99	0.98	1.01	1.01	1.02	0.98	0.97	0.98	1.02	1.02	0.92	0.95	0.99	1.00	0.99	1.01	0.95	0.95
M	n_p^*	0.01	0.00	0.01	0.00	0.00	0.00	0.01	0.01	0.01	0.00	0.00	0.03	0.02	0.01	0.00	0.01	0.00	0.02	0.02
A	n_p	0.01	0.02	0.03	0.02	0.02	0.02	0.03	0.03	0.03	0.02	0.02	0.04	0.04	0.03	0.03	0.03	0.03	0.05	0.05
R	n_T											Average 0.02								
K	n_T^*											Average 0.05								

Table 6.5. Cont.

F ᾱ	0.98	0.99	0.99	1.00	0.98	0.98	0.98	0.98	0.98	0.98	0.98	0.97	0.97	0.96	0.96	0.96	0.96
R ᾱ*	1.01	1.00	1.01	1.00	1.00	1.01	1.01	1.01	1.01	1.01	1.01	1.01	1.01	1.01	1.01	1.01	1.01
A α	0.95	0.96	0.91	0.92	0.95	0.94	0.92	0.93	1.00	1.04	1.04	1.00	1.00	1.02	1.01	1.01	0.97
N n_p*	0.01	0.01	0.03	0.03	0.01	0.01	0.02	0.02	−0.01	−0.02	−0.02	−0.01	−0.01	−0.03	−0.02	−0.01	0.00
C n_T*	0.02	0.01	0.04	0.04	0.02	0.02	0.04	0.03	0.00	−0.01	−0.01	0.00	0.00	0.00	0.00	0.01	0.02
E n_T*												Average −0.02					
												Average 0.01					

G ᾱ	0.99	1.00	1.00	1.00	0.99	0.99	0.98	0.99	0.99	0.99	0.99	1.00	1.00	1.00	1.00	1.00	1.00
E ᾱ*	1.03	1.04	1.03	1.03	1.03	1.03	1.03	1.03	1.03	1.04	1.04	1.04	1.05	1.04	1.04	1.04	1.04
R α	0.99	1.05	1.06	1.10	1.09	1.11	1.12	1.07	1.01	1.04	1.05	1.00	0.98	0.98	0.94	0.94	0.92
M n_p	0.00	−0.02	−0.02	−0.03	−0.03	−0.04	−0.04	−0.03	−0.01	−0.02	−0.02	0.00	0.01	0.00	0.02	0.02	0.03
A n_p*	0.01	0.00	−0.01	−0.02	−0.02	−0.03	−0.03	−0.01	0.00	0.00	0.01	0.01	0.03	0.01	0.04	0.04	0.05
N n_T												Average −0.01					
Y n_T*												Average 0.02					

I ᾱ									0.98	0.98	0.99	0.98	0.98	0.98	0.98	0.98	0.98
T ᾱ*	1.05	1.05	1.05	1.05	1.05	1.05	1.05	1.05	1.05	1.07	1.07	1.05	1.05	1.05	1.05	1.05	1.05
A α	0.79	0.77	0.80	0.83	0.82	0.86	0.86	0.86	0.89	0.90	0.91	0.91	0.90	0.91	0.82	0.83	0.85
L n_p*	0.07	0.08	0.07	0.07	0.06	0.06	0.06	0.05	0.05	0.02	0.03	0.03	0.02	0.03	0.05	0.06	0.05
Y n_T*	0.07	0.08	0.07	0.07	0.06	0.06	0.06	0.05	0.05	0.05	0.05	0.04	0.05	0.05	0.08	0.06	0.07
											Average 0.09						
											Average 0.15						

I ᾱ	0.98	0.98	0.99	0.98	0.98	0.98	0.98	0.99	0.98	0.98	0.98	0.98	0.98	0.98	0.98	0.98
R ᾱ*	1.03	1.03	1.02	1.03	1.03	1.03	1.03	1.03	1.04	1.04	1.04	1.04	1.04	1.04	1.04	1.04
E α	0.81	0.82	0.83	0.82	0.83	0.78	0.79	0.81	0.79	0.78	0.79	0.78	0.83	0.82	0.83	0.82
L n_p	0.06	0.06	0.05	0.06	0.05	0.06	0.07	0.06	0.06	0.07	0.06	0.06	0.05	0.06	0.07	0.06
A n_p*	0.07	0.07	0.06	0.07	0.06	0.07	0.08	0.07	0.08	0.08	0.08	0.08	0.08	0.08	0.09	0.08
N n_T											Average 0.09					
D n_T*											Average 0.12					

Table 6.5. Cont.

JAPAN

$\bar\alpha$	1.00	1.00	1.00	1.01	0.99	0.99	1.01	1.01	1.00	1.00	1.03	1.04	1.05	1.04	1.05	1.04	1.04	1.04	1.04
α^*	1.07	1.07	1.08	1.07	1.05	1.05	1.07	1.08	1.08	1.08	1.10	1.10	1.11	1.11	1.11	1.10	1.10	1.10	1.10
α	1.08	1.07	1.11	0.98	0.92	0.84	0.84	0.85	0.81	0.85	1.00	1.08	1.02	1.00	0.98	0.95	0.93	0.97	0.98
n_p^*	-0.03	-0.02	-0.04	0.01	0.02	0.05	0.06	0.06	0.07	0.07	0.01	-0.01	0.01	0.01	0.02	0.02	0.02	0.01	0.01
n_T^*	0.00	0.00	-0.01	0.03	0.04	0.07	0.08	0.08	0.10	0.08	0.02	0.01	0.02	0.02	0.03	0.03	0.04	0.03	0.03

Average 0.03 (n_p^*)
Average 0.06 (n_T^*)

NETHERLANDS

$\bar\alpha$	1.00	1.00	1.01	1.00	1.00	1.00	1.00	1.01	1.00	1.00	1.01	1.00	1.01	1.01	1.00	1.00	1.00	0.99
α^*	1.08	1.08	1.08	1.08	1.09	1.08	1.08	1.08	1.08	1.08	1.08	1.08	1.08	1.08	1.08	1.08	1.08	1.08
α	0.88	0.92	0.85	0.81	0.92	0.86	0.87	0.86	0.82	0.84	0.84	0.84	0.84	0.85	0.86	0.84	0.84	0.86
n_p^*	0.04	0.03	0.06	0.07	0.03	0.06	0.05	0.06	0.07	0.07	0.07	0.07	0.07	0.06	0.05	0.07	0.07	0.06
n_T^*	0.07	0.05	0.08	0.10	0.05	0.07	0.08	0.08	0.10	0.10	0.10	0.10	0.10	0.08	0.06	0.11	0.10	0.10

Average 0.08 (n_p^*)
Average 0.11 (n_T^*)

UNITED KINGDOM

$\bar\alpha$	1.00	1.00	1.00	1.00	1.01	1.00	1.01	1.01	1.00	1.01	1.00	1.00	1.01	1.01	1.01	1.00	1.00	1.00
α^*	1.08	1.09	1.08	1.08	1.08	1.09	1.08	1.08	1.08	1.08	1.08	1.09	1.08	1.08	1.08	1.09	1.08	1.08
α	0.92	0.87	0.88	0.92	0.89	0.92	0.91	0.86	0.90	0.85	0.88	0.90	0.91	0.91	0.86	0.83	0.87	0.89
n_p^*	0.03	0.05	0.04	0.03	0.04	0.03	0.03	0.05	0.04	0.06	0.05	0.04	0.03	0.03	0.05	0.06	0.05	0.05
n_T^*	0.06	0.08	0.07	0.05	0.06	0.05	0.05	0.07	0.06	0.08	0.07	0.06	0.05	0.05	0.07	0.09	0.08	0.08

Average 0.11 (n_p^*)
Average 0.18 (n_T^*)

Table 6.5. Cont.

UNITED STATES

$\bar{\alpha}$	1.02	1.04	1.04	1.04	1.04	1.03	1.02	1.02	1.02	1.02	1.03	1.03	1.02	1.03	1.02	1.03	1.02
$\bar{\alpha}^*$	1.08	1.10	1.09	1.09	1.09	1.09	1.09	1.09	1.09	1.09	1.09	1.09	1.09	1.09	1.09	1.09	1.09
α	1.15	1.07	0.94	0.92	0.90	1.00	1.02	0.98	0.87	0.94	0.96	0.98	0.97	0.98	0.97	0.91	0.95
n_p	0.03	−0.01	0.03	0.04	0.04	0.01	0.00	0.01	0.05	0.02	0.02	0.01	0.02	0.01	0.02	0.04	0.02
n_p^*	0.01	0.01	0.04	0.05	0.06	0.02	0.02	0.03	0.06	0.04	0.04	0.03	0.03	0.03	0.03	0.06	0.04
n_T								Average 0.10									
n_T^*								Average 0.19									

Key: $\bar{\alpha}$ ... *required* ratio of government tax revenue to government expenditure for neutral impact, based on *actual* propensities to consume.

$\bar{\alpha}^*$ ... *required* ratio of government tax revenue to government expenditure for neutral impact, assuming *notional* propensities to consume.

α ... *actual* ratios of government tax revenue to government expenditure.

n_p ... ratio of net *primary* impact of government expenditure and taxation to GDP at factor cost, based on *actual* propensities to consume.

n_p^* ... ratio of net *primary* impact of government expenditure and taxation to GDP at factor cost, assuming *notional* propensities to consume.

n_T ... ratio of net *total* impact of government expenditure and taxation to GDP at factor cost, based on *actual* propensities to consume.

n_T^* ... ratio of net *total* impact of government expenditure and taxation to GDP at factor cost, assuming *notional* propensities to consume.

cyclical fluctuation. This is not surprising since significant changes in the structure of taxation and expenditure are not to be expected in the short run or necessarily in the long run.

The $\bar{\alpha}$'s in Table 6.5. almost certainly understate the required ratio of revenue to expenditure for neutral government impact, for the reasons indicated earlier: the propensity to consume of the recipients of government transfer payments is likely to be higher than that of the economy as a whole while the propensity to consume of taxpayers is likely to be lower. We do not have direct estimates of the propensities to consume of transfer payment recipients or taxpayers for any country. However, to discover what difference might be made in our estimation of $\bar{\alpha}$'s by allowing different propensities to consume, we have made some admittedly heroic assumptions about them which we nonetheless hope to be reasonable, and then re-estimated. In general, in the case of each country we have assumed that the propensity to consume of transfer payment recipients is somewhat above, and the propensity to consume of taxpayers is somewhat below, the *average* of the annual ratios of consumption expenditure to disposable income for the latter part of the period 1955-68, taking into account some rather qualitative judgment of the progressiveness of the tax system:[10] the early years of the 1950s are ignored because clearly the behaviour of practically all economies was still being affected by the Second World War to some degree and very much so by the contemporary Korean War.

The estimated adjusted values of the $\bar{\alpha}$s (donated by $\bar{\alpha}^*$) appear immediately below the values of the unadjusted $\bar{\alpha}$'s in Table 6.5. It will be seen that a quite striking difference is made to our initial estimates by assuming even moderate differences between the different propensities to consume (the specific assumptions are set out in the notes at the end of this table). The U.K., for instance, for which we have assumed propensities to consume of 0.95 and 0.8 for transfer recipients and taxpayers respectively, would require a ratio of tax revenue to government expenditure of 1.08 as against an unadjusted ratio of about 1.01: the U.S., on the basis of rather similar assumptions, would require a ratio of around 1.13 instead of 1.03/1.04. Much less, but still significant, difference is made to the ratios for countries like France, Belgium and Italy which rely more heavily on indirect rather than progressive direct income taxes. While for obvious reasons these adjusted estimates have to be treated with reserve, there seems good reason for believing that in all countries the required ratios of revenue to expenditure for neutral impact would certainly lie above the unadjusted ratios set out in Table 6.6., and probably closer to the adjusted values.

$\bar{\alpha}$ provides an indication of the *required* ratio of tax revenue to expenditure to produce a neutral impact on the economy. A comparison between this and α (the *actual* ratio of general government tax revenue to expenditure) enables us to judge whether in fact government spending and taxing operations had a positive or negative impact on GDP. In the third row of each country section of Table 6.5., therefore, we include the actual annual values of α for each country. These are derived from O.E.C.D. National Accounts data.

It will be seen that as far as each country is concerned, α varies from year to year much more widely than does $\bar{\alpha}$. This, of course, is to be expected since the levels of expenditure and taxation are much more likely to change from year to year than is the structure of expenditure and taxation. In most countries α appears to be consistently smaller than $\bar{\alpha}$ (and $\bar{\alpha}^*$), indicating that the fiscal budget in these countries was exerting a net expansionary effect on total demand throughout the period. In Germany, α was larger than $\bar{\alpha}$ in the 1950s but smaller in the 1960s, indicating a reversal in the direction of fiscal policy: indeed, Germany appeared to pursue a strong expansionary fiscal policy in the mid 1960s. France and Belgium on the other hand, had higher α's than $\bar{\alpha}$'s in the 1960s but lower ones in the 1950s. In France, in particular, the ratio of tax revenue to government expenditure rose very sharply in 1959, and stayed high thereafter, clearly the consequence of the French government attempt to deal with the economic and monetary instability of the 1950s which culminated in the devaluation of the franc in 1958. No real long term trend in the value of α can be seen in the case of the U.K. and the U.S., where α generally lay below $\bar{\alpha}$ after the Korean War years.

The difference between α and $\bar{\alpha}$ provides an indication of the net *primary* impact of expenditure and taxation on the economy: more precisely, as a proportion of GDP, the net primary impact on the economy equals $v(\bar{\alpha} - \alpha)(u'c'' + u'')$ where v is the ratio of government expenditure to GDP at factor cost.[11] To the primary impact must be added the multiplier or secondary effects. (If α equals $\bar{\alpha}$, taxing and spending neutralised each other and secondary effects do not enter.)

For convenience, $v(\alpha - \bar{\alpha})(u'c'' + u'')$ which is N_p/Y, now to be denoted by n_p, is plotted for each of the countries in Figure 6.1. Both the unadjusted and adjusted the values of $\bar{\alpha}$ are used to give alternative estimates (n_p and n_p^*). (See Table 6.5., rows four and five of each country section).[12] It should be noted that despite the somewhat different method of estimation, the *short run* behaviour of the difference between α and $\bar{\alpha}$ is virtually the same in respect of any one country whether the adjusted or the unadjusted values of $\bar{\alpha}$ are used. This is because it is the variation in the value of α that principally determines the difference between α and $\bar{\alpha}$. Of course, there are differences *between* countries in the short run behaviour of $\bar{\alpha} - \alpha$, as there is in its size, and naturally the estimates of the primary first round impact are larger when the adjusted values of $\bar{\alpha}$ are used.

It is evident from the charts that there were significant differences between countries in the net *primary* impact of government expenditure

Table 6.6. O.E.C.D. Countries: Annual Percentage Change in Government Expenditure and Tax Revenue 1951-68

	1951	1952	1953	1954	1955	1956	1957	1958	1959	1960	1961	1962	1963	1964	1965	1966	1967	1968
BELGIUM																		
Total tax revenue	–	–	–	0.32	9.15	9.15	9.97	1.04	6.12	7.93	10.19	11.58	8.86	13.89	14.97	13.77	9.84	8.20
Total gov. expenditure	–										4.05	9.28	10.85	9.70	16.08	11.40	10.07	13.30
CANADA																		
Total tax revenue	33.71	9.90	3.26	-1.74	9.15	13.25	5.50	-1.06	12.33	6.45	5.51	9.99	6.22	13.86	12.25	16.11	11.55	13.44
Total gov. expenditure	25.25	25.05	6.19	3.43	5.21	9.77	8.75	12.04	6.37	8.87	7.63	8.21	4.93	7.63	9.79	14.92	13.26	10.67
DENMARK																		
Total tax revenue	15.12	10.33	9.90	6.16	9.04	7.33	8.45	7.18	11.97	7.74	9.03	19.55	12.90	14.37	17.64	17.89	10.57	20.01
Total gov. expenditure	19.13	11.11	7.26	6.37	7.24	12.45	9.08	6.43	7.64	6.98	20.99	16.36	8.51	13.46	18.13	16.10	17.65	17.21
FRANCE																		
Total tax revenue	24.17	20.05	8.86	5.42	6.35	12.40	13.38	17.48	12.57	8.09	12.24	12.61	14.98	12.79	8.45	8.19	7.20	10.30
Total gov. expenditure	23.27	25.64	7.56	2.40	7.21	15.71	11.17	9.62	7.85	8.17	12.81	16.79	15.52	11.46	8.79	9.15	9.37	12.72
GERMANY																		
Total tax revenue	26.86	19.22	10.10	6.10	11.19	10.91	10.52	6.85	9.99	20.67	13.02	10.04	6.27	8.51	7.28	7.87	2.21	7.76
Total gov. expenditure	19.57	18.08	6.37	6.68	9.35	9.88	15.47	13.55	7.21	18.72	13.81	15.11	8.61	8.49	12.02	7.46	6.65	5.29

Total tax revenue	8.48	14.75	5.65	2.67	4.40	6.79	3.78	1.86	4.34	4.31	12.18	6.05	12.12	18.36	10.33	13.86	11.50	—
Total gov. expenditure	—	—	—	—	—	—	—	1.01	2.82	7.73	14.46	7.35	11.08	18.71	11.05	7.32	12.93	—
ITALY																		
Total tax revenue	17.74	16.85	14.95	9.65	16.33	7.32	7.83	9.60	12.02	9.18	18.33	17.11	12.81	6.72	6.90	15.23	9.39	
Total gov. expenditure	20.79	11.85	10.79	11.10	10.87	7.53	8.09	9.06	8.17	8.56	15.38	17.83	11.75	17.44	8.20	8.64	11.26	
JAPAN																		
Total tax revenue	—	9.52	7.76	4.47	10.27	15.16	—	3.42	11.86	23.54	24.51	14.97	14.74	14.47	13.11	12.71	17.81	20.62
Total gov. expenditure	—	—	—	—	—	—	—	—	—	—	19.20	19.80	16.92	16.71	16.25	15.47	14.26	18.40
NETHERLANDS																		
Total tax revenue	14.89	10.22	-0.82	4.96	5.46	15.86	18.85	-2.38	7.11	12.87	9.79	6.14	11.89	19.59	16.63	14.51	13.86	13.27
Total gov. expenditure	15.59	6.12	12.85	10.90	15.45	16.57	17.85	2.59	1.61	11.33	9.18	7.39	16.54	19.58	14.61	14.55	13.34	11.09
U.K.																		
Total tax revenue	6.42	7.37	1.19	3.39	7.40	4.97	6.60	6.58	3.77	2.40	10.79	9.90	2.17	7.66	13.57	11.51	9.87	13.64
Total gov. expenditure	19.77	14.66	4.49	-2.00	3.51	8.49	3.91	5.71	5.78	6.66	9.02	7.54	10.88	3.22	15.36	4.16	14.55	11.18
U.S.																		
Total tax revenue	23.50	5.93	5.01	-4.91	11.92	8.59	6.06	-0.77	12.43	8.44	3.45	8.57	7.47	3.14	8.61	12.84	7.06	15.67
Total gov. expenditure	32.72	19.91	7.99	-3.67	1.33	6.33	10.85	10.97	2.67	3.70	9.47	7.17	4.37	5.53	6.67	13.74	14.44	11.35

Source: O.E.C.D. *National Accounts of O.E.C.D. countries 1950-68;*
O.E.C.D. *Economic Surveys of B.L.U.E. and Japan, 1970.*

and taxation on their economies. On this evidence, the net primary impact was highest in the Netherlands, the U.K., Canada and Italy, averaging six per cent of GDP or over during the period 1955 to 1968 if the adjusted values of $\bar{\alpha}$ are used and over four per cent if the unadjusted values are used. In the U.S., Austria and Denmark it was half or less than this. The impact varied over time.

In the U.S., it was well above average in the early 1950s at the time of the Korean War, and again in 1958 and 1967-8. In the U.K. the Korean War impact also stands out, as does the expansionary policy pursued by the government in 1963/4. In Germany, the net primary impact of government fiscal operations was significantly contractionary in the 1950s to the extent of three or four per cent of GDP, but it then became significantly expansionary in the 1960s to about the same extent. The reverse was true in France and Belgium: government fiscal policy turned from being moderately expansionary in the 1950s to being mildly contractionary or neutral in the 1960s, although in France towards the end of the period it became expansionary once more. In the Netherlands and to some extent in Italy we can discern a sustained expansionary effect throughout most of the mid and late 1960s.

To obtain an estimate of the net *total* impact we must multiply our primary estimate by the reciprocal of the term $1 - c(1 - r) + m$. (See equation (iv) b on page 123.) This term, however, requires us to know the value of r (the ratio of retained gross business profits (saving) to GDP at factor cost). Estimates of gross business saving on a comparable basis are available in the O.E.C.D. National Accounts Data for only four countries (the U.S., the U.K., Canada, and Netherlands): hence we have had to make use of other sources of data for the other countries, which may be less comparable. We also use the average of the annual ratios of personal consumption expenditure to disposable income and the average of the annual ratios of imports to GDP at factor cost and estimate an average value of the reciprocal term $1 - c(1 - r) + m$ (i.e. the multiplier)[13] denoted by k. The estimated values of k for each country are as follows:[14]

U.S.	5.2	Belgium	1.8
U.K.	2.5	Denmark	1.8
Germany	2.3	Netherlands	1.3
France	2.8	Sweden	2.1
Italy	2.8	Canada	2.4
Austria	2.0	Japan	2.7

Obviously, the size of k depends very largely on the ratio of imports to GDP (since the ratio of personal consumption to disposable income and the ratio of business saving to GDP at factor cost do not differ all that greatly between countries); and, apart from the U.S. and the Netherlands, (the former of which has a very low ratio of imports to GDP at factor cost while the latter has a very high one), it tends to lie in the neighbour-

FIGURE 6.1

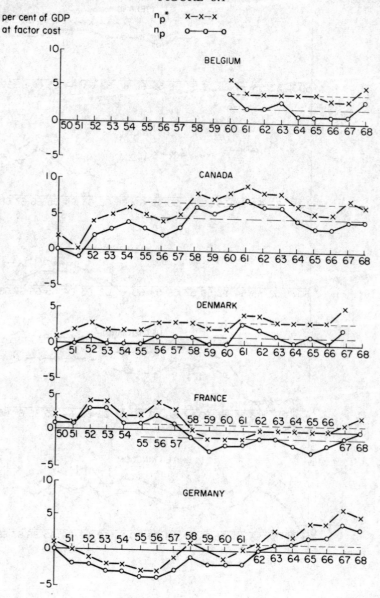

per cent of GDP
at factor cost

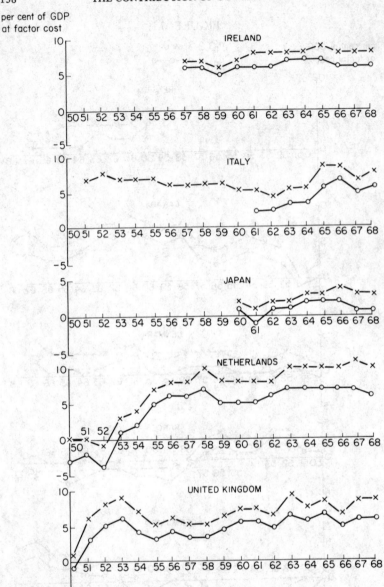

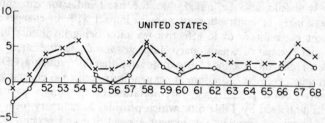

per cent of GDP
at factor cost

hood of 2 or 2½. Applying the appropriate value of k to the alternative estimates of n_p gives us alternative estimates of the *total* net impact of government expenditure and taxation on GDP as a proportion of GDP, (i.e. n_T and n^*_T): these are also to be found in Table 6.5. in the last two rows of each country section.

These estimates suggest that in some countries at any rate the total net contribution of government spending and taxation to GDP was very substantial — of the order of 15 per cent or more. In this category come the U.S., the U.K., Canada, and Italy. Somewhat below them at 10-12 per cent comes the Netherlands.[15] The net total contribution was much lower, at five per cent or less, in France, Germany, Austria, Belgium and Denmark, although the evidence seems to suggest that in Germany fiscal operations provided an important stimulus, possibly approaching ten per cent of GDP, in the latter part of the 1960s.

Clearly these estimates have to be treated with reserve. A difficulty is that the values of α are *ex post*. Since a large part of tax revenue and even a part of expenditure are dependent on GDP itself, the value α does not indicate accurately the impact of government *decisions* concerning its components. All that we can say is that if *ex post* the value of α was different from $\bar{\alpha}$, there is a presumption that government fiscal activity had a negative or positive effect on activity, the size of which is broadly related to the value of the difference between $\bar{\alpha}$ and α. Although speculative, the estimates can, if interpreted as broad indicators of magnitude only, probably provide a useful basis on which country comparisons can be made.

Care has to be used in interpreting year-to-year fluctuations in n_p. We can illustrate why by reference to the U.S. The chart for the U.S. shows a marked rise in n_p in 1958 and again in 1967 and an equally sharp fall in 1959 and 1968. The explanation of the sharp rises can be found in a large rise in government expenditure on both occasions while the sharp falls occurred because of a subsequent large rise in tax revenue.[16] Clearly a substantial part of the increase in tax revenue was a lagged response to the rise in GDP which was itself produced by the rise in expenditure a year earlier. Thus the indicated fall in net fiscal impact in 1959 cannot be interpreted simply as a government decision to deflate the economy.

It should also be noted that the fiscal indicator can show an expansionary or contractionary primary impact without changes in government expenditure or in effective tax rates being involved: for instance, a net primary expansionary impact would be indicated if private sector demand declined autonomously, thereby reducing GDP and tax revenue even if government expenditure remains constant; and, of course, conversely. Hence, interpretation of the charts on pages 137-8 will be helped by Table 6.6., which provides in summary form the annual percentage changes in government expenditure and revenue for each of our countries.

Inspection of Table 6.6. and the country charts together, however, does suggest that whenever a significant net primary expansionary impact is indicated the cause is practically always, in all countries alike, a significant rise in government expenditure rather than a decline in tax revenue; and whenever a net primary contractionary impact is indicated the cause is invariably a rise in tax revenue — which may follow a previous rise in government expenditure as suggested above in the case of the U.S. — rather than a fall in government expenditure. Government expenditure and tax revenue rose steadily in all countries throughout the period.

Fiscal impact and inflation

What light do these estimates of fiscal impact throw on the rate of inflation in the postwar period? Is it the case that countries in which, on average for the period as a whole, the fiscal impact appears to have been greatest, also suffered a higher average rate of inflation? Can variations in the rate of inflation experienced by each country be explained by variations in the degree of fiscal impact?

If we relate the average rate of inflation for the period 1954-68 (we omit the early years of the 1950s since these were distorted by the rapid rearmament build-up at the time of the Korean War — see Table 1.1.) with the estimated average total fiscal impact as set out in Table 6.5. on a country-by-country basis, there is clearly no evidence for concluding that countries with the highest net fiscal impact experienced the highest rates of inflation. The U.S., for instance, which had one of the highest if not the highest net fiscal impact, by no means suffered the highest average rate of inflation. Its inflation was not significantly different from Germany's, and was less than say France, both of which appeared to have had on average a lower net fiscal impact on their economic activity. Nor is it true that countries in which the ratios of government expenditure and tax revenue to GDP were the highest also experienced the highest average rates of inflation. Pretty well every country had ratios well above 30 per cent irrespective of whether their rate of inflation was above or below the average for all countries together.

There is perhaps a little more evidence to suggest that as far as any individual country is concerned, there was some loose connection between variations in net fiscal impact and variations in the inflation rate around the average. The Korean War period, 1950-53, is a clear instance, in the U.S. and the U.K. in particular, of a sharp rise in net fiscal impact going along with a higher rate of inflation. There was for a number of countries a longish period in the second half of the 1950s, extending in the case of some countries into the very early 1960s, when net fiscal impact and the rate of inflation were both below the average for the period as a whole — for instance, the U.S. (apart from 1958 mentioned earlier), the U.K., Austria, Italy and Canada. In Germany and France there was a significant about-face from the beginning to the end of the period in both net fiscal impact and rate of inflation. In the 1950s, Germany experienced both a negative fiscal impact and a very low rate of inflation: in the 1960s the fiscal impact became significantly and increasingly positive and the rate of inflation became higher. The opposite was true of France: before 1958 the net fiscal impact was substantial and the rate of inflation was very high; after 1958 fiscal impact became negative and the rate of inflation was lower. In practically all countries a tendency for the net fiscal impact to rise during the decade of the 1960s was associated with a gradual acceleration in the inflation rate. Hence we cannot dismiss government spending and taxing operations as an element underlying inflation, even during those years (1954-70) when it remained very moderate, although it seems reasonably clear that the different rates of inflation experienced by different countries cannot be explained simply, if at all, in these terms.

After 1970 there was a marked jump in net fiscal impact in a number of countries which clearly contributed to the sharp rise in the world's inflation rate.[17] Of particular significance is the sharp increase in net fiscal impact in the U.S. Owing to a substantial fall in the ratio of tax revenue to government expenditure, the net primary impact of fiscal operations probably doubled in 1970-71 as compared with preceding years; by 1971 it amounted to over six per cent of GNP. The total effect, including multiplier repercussions, increased correspondingly, although an increasing proportion of the expansion of aggregate demand emanating from the government sector found its way abroad as the U.S.'s trade balance worsened. Undoubtedly this was a strong contributory factor to the acceleration in world inflation in the early 1970s which we examine at greater length in Chapter 10. There was also a substantial rise in net fiscal impact in the U.K. and Italy also due to a fall in the ratio of tax to expenditure. In the U.K., the net impact measured over seven per cent of GDP in 1972 as compared with an average of four or five per cent in the preceding three years, and in Italy it amounted to over eight per cent in the same year. In other countries however — including Germany and France — government fiscal operations were no more expansionary than they had been earlier.

Conclusions

The conclusions to be drawn therefore is that government spending and taxing clearly had a significant impact on the level of economic activity in practically all of the countries we have examined, and at various times contributed to inflationary pressure. Nonetheless, the length and severity of postwar inflation, at least up to 1970, cannot be attributed mainly or even perhaps substantially to either the level of expenditure and tax revenue relative to GDP or to the balance between them; nor can the differences between the average rates of inflation experienced by different countries. The major contribution of government to inflation would appear to be indirect, arising from commitment to full employment and growth policies which, in the manner suggested in the early part of this chapter, materially influenced private sector attitudes in the market determination of wages and prices. Unfortunately, this contribution is even less amenable to quantitative investigation than is the direct contribution.

The Inflation-Unemployment Trade-off in O.E.C.D Countries 1954-68

Facts to be explained

In Chapters 2 and 3, we discussed the theoretical possibility of a trade-off between inflation and unemployment. In this chapter we develop a formal model which includes such a trade-off, and test it for a sample of 13 OECD countries for the period 1954-68. The post-1968 period will be analysed in a later chapter, because of the special nature of the inflationary experience which characterized it.

In retrospect, the period from 1954 to 1968 was one of relatively moderate inflation. For the group of countries considered here, the average rate of price increase as measured by the GDP price deflator only slightly exceeded 3.4 per cent per annum. There was considerable variation in average inflation rates between countries (from 2.2 to 4.8) as well as from year to year (from 1.5 to 4.7) for the group of countries as a whole.

Table 7.1. ANNUAL INFLATION RATES IN 13 O.E.C.D. COUNTRIES, 1954-68

	B	CA	DK	F	G	IR	I	J	NL	N	S	UK	US	Average
1954	0.9	2.5	2.4	1.0	0.1	-0.9	1.5	0.0	4.0	3.5	0.0	3.8	0.9	1.5
1955	0.4	-0.5	3.7	2.3	2.0	2.7	4.4	5.5	5.2	3.8	4.3	1.9	2.4	2.9
1956	3.5	4.3	4.8	4.9	2.9	2.8	3.9	3.1	4.0	6.3	5.4	6.4	3.3	4.3
1957	3.5	2.9	0.9	6.1	2.9	3.2	1.8	4.5	6.3	4.6	4.3	3.8	3.9	3.7
1958	1.5	1.8	1.8	11.8	3.6	6.3	2.6	-1.1	1.0	1.7	3.0	3.8	2.2	3.1
1959	0.6	2.8	3.9	6.4	1.3	2.1	0.0	2.3	2.0	2.6	0.9	1.3	1.9	2.2
1960	0.7	1.3	1.6	3.0	2.6	0.7	2.5	3.8	2.7	2.7	4.9	1.1	1.7	2.3
1961	1.2	0.6	4.7	3.3	4.3	2.6	2.7	6.8	2.5	2.4	3.3	2.9	1.2	3.0
1962	1.7	1.3	6.8	7.7	4.4	4.6	5.8	4.2	3.2	3.0	4.6	4.0	1.0	4.0
1963	2.9	2.0	5.7	6.6	2.9	2.7	8.6	4.4	5.2	2.5	3.5	1.6	1.4	3.8
1964	4.8	2.5	4.7	4.7	2.7	9.5	6.3	4.1	7.9	5.4	3.4	2.9	1.8	4.7
1965	5.1	2.9	7.3	3.8	3.6	4.4	3.9	5.5	5.8	4.8	5.7	4.8	1.8	4.6
1966	4.5	4.5	7.3	3.0	3.8	3.8	2.1	4.5	6.0	4.3	5.5	4.1	2.3	4.3
1967	3.0	3.8	6.0	2.7	0.6	3.1	2.8	4.2	3.8	3.9	4.9	2.7	2.9	3.4
1968	2.7	3.6	5.7	4.8	1.7	4.0	1.5	3.8	3.7	1.0	2.6	3.2	4.1	3.3
Average	2.5	2.4	4.5	4.8	2.6	3.4	3.4	3.7	4.2	3.5	3.8	3.2	2.2	3.4

B—Belgium, CA—Canada, DK—Denmark, F—France, G—W. Germany, IR—Ireland, I—Italy, J—Japan, NL—Netherlands, N—Norway, S—Sweden, UK—United Kingdom, US—United States

The annual inflation rates for each country separately, as well as the cross-country and cross-period averages, were presented in Table 5.1. The aim of this chapter is to explain the variation in annual inflation rates for each country individually, and, as a by-product, to throw light on the inter-country differences in average inflation rates. However, explanation of inter-country differences will be left to Chapter 8.

A general trade-off model

a. *The price function*
We start from the identity:

$$PY \equiv WL + RK + P_m M + T_i$$

where

P	is the price level
Y	is real gross output
W	is the wage rate
L	is employment
R	is return on capital
K	is the volume of capital
P_m	is the price level of imports
M	is the volume of imports
T_i	is the amount of indirect taxes

Gross output at current prices is defined as the sum of the wage bill, profits, imports, and indirect taxes. Taking first differences, this identity can be transformed into the following expression:

$$Y \Delta P + P \Delta Y = L \Delta W + W \Delta L + K \Delta R + R \Delta K + M \Delta P_m + P_m \Delta M + \Delta T_i$$

Dividing both sides by PY yields:

$$\frac{\Delta P}{P} + \frac{\Delta Y}{Y} = \frac{\Delta W}{W} \frac{WL}{PY} + \frac{\Delta L}{L} \frac{WL}{PY} + \frac{\Delta R}{R} \frac{RK}{PY} + \frac{\Delta K}{K} \frac{RK}{PY} + \frac{\Delta Pm}{Pm} \frac{PmM}{PY} + \frac{\Delta M}{M} \frac{PmM}{PY} + \frac{\Delta Ti}{Ti} \frac{T}{P}$$

Simplifying notation, this can be rewritten as:

$$p + y = \alpha w + \alpha l + \beta r + \beta k + \gamma p_m + \gamma m + \tau t_i$$

All lower case letters refer to percentage changes, and all Greek symbols to shares, e.g.

$$\alpha = \frac{WL}{PY}, \ \beta = \frac{RK}{PY} \text{ etc. subject to the constraint: } \alpha + \beta + \gamma + \tau = 1$$

It will be noted that these shares must be variable if the identity is to be preserved. On the other hand, if we regard the corresponding coefficients as constant parameters, the equation becomes a cost-determined price function. For this purpose, we transfer y to the right-hand side, and write it as $(\alpha + \beta + \gamma + \tau)y$. This allows the variables to be regrouped in the following way.

$$p = - [\alpha(y-1) + \beta(y-k) + \gamma(y-m)] + \alpha w + \beta r + \gamma p_m + \tau(t_i - y)$$

The first term can be considered as some weighted productivity term, which includes not only the growth rate of labour productivity (y-1), but also of capital (y-k) and of imports (y-m). Representing this overall productivity term by q, the price function then becomes:

$$p = (\beta r - q) + \alpha w + \gamma p_m + \tau(t_i - y)$$

Finally, we rewrite $\gamma p_m = \bar{p}_m$ and $t_i = \dfrac{\Delta Ti}{Ti} = \dfrac{\Delta \tau}{\tau} + p + y$ since $T_i = \tau PY$ so that $t_i - y = \dfrac{\Delta \tau}{\tau} + p$, and $\tau(t_i - y) = \Delta \tau + p\,\tau \cong \Delta \tau$ as τp is very small.[1]

The variable $\Delta \tau$ indicates the change in pressure of indirect taxation. The price function then takes the following form:

(i) $p \cong (\beta r - q) + \alpha w + \bar{p}_m + \Delta \tau$

The coefficients of import prices and of indirect taxation have thus been standardized to unity, which will prove convenient for international comparison of our econometric results.

b. *The wage function*

The wage function is specified in accordance with the theoretical discussion of the Phillips Curve in Chapter 3. The relative change in the nominal wage rate is expressed as a function of the net vacancy rate and of the expected inflation rate. The net vacancy rate is itself assumed to be a hyperbolic function of the unemployment rate:

(ii) $w = \eta v + \epsilon p^e$ where w   = rate of wage inflation

v   = net vacancy rate

p^e = expected rate of price inflation

(iii) $v = \varphi u^{-1}$ where u   = unemployment rate

The parameter φ is a friction parameter, related to the degree of imperfection in the labour market. Combining equations (ii) and (iii), we obtain a relationship between the rate of wage inflation and the unemployment rate. This relationship shifts with the expected rate of price inflation, as shown on Figure 7.1.

FIGURE 7.1

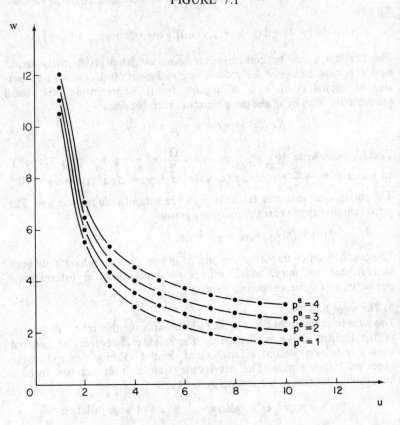

c. The price expectation function

The diagram shows that price expectations become relatively more important for higher rates of unemployment. However, this is only true when the expected rate of price inflation, as is the case in the diagram, is a given constant, independent of what happens to price inflation itself. It is more reasonable to assume an adaptive process for the formation of price expectations, where the latter depends partly on the current inflation rate and partly on past expectations:

$$\text{(iv)} \quad p^e = \mu p + (1-\mu) p^e_{-1}$$

Through p, and indirectly through w and μ, price expectations thus depend on the unemployment rate, so that in a fully determined system, price expectations are only an endogenous link in the process of price formation.

The complete model thus consists of the following equations:

$$p = (\beta r - q) + \alpha w + \bar{p}_m + \Delta\tau \qquad \text{price equation}$$

$$w = \eta\varphi u^{-1} + \epsilon p^e \qquad \text{wage equation}$$

$$p^e = \mu p + (1-\mu)p^e_{-1} \qquad \text{price expectation function}$$

As time series on r and q are not available, we shall assume these variables to be relatively constant. The term in brackets $(\beta r\text{-}q)$ may therefore be regarded as the constant term of the price equation. The solution of the model is then relatively straightforward, and can be expressed as follows:

$$p = \frac{\mu(\beta r - q)}{1-\alpha\epsilon\mu} + \frac{1-\mu}{1-\alpha\epsilon\mu} p_{-1} + \frac{\alpha\eta\varphi}{1-\alpha\epsilon\mu}\left[u^{-1} - (1-\mu)u^{-1}_{-1}\right]$$

$$+ \frac{1}{1-\alpha\epsilon\mu}\left[\bar{p}_m - (1-\mu)\bar{p}_{m-1}\right] + \frac{1}{1-\alpha\epsilon\mu}\left[\Delta\tau - (1-\mu)\Delta\tau_{-1}\right]$$

The first term, which is a function of r and q, can again be regarded as the constant term of the reduced form. There are then left three explanatory variables in addition to the lagged inflation rate — namely, the unemployment rate, import prices and changes in the pressure of indirect taxation. Corresponding to the value of μ, a different transformation is applied to these explanatory variables.

It should be noted that, as μ varies from zero to unity, the coefficient of the lagged inflation rate p_{-1} varies from unity to zero, the trade-off coefficient with respect to unemployment varies from $\alpha\eta\varphi$ to $\alpha\eta\varphi/1-\alpha\epsilon$, and the coefficient of import prices and of indirect taxation from unity to $1/1-\alpha\epsilon$. This information will be helpful in interpreting the econometric results which follow.

Estimation results

The reduced-form equation derived in the preceding section can only be estimated for alternative values of μ, varying between zero and unity. The best result can then be selected on the basis of multiple criteria, such as t- values, the corrected multiple correlation coefficient, the Durbin-Watson coefficient and the degree of multicollinearity. The data used for estimating the equation are summarised in an appendix at the end of this chapter. We first present our results for each country, and then comment on the conclusions that can be drawn from them generally.

The United States

In order to avoid too extensive a presentation, we produce only the results for three alternative values for μ, namely, one-third, two-thirds and unity. Actual calculations were also made with other values of μ, but for our purpose the results presented here are sufficient.

1955-68	Constant term	Lagged inflation rate	Unemployment (lagged 1 year)	Indirect taxation	$\bar{R}^2$	DW	COL
$\mu= 1/3$	0.85	0.64 (2.09)	1.88 (0.32)	0.00 (0.00)	0.20	0.93	0.88
$\mu= 2/3$	0.13	0.45 (1.40)	9.32 (1.32)	-0.25 (0.26)	0.32	1.21	0.79
$\mu= 1$	-1.70	0.12 (0.43)	18.44 (2.86)	0.14 (0.16)	0.58	2.02	0.68
$\mu= 1$	-1.85	not included	20.40 (4.70)	0.27 (0.36)	0.61	2.05	0.99

It will be seen that the results indicate a high sensitivity to the assumed value of μ. When μ is low, the coefficient of the lagged inflation rate is high, as expected, but the trade-off coefficient with respect to unemployment is not significant (t-values are indicated between brackets). Indirect taxes show no influence either. Import prices were not included here because of the small share of imports in GDP. As μ increases, the coefficient of determination corrected for degrees of freedom ($\bar{R}^2$), as well as the Durbin-Watson coefficient (DW) improve very rapidly. On the other hand, multicollinearity worsens (this is indicated by the COL-coefficient, which represents the square root of the determinant value of the correlation matrix). The best result is obtained for $\mu = 1$, where the coefficient of p_{-1} is in effect restricted to zero, by not including the variable.

Canada

In the case of Canada, a slightly different specification was used than for the other countries, in order to show the extreme dependence of its economy on that of the U.S. For this purpose, import prices were replaced by the U.S. price level. On the other hand, indirect taxes were dropped as an explanatory variable after preliminary calculations showed its coefficient to be erratic.

Again, the best results are obtained for values of μ close to unity. However, the improvement is hardly noticeable after $\mu = 2/3$. The most reliable estimate of the impact of the U.S. inflation rate on Canadian prices is 0.40, which confirms other estimates on the effect of inflation in the U.S. on Canada.[2]

1955-68	Constant term	Lagged inflation rate	Unem-ployment	U.S. Inflation rate	$\bar{R}^2$	DW	COL
$\mu = 1/3$	−0.16	0.39 (1.96)	19.73 (2.78)	0.69 (2.04)	0.68	1.51	0.66
$\mu = 2/3$	−1.29	0.20 (1.55)	19.47 (4.49)	0.52 (2.17)	0.82	1.92	0.72
$\mu = 1$	−1.81	0.07 (0.53)	17.31 (5.13)	0.34 (1.66)	0.82	1.99	0.73
$\mu = 1$	−1.69	n.i.	16.78 (5.41)	0.40 (2.50)	0.84	1.73	0.87

United Kingdom

As for the two preceding countries, a drastic improvement in the results takes place as μ increases. The major problem is that given $\mu = 1$, the unrestricted coefficient of p_{-1} becomes significantly negative. This is contrary to *a priori* expectations, and may indicate that the model is invalid. On the other hand, the coefficients of import prices and of indirect taxation seem plausible.

1955-68	Constant term	Lagged inflation rate	Unem-ployment (lagged 1 year)	Import prices (lagged 1 & 2 years)	Indirect taxes	$\bar{R}^2$	DW	COL
$\mu = 1/3$	1.56	0.07 (0.32)	6.71 (2.16)	0.58 (1.49)	0.59 (0.87)	0.38	2.49	0.84
$\mu = 2/3$	0.21	−0.16 (0.89)	8.56 (3.55)	0.67 (2.26)	0.78 (1.31)	0.62	2.49	0.83
$\mu = 1$	−1.56	−0.44 (3.14)	10.19 (5.95)	0.64 (3.29)	1.06 (2.21)	0.79	2.35	0.73
$\mu = 1$	−1.87	not included	8.34 (3.75)	0.49 (1.90)	1.01 (1.54)	0.61	2.85	0.82

Import prices were introduced simultaneously with a one and a two-year lag, and produced coefficients of similar order of magnitude. For simplification, we therefore used the sum of both relative changes as a single variable. The estimate where the coefficient of p_{-1} is restricted to zero is clearly unsatisfactory: the t-values fall drastically and negative autocorrelation becomes significant.

Ireland

The results for Ireland are quite unsatisfactory because of the poor explanatory record (low R^2) and the lack of significance of most regression coefficients. However, there is a clear improvement as μ varies from one-third to unity.

1954-69	Constant term	Lagged Inflation rate	Unemployment term	Import prices (lagged 1 year)	Indirect taxes	$\bar{R}^2$	DW	COL
$\mu = 1/3$	1.92	0.23 (0.85)	17.07 (0.38)	0.66 (1.37)	0.54 (0.50)	0.22	2.31	0.83
$\mu = 2/3$	0.56	0.12 (0.48)	24.97 (0.76)	0.72 (1.53)	0.99 (0.92)	0.33	2.41	0.89
$\mu = 1$	0.04	−0.02 (0.10)	23.04 (1.00)	0.73 (1.60)	1.26 (1.23)	0.42	2.42	0.87
$\mu = 1$	−0.92	not included	27.46 (1.30)	0.94 (2.47)	1.14 (1.27)	0.53	2.26	0.94

We shall use the estimates for $\mu = 1$ where the lagged inflation is dropped and all t-values are maximized. The highest significance is obtained for import prices. An attempt to replace import prices by the U.K. inflation rate, as we have done for Canada, did not produce good results.[3]

Japan

1955-68	Constant term	Lagged inflation rate	Unemployment	Import prices	Indirect taxes	$\bar{R}^2$	DW	COL
$\mu = 1/3$	1.43	0.48 (1.83)	1.92 (0.57)	3.28 (3.07)	−1.79 (2.09)	0.41	2.24	0.71
$\mu = 2/3$	2.01	0.27 (1.17)	1.19 (0.44)	3.44 (3.15)	−1.99 (2.08)	0.51	2.18	0.71
$\mu = 1$	2.92	0.05 (0.25)	0.62 (0.30)	3.37 (2.94)	−2.24 (1.88)	0.56	2.08	0.70
$\mu = 1$	2.78	not included	0.94 (0.64)	3.26 (3.45)	−2.33 (3.17)	0.71	2.05	0.87

The results for Japan follow the general pattern as they improve gradually when μ varies from one-third to unity. Yet, the trade-off coefficient itself never becomes significant. Its influence seems to be picked up by the constant term, which increases with μ. This may be the consequence of the fact that the unemployment rate has varied very little throughout the period (cf Table 7.5).

The results also indicate extremely high sensitivity to import prices as well as to indirect taxes, although the latter come out with a negative sign. Autocorrelation is never a problem, and multicollinearity is eliminated when the lagged inflation rate is dropped from the equation.

West Germany

1955-68	Constant term	Lagged inflation rate	Unemployment	Import prices (lagged 1 year)	$\bar{R}^2$	DW	COL
$\mu = 0.10$	0.95	0.57 (4.26)	2.51 (4.11)	0.73 (2.85)	0.71	2.07	0.95
$\mu = 0.20$	0.98	0.48 (3.76)	2.55 (4.21)	0.73 (2.79)	0.71	1.99	0.98
$\mu = 0.33$	1.05	0.37 (2.83)	2.46 (4.04)	0.74 (2.60)	0.69	1.79	0.98
$\mu = 0.50$	1.19	0.25 (1.71)	2.18 (3.54)	0.75 (2.28)	0.63	1.52	0.96

West Germany is the first country for which a relatively low value for μ appears to be optimal. The corrected $\bar{R}^2$ no longer increases for values for μ smaller than 0.20. All t-values are then significant, the Durbin-Watson is optimal, and multicollinearity is minimal.

Indirect taxes were not included, as their pressure was relatively constant throughout the period (nine per cent on the average).

Italy

1955-68	Constant term	Lagged inflation rate	Unemployment	Import prices (lagged 1 year)	Indirect taxes (lagged 1 year)	$\bar{R}^2$	DW	COL
$\mu = 0.10$	0.41	0.64 (3.22)	25.61 (2.22)	1.13 (1.60)	0.03 (0.05)	0.48	1.40	0.90
$\mu = 0.20$	0.20	0.55 (2.89)	24.66 (2.30)	1.16 (1.57)	0.04 (0.05)	0.49	1.30	0.94
$\mu = 0.33$	0.09	0.44 (2.26)	21.99 (2.28)	1.22 (1.50)	0.07 (0.09)	0.47	1.19	0.94
$\mu = 0.67$	0.16	0.27 (1.12)	15.07 (2.01)	1.24 (1.20)	0.27 (0.27)	0.38	1.10	0.81

The result for Italy is similar to that for Germany, with an optimal value for μ of approximately 0.20. For this value of μ, both the coefficients of lagged inflation rate and of the unemployment term are significant. All results indicate strong autocorrelation, however, which worsens with increasing value for μ.

The effect of indirect taxes is negligible, while that of import prices seems of the right order of magnitude. However, the t-value comes somewhat short of the significance barrier.

France

1955-69	Constant term	Lagged inflation rate	Unemployment term (lagged 1 year)	Indirect taxes	$\bar{R}^2$	DW	COL
μ= 0.10	1.49	0.57 (3.12)	5.60 (4.26)	−1.64 (1.58)	0.59	2.32	0.82
μ= 0.33	−0.27	0.46 (2.61)	6.08 (4.31)	−2.14 (2.00)	0.60	2.28	0.80
μ= 0.50	−1.61	0.37 (2.07)	6.42 (4.20)	−2.50 (2.22)	0.60	2.23	0.75
μ= 0.67	−2.89	0.27 (1.47)	6.41 (3.96)	−2.82 (2.31)	0.55	2.16	0.69

As was the case for Germany and Italy, the results for France indicate a relatively low value for μ. The optimal value of μ is somewhat difficult to determine because the estimates are quite similar to μ =0.5. Only after that does the corrected $\bar{R}^2$ start to decline.

Import prices were not included as an explanatory variable, because their behaviour reflects in part the successive devaluations of the French franc during the period. These devaluations, which were reflected in an increase of import prices, were the consequence of inflation, not the cause of it. Surprisingly, the coefficient of indirect taxes is strongly negative, although only significantly so for values of μ of 0.5 and higher.

Belgium

1955-68	Constant term	Lagged inflation rate	Unemployment term (lagged 1 year)	Import prices	Indirect taxes	$\bar{R}^2$	DW	COL
μ= 0.33	−0.57	0.58 (4.96)	18.08 (5.43)	0.80 (4.51)	−0.82 (2.47)	0.87	2.43	0.74
μ= 0.50	−0.71	0.39 (2.96)	17.23 (5.22)	0.79 (4.42)	−0.79 (2.36)	0.88	2.03	0.66
μ= 0.67	−0.73	0.26 (1.66)	15.39 (4.63)	0.80 (4.27)	−0.82 (2.33)	0.87	1.68	0.58
μ= 1	−0.40	0.15 (0.81)	10.77 (3.76)	0.88 (4.60)	−0.99 (2.73)	0.88	1.51	0.51

Belgium joins the ranks of the group of countries with a relatively low value for μ. As for France, the results are quite insensitive to variations in μ, however. We can select the optimal result mainly on the basis of the Durbin-Watson test, which equals 2 at μ = 0.50.

The coefficient of import prices is highly significant, and so is that of indirect taxes, despite its negative sign. Multicollinearity becomes a problem as μ increases.

Netherlands

1955-68	Constant term	Lagged inflation rate	Unem-ployment term (lagged 2 years)	Import prices	Indirect taxes	$\bar{R}^2$	DW	COL
$\mu = 1/3$	1.39	0.50 (2.73)	2.57 (1.54)	1.10 (3.56)	−0.61 (0.71)	0.67	1.87	0.69
$\mu = 1/2$	1.39	0.36 (2.01)	3.01 (1.85)	1.19 (3.92)	−0.42 (0.51)	0.70	1.87	0.68
$\mu = 2/3$	1.49	0.24 (1.31)	3.03 (1.96)	1.26 (4.17)	−0.28 (0.35)	0.71	1.87	0.65
$\mu = 3/4$	1.60	0.19 (1.00)	2.90 (1.93)	1.28 (4.26)	−0.20 (0.25)	0.71	1.86	0.63
$\mu = 1$	2.15	0.05 (0.24)	2.27 (1.64)	1.36 (4.39)	0.09 (0.12)	0.69	1.79	0.58

The Netherlands is the only country where a very long lag with respect to the unemployment situation seems to exist. The optimal value for μ is situated in the range between 2/3 and 3/4. The Durbin-Watson is of no help here to discriminate between results. On the basis of the t-values, it would seem possible to select 2/3 as the best guess for μ.

As was the case for Belgium, the coefficient of import prices is highly significant. The coefficient of indirect taxes is usually negative also, but never significant.

Sweden

1955-68	Constant term	Lagged inflation rate	Unem-ployment term (lag-ged 1 year)	Import prices (lagged 1 year)	Indirect taxes	$\bar{R}^2$	DW	COL
$\mu = 1/3$	2.38	0.26 (2.05)	1.63 (0.97)	1.20 (5.42)	1.28 (3.15)	0.76	1.90	0.76
$\mu = 2/3$	2.68	0.00 (0.00)	2.04 (1.53)	1.29 (6.38)	1.33 (3.15)	0.81	2.08	0.74
$\mu = 1$	3.18	−0.25 (2.07)	1.77 (1.70)	1.38 (6.85)	1.53 (3.36)	0.82	2.19	0.66

For Sweden the highest t-values are obtained for $\mu=1$. The overall correlation hardly increases after $\mu=2/3$. The Durbin-Watson is always satisfactory. The major problem is that the coefficient of the lagged inflation rate becomes negative at $\mu=1$. We found a similar result for the U.K. The unemployment trade-off is never significant, although it comes nearer to being so as μ increases.

The coefficients of import prices and of indirect taxes are clearly highly significant.

Denmark

1954-68	Constant term	Lagged inflation rate	Unem-ployment term (lagged 1 year)	Import prices	Indirect taxes	$\bar{R}^2$	DW	COL
$\mu= 1/3$	1.54	0.25 (1.23)	21.27 (2.46)	0.44 (1.08)	−0.05 (0.10)	0.47	2.60	0.86
$\mu= 2/3$	1.59	−0.13 (0.57)	21.77 (3.67)	0.70 (1.68)	0.12 (0.26)	0.64	2.63	0.65
$\mu= 1$	1.99	−0.54 (2.11)	20.61 (4.88)	0.98 (2.37)	0.45 (1.00)	0.74	2.67	0.46

The results are very sensitive to changes in μ. The optimal value is clearly $\mu=1$, as was the case for Sweden. However, for $\mu=1$ the coefficient of p_{-1} again becomes negative. Negative autocorrelation is also a problem. The unemployment trade-off is always significant, however. The t-values for the coefficients of import prices are somewhat lower, although significant for $\mu=1$.

The coefficient of indirect taxes is quite unreliable, although the estimate improves as μ approaches 1. Multicollinearity becomes severe also for higher values of μ.

Norway

1955-68	Constant term	Lagged inflation rate	Unem-ployment term	Import prices	Indirect taxes	$\bar{R}^2$	DW	COL
$\mu= 1/3$	1.33	0.46 (1.64)	2.08 (0.76)	0.58 (1.90)	0.68 (1.08)	0.29	2.33	0.81
$\mu= 2/3$	1.65	0.31 (1.26)	1.42 (0.57)	0.78 (2.70)	0.92 (1.42)	0.44	2.37	0.82
$\mu= 1$	2.31	0.11 (0.50)	0.96 (0.50)	0.91 (3.68)	1.18 (1.80)	0.57	2.22	0.80

The results for Norway follow the same pattern as for Sweden and Denmark. They improve rapidly as μ increases from one-third to unity. The unemployment trade-off is never significant, however. The highest t-value is obtained for import prices, followed by indirect taxes. Autocorrelation is never a problem, nor is multicollinearity.

Summary and interpretation of results

The overall explanatory power of the model can be considered satisfactory: it explains relatively well variations in each country's inflation rate in the period 1954-68. For seven countries out of thirteen, (Belgium, Canada, Denmark, France, Germany, U.K. and U.S.), the unemployment rate is the most important explanatory variable. This is confirmed by the so-called beta-coefficients, which reflect the relative importance of each explanatory variable in the process of inflation. Table 7.2. summarizes these coefficients for the optimal result arrived at for each country. The relative sizes of the coefficients under each independent variable is an indication of the relative importance of each variable.

Table 7.2. BETA-COEFFICIENTS OF THE EXPLANATORY VARIABLES IN THE TRADE-OFF MODEL

	Lagged inflation rate	Unemployment rate	Import prices	Indirect taxes
B	0.40	0.68	0.49	−0.25
CA	0.08	0.75	0.28	n.i.
DK	−0.60	1.11	0.46	0.14
F	0.57	0.79	n.i.	−0.37
G	0.55	0.61	0.41	n.i.
IR	n.i.	0.27	0.52	0.26
I	0.58	0.45	0.30	0.01
J	0.06	0.08	0.66	−0.35
NL	0.16	0.38	0.78	−0.04
N	0.10	0.10	0.78	0.35
S	−0.31	0.24	0.95	0.48
UK	−0.44	0.91	0.47	0.34
US	0.11	0.74	n.i.	0.03

The beta-coefficients of the lagged inflation rate practically coincide with the regression coefficient of this variable in the corresponding equation. This is a consequence of the definition of the beta-coefficient, which is the product of the regression coefficient and the proportion of the standard deviation of the independent variable and that of the dependent variable. Since the standard deviation of p cannot differ much from that of p_{-1}, the proportion is approximately one, and the beta-coefficient therefore coincides with the regression coefficient of the lagged inflation rate.

Of more interest are the beta-coefficients of the remaining explanatory variables, import prices and indirect taxes. Import prices are the most important variable for Sweden, Norway, The Netherlands, Japan and Ireland. Indirect taxes are in no case the most important variable, but they come second for Sweden, Norway, Japan and Ireland.

Our econometric results not only allow us to determine the contribution of each explanatory variable to annual variations in the rate of price inflation, but also its contribution to the *average* annual inflation rate recorded for each country during the period 1954-68. For this purpose, and to eliminate the influence of the lagged inflation rate, we computed first the steady-state equivalent of the optimal econometric result for each country. The average value of each explanatory variable was then multiplied by the corresponding steady-state coefficient. The results are shown in Table 7.3.

Table 7.3. CONTRIBUTION OF THE INDEPENDENT VARIABLES
TO THE AVERAGE INFLATION RATE 1954-68

	Constant term	Unemployment term	Import prices	Indirect taxes	Total explained price inflation (annual average)
B	-1.2	3.8	-0.1	0.1	2.6
CA	-1.7	3.4	0.9	n.i.	2.6
DK	1.3	2.8	0.1	0.1	4.3
F	-2.6	7.7	n.i.	0.2	5.3
G	1.9	0.8	-0.1	n.i.	2.6
IR	-0.9	4.1	0.1	0.1	3.4
I	0.4	2.6	-0.1	0.0	2.9
J	2.8	0.9	-0.3	0.4	3.8
NL	2.0	2.3	-0.1	0.0	4.2
N	2.6	0.8	-0.1	0.1	3.4
S	2.5	0.9	0.1	0.4	3.9
UK	-1.1	4.2	0.2	0.1	3.4
US	-1.9	4.1	n.i.	0.0	2.2
Average	0.4	2.9	0.1	0.1	3.5

Partly because of rounding errors, partly because of the steady-state formula used, the total explained price inflation sometimes differs slightly from the observed averages. The table clearly shows that despite the sometimes important contribution of import prices and indirect taxes to fluctuations in the inflation rate, the *average* influence of these variables was usually negligible. (The only exception is Canada, but here import prices were replaced in the estimating equation by the U.S. inflation rate). The reason is that import price levels were on the whole steady or even slightly decreasing during the period under consideration, so they could contribute very little to average inflation in the countries concerned. Indirect taxes had a noticeable impact only in Sweden. Here the reason is different: although in most countries the pressure of indirect taxation increased during the period as a whole, the estimated regression coefficients were often small and erratic, so that our estimate of their average contribution is also small and unreliable.

The effect of average unemployment rates on inflation is difficult to establish because of the presence of the constant term, which absorbs part of the influence of the trade-off coefficient, and therefore does not correspond to its definition implied by the theoretical model. Still, the econometric results are useful to correct the observed inflation rates for the estimated influence of import prices and indirect taxes. We can then relate the corrected average inflation rates ($\hat{p}$) to average unemployment rates ($\bar{u}$). This is done in Fig. 7.2.

FIGURE 7.2

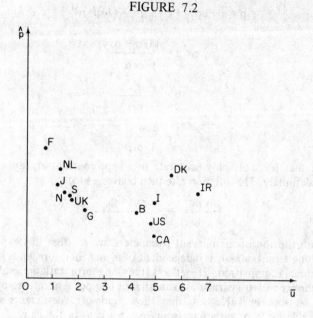

F	France	NL	Netherlands	DK	Denmark
G	Germany	S	Sweden	I	Italy
J	Japan	UK	United Kingdom	C	Canada
N	Norway	B	Belgium	US	United States
				IR	Ireland

This figure indicates that it is not possible to explain inter-country differences in inflation simply by inter-country differences in unemployment levels. At best such a relationship might exist for the group of countries at the left, ranging from France (F) to Germany (G); if so, the other countries would appear to lie on different trade-off curves. This is confirmed by the econometric results recorded, which show much higher trade-off coefficients for the six countries at the right (Belgium, Canada, Denmark, Ireland, Italy, United States) than for those at the left of the diagram. The estimated trade-off coefficients, however, are not directly comparable, since they depend on the assumed values of μ. It is therefore preferable first to translate all estimated short term trade-off coefficients into their long term equivalent. This can be done as follows.

Assume import prices and the pressure of indirect taxation are constant. The reduced form of the equation can then be written as:

$$p = a + bp_{-1} + c \; [\; \mu^{-1} - (1-\mu) \, \mu_{-1}^{-1} \;]$$

$$\text{where } a = \frac{\mu(\beta\eta - q)}{1-\alpha\epsilon\mu}$$

$$b = \frac{1-\mu}{1-\alpha\epsilon\mu}$$

$$c = \frac{\alpha\varphi\eta}{1-\alpha\epsilon\mu}$$

Assume that the unemployment rate u is kept constant at, say, one per cent, indefinitely. The inflation rate then converges to:

$$\frac{a + \mu c}{1-b} = \frac{\alpha\varphi\eta + \beta\eta - q}{1-\alpha\epsilon}$$

After substitution of the relevant parameters, we see that this expression of the long term trade-off is independent of μ, and therefore lends itself to international comparison. It reflects the long-term inflation rate that would correspond to a permanent situation of one per cent unemployment. It can be seen in Table 7.4. that these trade-off coefficients show a considerable range of variation, from 26.5 per cent in the case of Ireland to 2.5 per cent in the case of France.

Table 7.4. LONG TERM TRADE-OFF COEFFICIENTS AND UNEMPLOYMENT RATES

	Optimal μ	$\dfrac{a + \mu c}{1 - b}$	Minimum unemployment	Average unemployment
Belgium	0.5	13.0	2.2	4.4
Canada	1	16.7	3.4	5.1
Denmark	1	14.7	2.4	5.8
France	0.5	2.5	0.4	0.7
Germany	0.2	2.9	0.6	2.3
Ireland	1	26.5	5.5	6.9
Italy	0.2	11.4	2.5	5.1
Japan	1	3.7	0.8	1.2
Netherlands	0.67	4.6	0.8	1.3
Norway	1	3.7	1.0	1.5
Sweden	1	4.0	1.1	1.7
United Kingdom	1	6.0	1.2	1.8
United States	1	19.0	3.6	5.0

The relationships between the estimated trade-offs and the unemployment rates revealed in this table are very interesting. It can be seen that the countries with low coefficients are relatively low-unemployment countries (from U.K. to F) whereas high trade-offs are observed for high-unemployment countries.

The relationship is especially close with respect to the minimum unemployment rate which was observed for each country during the period under study, as Figure 7.3 shows.

FIGURE 7.3

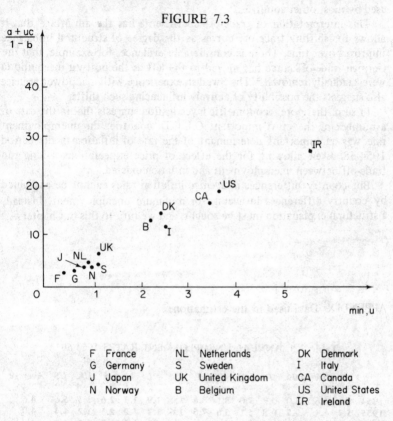

F	France	NL	Netherlands	DK	Denmark
G	Germany	S	Sweden	I	Italy
J	Japan	UK	United Kingdom	CA	Canada
N	Norway	B	Belgium	US	United States
				IR	Ireland

The apparent straight line relationship between the estimated long term trade-off coefficient and the minimum unemployment rate suggests a structural interpretation of the former. Apart from statistical measurement aspects, the minimum unemployment rate must be related to the degree of structural disequilibrium of the labour market. This interpretation is supported by the fact that most of the countries with apparent high trade-offs are well known to have faced structural unemployment problems during the period under study. The best example is Italy, where migration from the south to the north was prohibited until 1961. Linguistic problems in Belgium and Canada have also tended to segment the labour market. Denmark's geographical structure, and Ireland's large rural concentration, may also help to explain their high trade-offs. Finally, in the U.S. the old racial problem and the related discriminatory hiring practices in the labour market may still be playing a role in keeping the minimum unemployment rate at a relatively high level. Furthermore, it is well known that the U.S. unemployment rate is over-estimated when compared to the definition used by most other countries.[4]

This interpretation of trade-off coefficients has the advantage that it allows for shifting trade-off curves as the degree of structural imbalance improves over time. There is considerable evidence, for example, that the German trade-off curve has moved to the left as the postwar disequilibria were gradually removed.[5] The Swedish experience with manpower policies also suggests the possibility of actively influencing such shifts.

In sum, therefore, econometric investigation suggests that in the case of a number of the most important O.E.C.D. countries the unemployment rate was an important determinant of the rate of inflation in the period 1954-68. Even allowing for the effect of price expectations a long run trade-off between unemployment and inflation existed.

But country differences in *average* inflation rates cannot be explained by country differences in average or minimum unemployment. Instead, a structural explanation must be sought, and we turn to this in Chapter 8.

APPENDIX: Data used in the estimations.

Table 7.5. ANNUAL UNEMPLOYMENT RATES 1954-68

	B	CA	DK	F	G	IR	I	J	NL	N	S	UK	US	Average
1954	8.4	4.6	8.0	0.9	7.0	8.1	8.8	1.4	1.9	1.3	2.6	1.5	5.6	4.6
1955	5.7	4.4	9.7	0.8	5.1	6.8	7.6	1.6	1.3	1.2	2.5	1.2	4.4	4.0
1956	4.6	3.4	11.1	0.6	4.0	7.7	9.4	1.5	0.9	1.4	1.7	1.3	4.2	4.0
1957	3.9	4.6	10.2	0.4	3.4	9.2	8.2	1.4	1.2	1.4	1.9	1.5	4.3	4.0
1958	5.5	7.0	9.3	0.5	3.5	8.6	6.6	1.4	2.3	2.3	2.5	2.0	6.8	4.5
1959	6.3	6.0	6.6	0.6	2.4	8.0	5.6	1.5	1.8	2.2	2.0	2.2	5.5	3.9
1960	5.4	7.0	4.3	0.7	7.2	6.7	4.2	1.1	1.2	1.7	1.4	1.6	5.6	3.2
1961	4.2	7.1	3.9	0.6	0.8	5.7	3.5	1.0	0.9	1.2	1.2	1.5	6.7	2.9
1962	3.3	5.9	3.3	0.6	0.7	5.7	3.0	0.9	0.8	1.4	1.3	2.0	5.6	2.7
1963	2.7	5.5	4.3	0.7	0.8	6.1	2.5	0.9	0.9	1.7	1.4	2.4	5.7	2.7
1964	2.2	4.7	2.9	0.6	0.7	5.7	2.7	0.8	0.8	1.4	1.1	1.8	5.2	2.4
1965	2.4	3.9	2.4	0.7	0.6	5.5	3.6	0.8	0.9	1.2	1.1	1.5	4.5	2.2
1966	2.7	3.6	2.6	0.7	0.7	6.1	3.9	0.9	1.1	1.1	1.4	1.6	3.8	2.3
1967	3.7	4.1	3.2	1.0	2.1	6.7	3.5	1.2	2.0	1.0	1.8	2.5	3.8	2.8
1968	4.5	4.8	5.2	1.3	1.6	6.4	3.5	1.2	1.9	1.5	2.0	2.5	3.6	3.1
Average	4.4	5.1	5.8	0.7	2.3	6.9	5.1	1.2	1.3	1.5	1.7	1.8	5.0	3.3

Table 7.6. ANNUAL RATE OF INDIRECT TAXES 1954-68
(First differences)

	B	CA	DK	F	G	IR	I	J	NL	N	S	UK	US	Average
1954	0.1	0.2	−0.5	−0.3	0.0	0.0	0.8	1.0	−0.2	0.0	0.3	0.1	0.0	0.1
1955	0.1	0.2	2.1	−0.5	0.0	−0.4	−0.3	−0.9	−1.0	0.2	0.4	0.2	−0.1	0.0
1956	−0.1	−0.1	−0.1	−0.3	−0.4	0.3	0.4	−0.1	−0.6	0.0	0.0	−0.3	0.1	−0.1
1957	0.1	0.2	0.0	0.5	−0.3	0.6	−0.5	−0.1	−1.2	−0.1	0.0	−0.4	0.1	−0.1
1958	0.1	−0.3	0.4	0.2	−0.2	0.2	0.2	0.0	−0.3	0.9	0.0	−0.1	0.1	0.1
1959	0.7	0.4	0.4	0.8	0.4	−0.2	0.3	0.4	0.5	0.3	0.3	0.1	0.2	0.4
1960	0.2	0.1	0.1	−0.6	−0.2	−1.1	0.1	−0.5	0.2	−0.3	1.3	−0.5	0.4	−0.1
1961	1.0	0.2	−0.7	−0.1	0.1	−0.7	−0.2	−0.3	0.3	0.3	0.1	−0.2	0.0	0.0
1962	−0.2	0.6	0.7	0.0	0.0	−0.3	0.3	−0.2	0.1	0.2	0.9	0.2	0.0	0.2
1963	0.1	−0.2	0.9	0.2	−0.4	0.6	−0.5	−0.3	0.1	−0.5	0.2	−0.2	0.2	0.0
1964	−0.1	0.5	0.0	0.3	−0.1	0.5	0.2	−0.4	−0.1	0.7	−0.1	0.5	−0.1	0.1
1965	−0.2	0.3	0.4	−0.3	0.0	0.1	−0.5	−0.1	0.2	−0.4	0.1	0.5	0.0	0.0
1966	0.8	0.0	0.8	0.0	0.0	1.1	0.5	−0.3	0.4	0.5	0.9	0.7	−0.6	0.4
1967	0.6	0.3	0.1	−0.3	0.4	−0.3	0.1	−0.2	0.3	0.1	0.2	−0.3	0.1	0.1
1968	−0.5	0.0	0.9	−1.2	−1.2	0.3	−0.4	−0.2	0.5	−0.5	0.4	1.1	0.0	0.1
Average	0.2	0.2	0.4	−0.10	−0.14	0.05	0.03	−0.15	−0.05	0.1	0.3	0.1	0.03	0.08

Table 7.7. ANNUAL WEIGHTED IMPORT PRICE ($p_m \frac{M}{Y}$) 1954-68
(Relative changes) *

	B	CA	DK	F	G	IR	I	NL	N	S	UK	US	Average
1954	−1.0	0.0	−1.0	−0.2	−0.1	0.2	−0.3	−0.7	−1.7	−0.2	−0.2	0.1	−0.4
1955	0.0	0.2	0.3	−0.2	0.3	1.2	0.0	0.4	1.1	1.2	−0.6	0.0	0.3
1956	0.9	0.5	1.4	0.7	0.3	0.6	0.3	1.2	2.1	1.4	0.4	0.1	0.8
1957	0.9	0.7	0.7	1.3	0.2	1.5	0.6	2.0	1.7	0.2	0.4	0.0	0.8
1958	−2.1	0.0	−2.6	0.7	−1.5	−1.5	−1.2	−2.2	−2.5	−2.2	−1.5	−0.2	−1.3
1959	−0.6	−0.2	−0.8	1.2	−0.8	−0.8	−0.7	−1.2	−1.8	−0.5	−0.2	0.0	−0.5
1960	0.0	0.2	0.4	0.5	0.0	0.6	−0.1	0.0	0.4	0.0	0.2	0.0	0.2
1961	0.7	0.0	−0.4	−0.4	−0.9	0.4	−0.3	−0.9	−0.4	−0.5	−0.4	−0.1	−0.2
1962	−1.1	0.8	0.8	0.0	−0.3	0.0	0.0	−0.5	−0.4	−0.3	−0.2	−0.1	−0.1
1963	0.0	0.8	0.8	0.1	−0.3	0.7	0.2	0.5	0.4	0.3	0.9	0.0	0.3
1964	0.7	0.2	0.5	0.3	0.0	0.4	0.5	1.0	0.4	1.1	0.9	0.1	0.5
1965	−0.4	0.0	0.5	0.3	0.9	1.0	−0.3	0.5	0.0	0.3	0.0	0.1	0.2
1966	0.4	0.2	0.5	0.2	0.0	−0.3	0.5	0.5	0.8	0.4	0.1		0.3
1967	−0.4	0.2	0.0	0.1	−0.3	0.0	0.0	−0.5	−0.5	0.0	0.0	0.0	−0.1
1968	0.4	0.5	0.8	−0.6	−0.6	3.9	−0.2	−1.7	−1.4	0.3	2.3	0.1	0.3
Average	−0.1	0.3	0.1	0.3	−0.2	0.5	−0.1	−0.1	−0.1	−0.1	0.2	0.0	0.06

8
Structural Factors in O.E.C.D Inflation

In the previous chapter we arrived at the conclusion that differences in unemployment levels could not satisfactorily explain international differences in price inflation. This conclusion was implied by our finding that over the period 1954-68 each country faced a different trade-off curve, which was determined by the minimum unemployment rate which the country had experienced.

In this chapter we examine an alternative hypothesis — the so-called structural or productivity-gap inflation theory, — which has rapidly gained acceptance in recent literature, especially in its Scandinavian versions.[1] In practice, all versions, old and new, have in common a breakdown of the economy into two basic sectors, one of which is characterized by rapid productivity growth, while the other registers much more modest productivity gains. However, the pace of money wage increases is set by the sector with the most rapid productivity advances. These wage increases are transmitted to the rest of the economy, under pressure from trade unions.[2] Normally, this will cause or add to price inflation in the lagging sector, as well as in the economy as a whole.

The originality of the Scandinavian versions lies in the link of the high productivity sector with the world economy: it is this sector which has to compete on the international market, either through exports or import substitution. The rest of the economy comprises those sectors which are either protected artificially from foreign competition or whose output is not normally traded internationally.[3]

The traditional model

The traditional structural inflation model can be summarized in the following four equations. The first equation states that the rate of wage inflation in the high productivity growth sector (which for brevity we shall call the advanced) sector is equal to the growth rate of the money value of productivity in the sector, which can be decomposed into the sector's rate of price inflation plus the growth rate of physical productivity:

(i) $\quad w_c = p_c + q_c$ where $\quad w_c$ = rate of wage inflation in advanced sector.

$\quad q_c$ = rate of physical productivity growth in advanced sector.

$\quad p_c$ = rate of inflation in advanced sector.

The second, and crucial hypothesis, is that the rate of wage inflation in the lagging sector is equal to the corresponding rate in the advanced sector:[4]

(ii) $w_s = w_c$ where w_s = rate of wage inflation in
                                      lagging sector.

The third hypothesis concerns price formation in the lagging sector.

(iii) $p_s = w_s - q_s$ where q_s = rate of physical productivity
                                      growth in lagging sector.

                                 p_s = rate of inflation in the
                                      lagging sector.

The overall rate of price inflation can then be expressed as a weighted average of the sectoral inflation rates:

(iv) $p = \pi p_c + (1 - \pi) p_s$ where p = overall rate of price inflation.
                                 and π and $(1 - \pi)$ are the relative weights
                                 of the advanced and lagging sectors.

The reduced form of this submodel is the following:

(I) $$p = p_c + (1 - \pi)(q_c - q_s)$$ where, by assumption, $q_c > q_s$

The Scandinavian version

In the reduced form of this model, p_c must be regarded as an exogenous variable, determined outside the model. In most expositions of structural. inflation, p_c is arbitrarily set equal to zero.[5] This is convenient because the overall inflation rate then depends only on the gap in productivity growth between the advanced and lagging sectors, and international differences in inflation can be entirely explained by different productivity gaps. However, it is not a satisfactory solution from the economic viewpoint. There are in fact only two possibilities: either p_c is determined within the model, and therefore becomes an endogenous variable; reduced form (I) is then no longer valid, and is an intermediate relationship only; or p_c is determined outside the model, e.g. through export prices. This is essentially what the Scandinavian model assumes: it identifies the advanced sector with the internationally competitive sector, so that p_c coincides with p_x, the growth rate of export prices. Thus we have:

(v) $p_c = p_x$

The lagging sector is in turn identified with the non-competitive or sheltered sector. If we substitute the additional equation (v) in reduced form (I), we obtain:

(II) $p = p_X + (1-\pi)(q_c - q_s)$

or in its more implicit form:

(II) $$p - p_X = (1-\pi)(q_c - q_s)$$

This result allows to regress international differences in the gap between overall price inflation and export price inflation against international differences in the productivity gap, (assuming that the parameter $1-\pi$ does not differ very much between countries.) If, in addition, p_X were equal for all countries, the same equation would again provide an explanation of why inflation rates differ. This hypothesis will be taken up near the end of this chapter, where the determination of export prices will be discussed. In the meantime we shall work with (II), and begin by examining a number of complications.

Possible extensions
It will be observed that the price functions implied by (i) and (iii) are somewhat different from those used in the previous chapter. In order to establish the link, let us reconsider the identity:

$$p + y = \alpha(w+1) + \beta(r+k) + j\ (p_m + m) + \tau t_i$$

This equation establishes the equality of the value of gross output to the sum of its components, after transformation of all variables into relative changes (see Chapter 7, p. 144).

Since the Scandinavian model neglects import prices and indirect taxes,[6] let us also drop the last two terms of the equation above. The identity can be rewritten as a price function:

$$p = \alpha(w+1-y) + \beta(r+k-y) \qquad \text{where } \alpha + \beta = 1$$

Defining the growth rate of labour productivity by q_l and that of capital by q_k, it follows that:

$$p = \alpha(w-q_1) + (1-\alpha)(r-q_k)$$

The rate of price inflation can thus be expressed as a weighted average of the relative increase of unit labour cost and of unit capital cost.

Let us express the relationship between the two relative increases by the formula:

$$r - q_k = (1-\delta)(w-q_1)$$

This formula defines possible changes in income distribution: when $\delta = 1$, the income distribution is fixed; when $\delta > 0$, the distribution changes in favour of wage income. In general, therefore, our price function can always be written as:

$$p = (w-q_1) \, [1-(1-\alpha)\delta] \qquad \text{where } \eta = 1-(1-\alpha)\delta$$
$$\eta \, (w-q) \qquad\qquad\qquad q = q_l$$

The parameter η is the so-called mark-up elasticity, which, through δ, is related to changes in income distribution (for $\delta > 0$, $\eta < 1$). In the Swedish study, it is indicated that η is equal to one for the sheltered sector, but smaller than one for the competitive sector. In the Norwegian report, η is also smaller than one for the sheltered sector. If we solve the model in general with η_c and η_s different from one, we obtain as reduced form:

$$\text{(II) } bis \quad p = [\pi + (1-\pi) \frac{\eta_s}{\eta_c} \,] \, p_X + (1-\pi)\eta_s \, (q_c - q_s)$$

This result indicates that it is the mark-up elasticity of the sheltered sector which determines the slope of the regression coefficient with respect to the productivity gap. If we want an expression similar to (II) with p_X transferred to the left-hand side, we have to assume $\eta_c = \eta_s = \eta$

$$\text{(II) } bis \quad \boxed{p - p_X = (1-\pi) \, \eta \, (q_c - q_s)}$$

Our second extension concerns the wage equations. In fact there is no wage equation for the competitive sector, since wages are determined through the inverted price equation (i). Without destroying the rationale of the model, it is therefore impossible to introduce any other explanatory variable, such as unemployment, in this equation. It could be done, however, in equation (ii), which describes the transmission of wage increases to the sheltered sector:

(ii) $w_s = w_c \, \varphi u^{-1}$ where u = unemployment rate
                                          φ = structural parameter, reflecting the degree of imperfection of the labour market.

The rate of wage inflation in the competitive sector will be fully transmitted to the sheltered sector only if $u = \varphi$, where φ can be interpreted as some minimum unemployment rate experienced by the economy. For all values of u above this minimum, w_s will be smaller than w_c. Unfortunately, the non-linearity of this relationship causes the reduced form of the model to lose its attractive simplicity. It can now be written as:

$$p = \pi p_X - (1-\pi)q_s + (1-\pi) \, (p_X + q_c) \, \varphi \, u^{-1}$$

Only if the growth rates of export prices and of productivity are relatively constant over time, will this equation behave like some sort of trade-off relationship.

The data

Before testing the reduced-forms (II) and (II) *bis*, we have to examine some of the data problems we are facing. As in Chapter 8, we shall test our theory on a sample of 13 O.E.C.D. countries and for the period 1954-68. The behaviour of the model during the post-1968 period will be examined in Chapter 10. A major difference with the approach of the previous chapter, however, is that we shall test the theory directly on a cross-section basis: indeed, since the phenomenon which we are trying to measure is a structural one, time series probably does not contain enough information for testing on a country-by-country basis. Our observations are therefore all averages for the period 1954-68 of the different variables concerned.

a. The dependent variables

Our dependent variable is $p-p_x$, i.e. the difference between the average inflation rate of GDP and the average growth rate of export prices, the latter expressed in domestic currency. However, since the Scandinavian model neglects import prices and indirect taxes, we are interested in obtaining a domestic inflation rate $\hat{p}$, which has been corrected for the influence of these explanatory variables. Our calculations of Chapter 7 allow us to calculate such a net inflation rate, as in Table 8.1.

Table 8.1. GROWTH RATES OF GDP-PRICE LEVEL AND
OF EXPORT PRICES 1954-68

	p	$\hat{p}$	p_x	$\hat{p} - p_x$
Belgium	2.5	2.5	− 0.1	2.6
Canada	2.4	1.5	1.3	0.1
Denmark	4.5	4.3	0.6	3.7
France	4.8	4.6	2.3	2.3
Germany	2.6	2.7	0.3	2.4
Ireland	3.4	3.5	1.3	2.2
Italy	3.4	3.5	− 0.9	4.4
Japan	3.7	3.6	− 0.6	4.3
Netherlands	4.2	4.3	0.1	4.2
Norway	3.5	3.5	0.4	3.1
Sweden	3.8	3.3	0.8	2.5
United Kingdom	3.2	2.9	2.0	0.9
United States	2.2	2.2	1.2	1.0

p = average rate of price inflation (GDP)
$\hat{p}$ = id., corrected for changes in import prices and indirect taxation.
    In the case of Canada import prices have been replaced by US-inflation rate
p_x = growth rate of export prices, national currency

In Table 8.1. we notice that the gap between domestic inflation and export prices is particularly important for Italy, Japan and the Netherlands This is due to the fact that the export price level for these countries either fell or remained constant during the period under consideration. On the other hand, the gap is of moderate size in the case of Belgium, France, Germany, Ireland, Norway and Sweden; but it is rather narrow for Canada, the United States and the United Kingdom, where export prices rose rather rapidly. The gap-estimate for Canada is probably too low, as a consequence of over-correcting the domestic inflation rate by using the U.S. inflation rate in place of import prices in the price equation (see p. 156, Chapter 7). It might therefore be preferable to use the non-corrected rate, thus bringing the gap $p- p_x$ to one per cent, the same as for the U.K. and the U.S.

b. The independent variable

Our independent variable is the gap in productivity growth between the competitive and sheltered sectors of the economy. For the purpose of our cross-section approach, it seems advisable to follow an identical sectoral breakdown for each of the countries in our sample. The breakdown suggested in the Swedish study[7] appeared impossible to employ at the international level because of definitional problems. Instead, we have used the following division, which is based on the standardized national accounts of the O.E.C.D. and the employment statistics of the I.L.O.

Competitive Sector	Sheltered Sector
1. Agriculture, forestry, fishing.	4. Construction.
2. Mining and quarrying.	5. Public utilities (water, gas, etc.)
3. Manufacturing.	6. Transport and communication.
	7. Commerce.
	8. Services.
	9. Miscellaneous.

The most obvious difference with the Swedish definitions lies in the inclusion of agriculture in the competitive sector, thus increasing the latter's importance to between 40 and 50 per cent of GDP, whereas it represented less than one-third in the Swedish study. However, the inclusion of agriculture can be defended on at least two grounds. First, although in most countries agriculture is protected in some way or another (for example, price support mechanisms, import controls, or both), price formation for agricultural products is essentially different from that in most branches of the sheltered sector. In a way, it can be argued that agricultural prices are determined *exogenously*. The same is true for prices in the competitive sector, which we assumed to be determined by the world market. From the viewpoint of the structure of the model, where the chain of causality runs from prices to incomes for the competitive sector, it seems logical to include agriculture in the same group as mining and manufacturing.

The second reason for including agriculture in the competitive sector is purely empirical, viz. in most countries the growth rate of productivity in agriculture is close to the average productivity growth of industries in the competitive sector. In a few countries, productivity gains in agriculture have even exceeded the average increase measured for a more narrowly defined competitive sector. Statistically speaking we therefore obtain a more homogeneously defined sector when we include agriculture in the competitive sector than when we exclude it.

Unless otherwise indicated, all productivity growth rates were calculated for the period 1954-68. The major exception is Ireland for which the required statistics were available only from 1958 onwards. The calculated growth rates are presented in Table 8.2.

Table 8.2. GROWTH RATES OF LABOUR PRODUCTIVITY IN COMPETITIVE AND SHELTERED SECTORS (averages for the period 1954-68)

	q_c	q_s	$q_c - q_s$
Belgium	4.1	1.8	2.3
Canada	4.1	0.0	4.1
Denmark	3.9	1.3	2.6
France	6.4	2.7	3.7
Germany	6.2	3.6	2.6
Ireland (58-68)	5.6	2.6	3.0
Italy	7.3	2.4	4.9
Japan	12.9	10.7	2.2
Netherlands	5.2	2.3	2.9
Norway	3.9	3.0	0.9
Sweden (56-68)	5.1	1.5	3.6
United Kingdom	3.0	1.1	1.9
United States	3.1	1.8	1.3

The range of productivity growth for the competitive sector is considerable, from 3 per cent in the U.K. to 13 per cent in Japan. The average for the 13 countries is about 5 per cent. Somewhat surprisingly, the corresponding range for the sheltered sector is equally large, from zero for Canada to 11 per cent in Japan. The scatter diagram (see Figure 8.1.) even suggests a positive correlation between the productivity growth rates in the two sectors.

This is an interesting finding, since it is generally thought that productivity cannot increase very much in the service sector, which represents a substantial share of the sheltered conglomerate. It may indicate that not only does there exist a wage spillover between the competitive and sheltered parts of the economy, but a productivity spillover as well. This somewhat weakens the case for productivity inflation, which supposedly results from rapid productivity growth in the advanced sector of the economy.

FIGURE 8.1

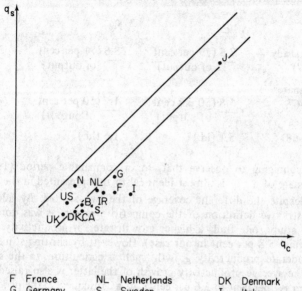

F	France	NL	Netherlands	DK	Denmark
G	Germany	S	Sweden	I	Italy
J	Japan	UK	United Kingdom	CA	Canada
N	Norway	B	Belgium	US	United States
				IR	Ireland

Some of the estimated productivity growth rates for the sheltered sector do appear to be unrealistic. This is surely the case for Canada, where a productivity growth of zero per cent seems too low; and also Norway, where it seems rather high (three per cent). In the case of Norway this may be the consequence of including transportation in the sheltered sector, despite the fact that perhaps two-thirds of it is shipping, which really belongs to the competitive sector. The Canadian case is well documented, although not satisfactorily clarified.[3] It is surprising that the productivity growth rate in the sheltered sector is so much lower than in U.S., whereas the contrary is true for the competitive sector. However, these odd results serve to remind us that the whole concept of productivity growth in a sector dominated by services is not a particularly reliable one, owing to the difficulties associated with measuring output. Some national accounts estimates are actually based on an *assumption* regarding productivity growth which is likely to differ from country to country.

Apart from such measurement errors, which in principle are random, systematic errors may result from our quite arbitrary definition of the competitive sector. We can check for the importance of this by comparing our estimates for Sweden with those presented in the original Swedish study, which refer to the period 1960-67. Recalculating our own figures for the same period, we have the following comparison:

Sweden	q_c	q_s	$q_c - q_s$
Swedish study (1960-67)	7.5 (29 per cent of output)	3.6 (71 per cent of output)	3.9
Our estimates a) 1960-67	5.8 (50 per cent of output)	1.7 (50 per cent of output)	4.1
b) 1956-68	5.1 (id.)	1.5 (id.)	3.6

It is encouraging to observe that, for a comparable period (1960-67), our estimate of $q_c - q_s$ is almost identical to that presented in the Swedish study, despite the different coverage of the two sectors. By adopting a more restrictive definition of the competitive sector, as was done in the Swedish study, one finds a higher growth rate for productivity (7.5 per cent against 5.8 per cent in our case). However, by shifting some sectors with moderate productivity growth, such as agriculture, to the sheltered sector, the average productivity growth of the latter is also raised (in this case from 1.7 per cent to 3.6 per cent). As a consequence, the productivity gap $q_c - q_s$ between the two sectors does not change very much (3.9 versus 4.1). If this Swedish example is at all representative, we may not need to worry too much about systematic errors arising from sectoral definitions.

Before we can proceed with a formal test of our main hypothesis, we still need *a priori* estimates of the parameters $(1-\pi)$ and η. The first is easy to calculate, since it represents the average share of the sheltered sector in total private GDP. The results of this calculation are presented in the last column of Table 8.3. It will be observed that the share of the sheltered sector varies from 42 per cent (W. Germany) to 59 per cent (United States). On account of this we would expect W. Germany to be less sensitive to productivity inflation than the U.S.

The mark-up elasticity η is more difficult to measure. According to our earlier derivation, we can write

$$p = \eta (w-q)$$

On the other hand, if we define the wage share by $S = WL/PY$ it follows, after transformation to relative changes, that

$$s = w + 1 - p - y = w - p - q$$

Substitution yields

$$s = w - q - \eta (w-q) = (1-\eta)(w-q)$$

Dividing both sides by $p = \eta (w-q)$, we find

$$\frac{s}{p} = \frac{1-\eta}{\eta} \text{ or } \eta = \frac{1}{1 + \dfrac{s}{p}}$$

This means that it is possible to derive an estimate of η if one knows the growth rate of the wage share, s, on the one hand, and the inflation rate p on the other, in this case corrected for the influence of import prices and indirect taxes. The results are presented in Table 8.3.

Table 8.3. CALCULATIONS OF MARK-UP ELASTICITIES η AND OF $(1 - \pi)$

	s	p	s/p	$\eta = \dfrac{1}{1 + s/p}$	$1 - \pi$
Belgium	1.0	2.5	0.40	0.71	0.51
Canada	0.7	(2.4)	0.29	0.78	0.55
Denmark	1.1	4.3	0.26	0.79	0.54
France	0.6	4.6	0.13	0.88	0.44
Germany	0.5	2.7	0.19	0.84	0.42
Ireland	1.1	3.5	0.31	0.76	0.46
Italy	1.2	3.5	0.34	0.75	0.48
Japan	0.6	3.6	0.17	0.85	0.50
Netherlands	1.2	4.3	0.28	0.78	0.49
Norway	0.8	3.2	0.23	0.81	0.52
Sweden	1.1	3.3	0.33	0.75	0.50
U.K.	0.5	2.9	0.17	0.85	0.51
U.S.	0.4	2.2	0.18	0.85	0.59

In principle, we are interested in measuring the mark-up elasticity for the competitive and sheltered sectors separately, but the lack of wage share data for these sectors makes this impossible.

Verification of the structural hypothesis

In our theoretical section, we have derived two basic expressions for the reduced form:

(I) $\qquad p = (1-\pi)(q_c - q_s) \qquad$ assuming $p_c = 0$

(II) $\qquad p - p_x = (1-\pi)\,\eta\,(q_c - q_s)$

The first type of reduced form, which represents the "pure" structural inflation hypothesis, relates international differences in the inflation rate to different productivity gaps only.

The second type of reduced form, which represents the Scandinavian version of the structural model, has as dependent variable the difference between p and p_x. Each type was tested in three versions, of which the last two make use of the a priori estimates of $(1-\pi)$ and η respectively.

Reduced form I   *Reduced form II*
(pure structural model)   (Scandinavian model)

$\hat{p} = 2.53 + 0.31 \, (q_c - q_s)$ $R = 0.42$ $\hat{p} - p_x = 1.29 + 0.50 \, (q_c - q_s)$ $R = 0.38$
                                          $t = 1.53$ $t = 1.3.$

$\hat{p} = 2.60 + 0.56 \, (1-\pi) \, (q_c - q_s)$ $\hat{p} - p_x = 1.25 + 1.04 \, (1-\pi) \, (q_c - q_s)$

                                          $R = 0.34$ $R = 0.3($
                                          $t = 1.20$ $t = 1.2\mathcal{9}$

$\hat{p} = 2.44 + 0.85 \eta \, (1-\pi) \, (q_c - q_s)$ $\hat{p} - p_x = 1.34 + 1.22 \eta \, (1-\pi) \, (q_c - q_s)$
                                          $R = 0.39$ $R = 0.3.$
                                          $t = 1.40$ $t = 1.2.$

Neither the results for the pure structural model, nor those for the Scandinavian version allow us to reject the null hypothesis which would imply that there is no connection with the productivity gap. The t-values corresponding to the measured correlation coefficients never reach the 95 per cent significance level.

The Scandinavian version appears to perform no better than the simple structural model: as a matter of fact, R is slightly lower in two estimates out of three for reduced form II. The use of *a priori* information concerning $(1-\pi)$ and η does not improve the results either, on the contrary, they are slightly worse. In other words, it seems better to assume that all countries have the same mark-up elasticity and the same relative share for the sheltered sector, than to use the *a priori* information which we have estimated.

Despite the fact that the regression coefficients are not significant, it must be admitted that their order of magnitude conforms to *a priori* expectations. The coefficient of $\eta \, (1-\pi) \, (q_c - q_s)$ is *a priori* equal to unity. The estimate of reduced form I puts it at 0.85 and that of reduced form II at 1.22, both not greatly different from 1. The structural hypothesis may therefore remain basically correct, although it is not a significant factor in explaining inter-country differences in inflation.

It will be noticed that in reduced form I, the constant term is approximately 2.5 in all three results; and it will be recalled that in the theoretical reduced form, the constant term stands for p_c, the rate of price inflation in the advanced sector. The estimate of 2.5 per cent per annum is of course some kind of average for the 13 countries in the sample, and is itself subject to considerable variation. However, it allows us to reject the hypothesis that $p_c = 0$. This is an important conclusion, since it implies that the rate of wage inflation must have exceeded the rate of productivity growth in this sector (i.e. w_c must have been greater than $q_c)^9$. On the other hand, the continued presence of a constant term of the order of 1.3 per cent per annum average in reduced form II, after subtraction of p_x, indicates that the assumption $p_x = p_c$, on which the Scandinavian

FIGURE 8.2

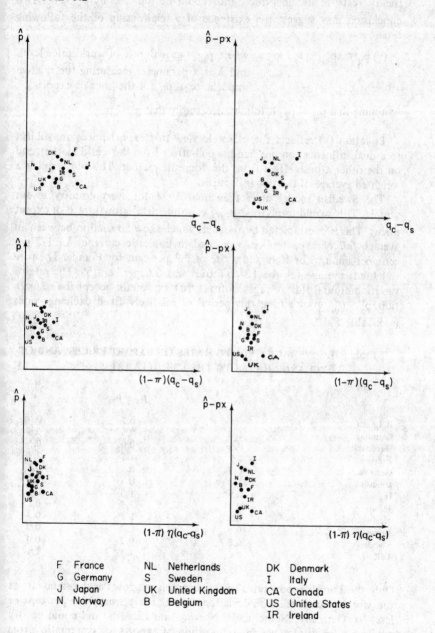

F	France	NL	Netherlands	DK	Denmark
G	Germany	S	Sweden	I	Italy
J	Japan	UK	United Kingdom	CA	Canada
N	Norway	B	Belgium	US	United States
				IR	Ireland

theory rests, is also incorrect, and should be replaced by $p_x < p_c$. This conclusion may suggest the existence of a relationship of the following type.

(v) $p_x = \lambda p_w + (1-\lambda)p_c$ · where p_w = growth rate of world price level, and λ is a parameter measuring the relative importance of p_w for the price of exports.

Assuming that $p_w < p_c$, it follows necessarily that $p_x < p_c$.[10]

Equation (v) reflects the plausible view that export prices are subject to a dual influence: on one hand, a pull-effect from the world market, and on the other a push-effect from the domestic market. The end result is a weighted average of the two influences.

The Swedish model in fact assumes $\lambda = 1$ for every country in our sample. This would imply $p_x = p_w$, i.e. an identical growth rate of export prices. This is contradicted by the facts which show a variation between an average *fall* of export prices measured in domestic currency of 1.2 per cent per annum for Italy and a *rise* of 2.3 per cent for France. The (unweighted) average for the 13 countries was 0.6 per cent.[11] The rate of variation around this average confirms that we cannot accept the assumption $p_x = p_w$, even during this period of relatively fixed exchange rates (see Table 8.4.).

Table 8.4. AVERAGE GROWTH RATES OF EXPORT PRICES, AND OF EXCHANGE RATES TO THE US-DOLLAR (1954-68)

	p_x	$p_x - p_w$	t
Belgium	− 0.1	− 0.7	0.0
Canada	1.4	0.8	0.6
Denmark	0.6	0.0	0.5
France	2.3	1.7	2.3
Germany	0.3	− 0.3	− 0.3
Ireland	1.3	0.7	1.1
Italy	− 0.9	− 1.5	− 0.1
Japan	− 0.7	− 1.3	− 0.1
Netherlands	0.1	− 0.5	− 0.3
Norway	0.4	− 0.2	0.0
Sweden	0.8	0.2	0.0
U.K.	2.0	1.4	1.1

Only the Danish export price level seems to have grown at the same rate as the world price level. The deviation was relatively small (0.5 per cent or less) for Germany, Netherlands, Norway and Sweden, and could be still explicable by differences in composition of exports, or systematic errors in the measurement of the export price index.

It is of interest to observe the relationship between relative changes in exchange rates (t) and each country's growth rate of export prices (Figure 8.3.). Even during this period of relative stability of exchange rates, the major adjustments that were required did take place, although in the case of some countries only at the very end of the period (for instance, the U.K. and Ireland in 1967).

FIGURE 8.3

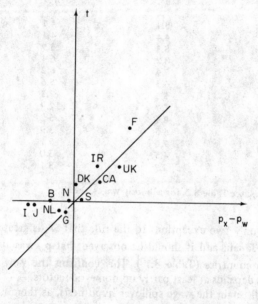

Non-symmetric distribution of the observations around the 45°-line at the lower part of the diagram indicates a clear reluctance on the part of some countries to revalue (with the exception of W. Germany and the Netherlands). In general, however, it seems justified to specify the relationship:

$$(vi) \qquad t = p_x - p_w$$

A Modified Structural Model

The results of our empirical investigation so far, while they do not force us to reject the productivity gap theory *per se*, are clearly inconclusive for explaining differences in international inflation rates. Is it possible to modify the structural model so as to add to our understanding of world inflation from 1954 to 1968? We can begin with our first equation, rewritten in the price equation form, from which it was originally derived:

$$(i) \; bis \qquad p_c = w_c - q_c \qquad \text{where normally } w_c > q_c$$

There exists some information concerning the extent to which the growth rate of wages has exceeded productivity growth in the competitive sector, which we summarize in Table 8.5. below.

Table 8.5. GROWTH RATES OF NOMINAL WAGES AND LABOUR PRODUCTIVITY IN THE COMPETITIVE SECTOR, 1954-68

	w_c	q_c	$w_c - q_c$
Belgium	6.4	4.1	2.3
Canada	4.4	4.1	0.3
Denmark	8.3	3.9	4.4
France	8.2	6.4	1.8
W. Germany	7.4	6.2	1.2
Ireland	6.3	5.6	0.7
Italy	5.5	7.3	− 1.8
Japan	7.7	12.9	− 5.2
Netherlands	8.1	5.2	2.9
Norway	6.5	3.9	2.6
Sweden	7.0	5.1	1.9
U.K.	4.5	3.0	1.5
U.S.	3.7	3.1	0.6

Notes: for q_c see Table 8.2; for w hourly wages, see IFS

There are only two exceptions to the rule that w_c is greater than q_c, viz. Italy and Japan; and it should be observed that p_x was also negative for these two countries (Table 8.1.). This confirms the view that the price of exports depends at least partly on domestic factors.

We shall retain the wage spillover hypothesis, as there is no reason for not doing so for the time being:

$$\text{(ii) } bis \qquad w_s = w_c$$

The third equation is the price equation for the sheltered sector, as before:

$$\text{(iii) } bis \qquad p_s = w_s - q_s$$

The fourth equation, which is the definitional equation, also remains unchanged.

$$\text{(iv) } bis \qquad p = \pi p_c + (1-\pi) p_s$$

The fifth equation is the export price function, mentioned above:

(v) $\qquad p = \lambda p_w + (1-\lambda) p_c$ where λ is the parameter measuring the relative importance of p_w for the price of exports.

Finally:

$$(vi) \qquad t = p_X - p_W$$

The model is now composed of 6 equations and 10 variables which leaves room for four exogenous variables (p_W, q_c, q_s and w_c). The major difference from the previous models is that w_c is now an exogenous variable, whereas in the previous models it was endogenous. It is of course possible to extend the model by introducing a wage equation of the type discussed in Chapter 7, but this is not necessary for our present purposes.

Arrow diagrams may bring out more clearly the difference in structure of the model presented here from that of the Swedish model examined earlier.

FIGURE 8.4

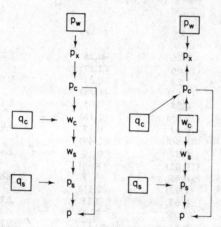

The variables enclosed in a square box are exogenous. Solving the general model for p and p_X, respectively, we find:

$$p = w_c - \pi q_c - (1-\pi) q_s$$
$$p_X = p_W + (1-\lambda) (w_c - q_c)$$

and

$$(III) \qquad p - p_X = \lambda (w_c - q_c - p_X) + (1-\pi) (q_c - q_s)$$

This result explains why our empirical investigation of reduced form II yielded a positive constant term. If our modified structural model is correct, it means that on the average, for our group of 13 countries as a whole, the growth rate of wages w_c exceeded the sum of the growth rate of productivity plus the growth rate of world prices. Reduced form III also explains why the correlation coefficient obtained with II was so low:

it is because of the variability of the term $\lambda (w_c - q_c - p_w)$ which was interpreted as a constant. This term varies for two reasons; first as a consequence of the degree of variation in $(w_c - q_c)$ as shown in Table 8.5., and second as a consequence of the variability of λ, which varies also from country to country.

In order to obtain an estimate of λ we have tested the export price function (v) on time series for each country separately. The results are given in Table 8.6. The equation tested was the logarithmic form of the reduced-form equation $p_x = \lambda p_w + (1 - \lambda) (w_c - q_c)$ on which we had imposed restrictions first, that the constant term was zero *and* second, that the sum of the regression coefficients should be one.

Table 8.6. EXPORT PRICE FUNCTIONS FOR O.E.C.D. COUNTRIES

$$\text{Log } P_x = \lambda \log P_w + (1 - \lambda) \log \frac{W_c}{Q_c}$$

	λ	$1 - \lambda$	DW	COL
Belgium*	1.26 (10.86)	−0.26 (2.27)	1.28	0.47
Canada**	1.24 (9.12)	−0.24 (1.74)	1.36	0.89
Denmark*	0.95 (22.65)	0.05 (1.18)	2.10	0.65
France*	0.63 (2.50)	0.37 (1.49)	0.53	0.99
W. Germany*	0.87 (10.01)	0.13 (1.48)	2.43	0.96
Ireland*	0.43 (1.92)	0.57 (2.58)	0.86	0.38
Italy	0.65 (5.04)	0.35 (2.75)	2.23	0.99
Japan*	0.83 (19.96)	0.17 (4.01)	1.71	0.69
Netherlands	1.15 (22.62)	−0.15 (2.99)	1.84	0.58
Norway*	1.37 (14.36)	−0.37 (3.86)	2.18	0.80
Sweden*	0.78 (4.70)	0.22 (1.32)	2.07	0.98
United Kingdom**	0.61 (2.81)	0.39 (1.97)	1.47	0.83
United States*	0.90 (5.71)	0.10 (0.65)	1.77	0.98

* second iteration   ** third iteration

We see that about half of our sample of 13 countries have an estimated value of λ above or close to unity. As one would expect, most small countries are included in this group, with Ireland being a conspicuous exception outside it. Estimated λ is also relatively high in the case of Germany, Japan and the U.S., but it is low in the case of France, Ireland and the U.K.: all these latter countries altered their exchange parities significantly at some time or another in the period.

It is instructive to associate the estimated values of λ with both the behaviour of export prices in domestic currency relative to the world price level and the behaviour of wage rates and productivity growth in the competitive sector of the countries we are examining, as is done in Table 8.7. It will be seen that export prices of most of the countries with an estimated λ above or close to unity rose more slowly than the world price level while the opposite was true for those countries which had a relatively low λ.

The most significant thing to be noted from Table 8.7. however is that two countries — Italy and Japan — enjoyed a significant and steady *fall* in the domestic currency price level of their exports and these were both countries (and they were the only two countries) in which productivity growth in the competitive sectors of their economies exceeded the rate of increase of money wages paid in these sectors. The difference was very great, and in the case of Japan exceeded five per cent per annum. It seems a plausible hypothesis therefore that these two countries, whose export volume grew very fast in the 1950s and 1960s, were price leaders in world trade, thereby determining to a significant degree the behaviour of the world price level.

Table 8.7. EXPORT PRICES IN RELATION TO THE WORLD PRICE LEVEL COMPARED WITH DOMESTIC COSTS IN COMPETITIVE SECTORS, O.E.C.D. COUNTRIES 1954-68

	λ	p_x	$(p_x - p_w)$	$(w_c - q_c)$
		per cent per annum		
Belgium	1.26	− 0.1	− 0.7	2.3
Canada	1.24	1.4	0.8	0.3
Denmark	0.95	0.6	0.0	4.4
Netherlands	1.15	0.1	− 1.5	2.9
Norway	1.37	0.4	− 0.2	2.6
Sweden	0.78	0.8	0.2	1.9
France	0.63	2.3	1.7	1.8
Germany	0.87	0.3	− 0.3	1.2
Ireland	0.43	1.3	0.7	0.7
Italy	0.65	− 0.9	− 1.5	− 1.8
Japan	0.83	− 0.7	− 1.3	− 5.2
United Kingdom	0.61	2.0	1.4	1.5
United States	0.90	1.2	0.6	0.6

They were not countries, it should be emphasized, whose average price level as measured by the GDP deflator rose exceptionally slowly compared to other countries. Nor were they countries in which money supply growth was significantly restrained as compared with other countries; on the contrary, as Table 5.12. indicates, money supply growth was exceptionally fast in both countries. The explanation must be that owing to an exceptionally fast growth of productivity in the manufacturing sectors of their economies, they were able to satisfy in abundant fashion the real income expectations of the working population and meet in a non-inflationary way the pressures imposed by trade unions. The situation changed markedly in the early 1970s for reasons we discuss in Chapter 10.

Conclusions

Judging by the results of Table 8.6. there is a majority of O.E.C.D. countries, including most of the smaller ones, for which the basic assumption of the Scandinavian structural model, viz that export prices follow world prices rather than domestic cost pressures (i.e. λ close to unity) appears broadly correct. But there was a minority of countries whose export prices (domestic currency) rose at a faster rate than the world price level of traded industrial goods, and whose exchange rates therefore had to give at some time or another in the period we are examining. Due to this and perhaps other factors, a test of the Scandinavian version of the structural hypothesis for explaining inflation did not yield significant results: inter-country differences in inflation rates cannot be explained simply in terms of the differences in the productivity gap between the competitive (advanced) and sheltered (lagging) sectors of the economy. This does not mean of course that productivity gap differences had no effect on the different inflation rates. The measured regression coefficient does correspond to what we might expect.

The reason for the failure of the Scandinavian model to stand up to test is brought out in the reduced form of a more general version of the structural model which includes an additional exogenous term, namely the excess of money wage rate increase over productivity growth in the competitive sector. Taking as one exogenous variable the sum of this excess and the rate of increase of the world price level, this complex variable differed considerably among O.E.C.D. countries and therefore contributed to the differences in overall inflation rates. The variance in the excess of money wage increase over productivity increase in the competitive sector may perhaps be explained by variance in minimum and/or average unemployment levels and by trade union aggressiveness discussed in earlier chapters of this book. This would leave the rate of increase of the world price level to be explained. Monetarists would like to explain this by reference to the rate of increase of world money supply, but for reasons we have examined elsewhere,[12] we believe money supply to be a passive rather than a determining element in the situation.[13]

An alternative and to our mind more satisfactory explanation is to be found in the very fast rate of productivity growth in the export sectors of Japan and Italy in the 1950s and 1960s which significantly (in the case of the former country, greatly) exceeded the increase in money wages. Export prices of these two countries fell and their export volumes expanded massively. The growing weight of these two countries in world trade imposed competitive pressures on other industrial countries, the big as well as the smaller, which were forced to follow the formers' price leadership. Some countries like Germany did so without difficulty; others like the U.K. and France accepted a slower rate of growth of their economies or devalued their exchange rates or did both. Export prices generally kept pace with the world price level in the former group of countries but rose faster in the latter group. The different behaviour of competitive sector prices was reflected in overall inflation rates, although country differences in the size of the sectoral productivity gap also contributed to country differences in the overall inflation rates.

9
Inflation in Less Developed Countries

It will not be possible to describe and analyse postwar inflation in the less developed world in the same detail we have employed for O.E.C.D. countries. We shall content ourselves with describing the inflationary factors which assume particular importance in less developed countries generally. However, we shall conclude the chapter with a somewhat closer examination of Latin America since this region has been more plagued by inflation than elsewhere.

We noted in Chapter 1 the commonly held fallacy that less developed countries tend to suffer more from inflation than do the richer, more developed ones. Table 1.1 shows that this is not the case. Leaving aside a few very high inflation countries in Latin America, the average rate of inflation among less developed countries has been remarkably similar to that of the main industrial countries and somewhat lower than that experienced by other developed countries, including some important producers of primary products.

In a world of fixed exchange rates and more or less free trade, some synchronization of price developments throughout the world is to be expected.[1] Countries whose domestic rates of inflation have far exceeded the world average are precisely those whose exchange rates have been far from stable and/or which have tended to develop behind tariff barriers which have been substantially raised relatively to those imposed by the rest of the world generally.

Of course, the fact that domestic inflation cannot greatly exceed the world average unless the country's rate of exchange depreciates does not mean that the direction of causation lies from the latter to the former: in general, higher inflation has forced the exchange depreciation which has then contributed to the inflationary process.

Leaving aside until later the discussion of these high inflation countries, the nature of the inflationary forces operating in less developed countries is likely to be broadly the same as those operating in the developed countries, i.e. a mixture of demand and cost pressures which in any given inflationary environment are usually difficult to disentangle. As with developed countries, if the inflation is to continue for any length of time it must be supported by a continuing rise in the quantity of money: indeed, the relationship between the quantity of money and the price level may be a good deal closer in less developed countries than in the developed ones, simply because the former are likely to possess a much less sophisticated financial structure and consequently fewer money substitutes. In these circumstances, the velocity of circulation of money is likely to be more stable, being determined by the transactions needs of the economy. Aside from this, it remains true that the nature and causes of the inflationary pressures in less developed countries may possess characteristics peculiar to themselves, therefore involving different policy prescriptions.

Cost and demand pressures in less developed countries

Cost pressures emanating from the side of wages might be thought to be a good deal less strong in less developed countries than in the developed ones: moreover, given that a much larger proportion of gross domestic product originates in the primary production sector of the economy and a small proportion in the manufacturing and industrial sectors, the phenomenon of administered pricing and administered price inflation described in Chapter 2 can be expected to be less relevant in the less developed countries. Agricultural and primary product prices tend to be more flexible than manufactured goods prices, responding much more directly to changes in the pressure of demand. But while we can expect the prices of these commodities to rise more quickly and more sharply than manufactured goods prices in response to an increase in demand, they are also more likely to fall in conditions of excess supply. Hence, although we should expect prices to be more unstable in less developed countries than they are in developed countries, there is no reason on this score alone to expect the long term rate of inflation to be higher in the former than in the latter.

Wage pressure on prices can be expected to be lower in less developed countries because unemployment, both disguised and actual, tends to be a good deal higher in the typical less developed country, which can be expected to reduce labour's bargaining power. Moreover, because of the higher proportion of labour employed in agricultural and primary production, trade union organization is likely to be less strong and efficient. We would therefore expect demand pressures to present a more important force behind inflation than cost pressures.

The expectation that because of higher unemployment and less effective trade union organization money wages and real wages would tend to rise less fast in less developed countries than in the developed ones is, however, not borne out by experience. In a detailed examination of 35 countries (of which 16 were under-developed, 14 were characterized as advanced market economies and 5 as planned economies), supplemented by a less detailed study of 58 more of which 34 were less developed, Professors Turner and Jackson concluded that in the period 1956-65 there was an extraordinary similarity in the price and wage behaviour in all countries whether developed or not. The table below is adapted from their article.[2]

CHANGES IN WAGES AND CONSUMER PRICES 1956-65

% increase p.a.

Mean of Country Averages	Money Wages	Prices	Real Wages
Section I (35 countries)			
Advanced "Market" Economies (14)	7.0	3.1	3.8
"Planned" Economies (5)	7.3	2.5	4.7
Less Developed Economies (16)	5.8	2.5	3.4
Overall Average	6.5	2.7	3.7
Section II (59 countries)			
Advanced "Market" Economies (19)	6.4	3.0	3.3
"Planned" Economies (5)	7.3	2.5	4.7
Less Developed Economies (35)	8.6	5.3	3.3
Less Developed Economies (32) (excluding hyper-inflationary countries of Latin America)	6.6	3.4	3.3

It will be seen that excluding the high inflation countries, money wages in both developed and less developed countries rose at an annual rate of about 6½ per cent, while prices (cost of living) rose at an annual rate of 3½ per cent. In other words, real wages in both categories of country rose at about 3–3½ per cent per annum, a rate of increase which roughly corresponds to the annual rate of growth of productivity in advanced industrial countries and in the modern and advanced sectors of less developed countries. It is true that deviations from these country-wide uniformities appear to be more pronounced in the poor countries than in the richer ones. The inter-industry dispersal of wage movements is on average considerably greater in the poorer ones than in the richer ones, and there are considerable differences in this respect even among the less developed countries themselves. Also inter-industry wages are much less equal.

Nonetheless, Turner and Jackson argue that the data fit a simple wage leadership/cost-inflation model for the world as a whole, the essential nature of which was outlined in Chapter 2 in the context of a closed developed economy. The model may be summarized as follows: where productivity is rising fast, firms find it easier and more convenient to raise wages than to lower prices, so that wages rise in line with productivity in these industries; wage increases in one industry tend to stimulate pressures for similar increases in other industries; and where wage increases exceed productivity growth the difference is passed on in the form of higher prices. As a consequence of these behavioural patterns, money wages in general tend to rise in line with the output per head in the fastest productivity growth industries, so that in those industries where productivity growth is less fast, the average price level tends to rise. Given wide dispersal among industries, the faster grows average productivity, the faster is the rate of increase of annual money wages and, therefore, of the price level.

The mechanism probably works less simply in less developed countries than it does in the developed ones, since, as has just been noted, there is a greater disparity in wage movements among different industries in these countries: unlike the developed countries the *average* wage increase across the economy as a whole does not approximate to the rate of growth of output per head in the fastest productivity growth industries but something less than this. This fact would imply that the typical less developed country would suffer a lower rate of inflation overall than does the typical developed country; but this is contrary to the evidence. Turner and Jackson believe that the contradiction can be resolved by supposing that on average the forces opposed to wage push overall are weaker in less developed countries than in the developed ones. Be that as it may, what is clear is that the existence of considerable surplus labour in the form of actual or disguised unemployment in the rural sector of under-developed economies, does not prevent a substantial rise in money and real wages in the modern industrial sectors of the economy. The reason may be that although trade union organization in these countries may be less strong in the orthodox sense than it is in the developed countries, urban employees often represent a significant political force able to embarrass the government of the day and thus secure wage legislation favourable to urban workers. In this they are helped not only by the fact that government is itself a key employer of labour, but also by the fact that foreign-owned companies tend to occupy a relatively import-ant place in the modern sectors of the poorer countries. Not only are foreign-owned companies vulnerable to political pressure from the countries in which they are located, they are also accustomed to paying higher money wages in their home economies, and indeed may be under pressure from their employees in these home countries to pay similar wages else-where overseas, ostensibly as part of local worker sympathy for labour conditions abroad, but perhaps more realistically to eliminate the compet-ition of cheap labour.

Turner and Jackson's analysis suggests that the world as a whole suffers from 'productivity-gap' or 'wage-transfer' inflation as described in Chapter 8. Less developed countries which have experienced some industrial development are importers of it. In this sense they can be said to be suffering from the same kind of moderate inflationary pressure which affects developed countries. But less developed countries, including those with some significant industrial development, do possess peculiar character-istics which can modify or intensify the common inflationary experience as it operates in their own countries, and even provide independent causes of domestic inflation. We go on to note some of these characteristics.

Open economies

Many less developed countries tend to have large foreign trade sectors. This is less a consequence of their stage of development than of their size, for there are many small developed countries as dependent, if not more dependent, on foreign trade as the typical less developed country: but there are many more small less developed countries than there are small developed ones. Economies which do have large foreign trade sectors are clearly more vulnerable to economic events external to themselves: on the other hand, if their economies are small the impact they have on the rest of the world is insignificant. Thus, the bigger developed countries set the pace, and the price and income behaviour of less developed countries follows behind.

Events overseas affect the economies of small less developed countries through changes in demand for their exports, which affect both volume and prices, and through changes in the price and volume of imports. An increase in export demand raises incomes, both wages and profits, setting up the usual multiplier effects on consumption and, if the boom in exports is strong enough, on investment expenditure as well. There are, of course, leakages in the system which tend to moderate the size of the secondary multiplier effects. The important ones are taxation, which in many less developed countries tends to fall quite heavily on export incomes, and spending on imports; but even so, a significant export boom will tend to raise the demand for labour and other factor and material inputs of a non-traded sort, producing a sympathetic rise in the domestic price level. The impact of all this will be a good deal greater in an economy in which exports are 30 or 40 per cent of national product than in one in which they are only ten per cent. The rise in export demand may express itself solely in a rise in export prices rather than in volume (if for example the short-run supply curve of exports has virtually zero elasticity), in which case the impact on the general price level may be direct, rather than through the secondary effects associated with the multiplier. Exports may enter in an important way in home consumption, so that there is a direct rise in the price level of a component of home consumption[3] which then provokes income and wage reactions and subsequently the wage-price spiral. Substitution effects may set up secondary excess demands elsewhere in the economy, causing a rise in the price level of non-traded goods. Similarly, rising import prices triggered off by events overseas have corresponding effects on the price level of under-developed countries.

This raises the question of how far these autonomous inflationary pressures arising abroad could be offset, or at any rate contained by, a system of more flexible exchange rates? Is it necessary for the typical less developed country to import so much inflation from abroad? Could a small, less developed country isolate its economy from a rise in prices abroad by altering its exchange rate?

If the effects of an autonomous rise in export and import prices on the domestic price level are to be exactly neutralized, the country's exchange rate must appreciate by the amount required. Can we rely on the mechanism of a free foreign exchange market to produce this result? The answer clearly depends on what happens to the country's terms of trade. We can distinguish three cases.

Assume first that as a result of forces operating externally to the economy import and export prices rise proportionally, leaving the terms of trade unchanged. The value of exports will rise in at least the same proportion as the rise in export prices; the value of imports, however, will rise at most in proportion to the rise in import prices and may even fall if domestic demand for imports is sufficiently elastic. Hence, assuming an initial balance in trade, there will be an excess supply of foreign exchange (i.e. an excess demand for domestic currency) which will cause an appreciation of the country's exchange rate which will continue until the value of domestic currency in terms of foreign currency has risen in exactly the same proportion as the autonomous rise in foreign trade prices. Domestic prices will therefore be unaffected. All this assumes, of course, that, after the initial rise, export and import prices expressed in foreign currency are unaffected by what is happening in the country in question, which is plausible for small countries but not necessarily for large ones, and also that wages in the country in question remain unchanged.

Suppose now that the autonomous rise in export and import prices is such that the terms of trade improve, i.e. export prices rise by more than import prices. Given the same assumptions as before, the balance of trade will improve, excess supply of foreign exchange will appear in the exchange market, and the country's exchange rate will appreciate. The appreciation will continue until there is a fall in the price of imports in terms of domestic currency and may continue beyond this point until export prices in terms of home currency have also fallen, before equilibrium in the foreign exchange market has been reached. A fall in the average price level of traded goods will tend to provide the basis for a shift of resources to the non-traded sector of the economy; but even if a rise in the price level of non-traded goods is required to facilitate the shift, there remains the possibility that the average price level will fall, depending on the magnitude of the direct relationship between imported and exportable raw materials and costs and prices in the using industries.

Finally, consider the case in which the terms of trade worsen as both import and export prices rise. In this case either an excess supply or an excess demand for foreign exchange could appear. If both the demand for import and export prices rise. In this case either an excess supply or an excess demand for foreign exchange could appear. If both the demand for imports and the supply of exports have zero elasticity, then the terms of trade would worsen and the rate of exchange would depreciate. In this case the rise in export and import prices in terms of home currency would be amplified and the inflationary impact on the domestic price level would therefore be greater. But if the elasticity of export supply is positive while the elasticity of demand for imports is sufficiently negative, an improvement in the trade balance and an appreciation in the exchange rate would result. But given the worsening in terms of trade, import prices in terms of home currency will, in the new equilibrium position, always be higher than initially, although given a sufficiently high elasticity of supply of exports, export prices in terms of domestic currency could show a fall. The precise outcome depends on the magnitude of the worsening in the terms of trade, on the elasticity of demand for import goods, on the elasticity of supply of export goods and on the initial balance of trade.

We can conclude that a floating exchange rate system or appropriate manipulation of the exchange rate by government to maintain equilibrium in the balance of payments can in principle enable a small country to isolate its domestic price level from inflationary events overseas. This is more likely to be achieved if the inflationary impulse from overseas either leaves the small country's terms of trade unchanged or brings about a substantial improvement in them. The less likelihood of the domestic price level remaining unaffected, the greater is the worsening in the terms of trade. Very few, if any, less developed countries in the postwar period have in fact manipulated their exchange rates so as to insulate their economies from inflationary events overseas. The main reason for this is their adherence to the Bretton-Woods system of par values. Countries which changed their exchange rates frequently or allowed them to float did not do so to avoid importing inflation from overseas, but largely because of internally generated inflationary pressures and consequential disequilibrium in their balances of payments. As a consequence, exchange rate changes have exacerbated rather than mitigated inflation.

Government sector and credit creation

The typical less developed country differs from the typical developed country in that government plays a more important and leading role in economic activity. In all countries, of course, the adoption of full employment and growth objectives and Keynesian-type economic policies generally has led to growing intervention of government; but in developed economies, even those such as the United Kingdom and France in which nationalization of industry has gone a considerable way, by far the largest part of economic activity is still controlled and financed by private enterprise. The private enterprise sectors of most less developed countries are very much weaker, and governments have thought it necessary to take a leading role, not only in areas traditionally reserved for government intervention (education, health, social infrastructure generally), but also in others of more productive activity, in particular in the provision of physical infrastructure, such as transport and power, etc. The explanation of this larger involvement in economic activity lies only partly in the apparent failure of private enterprise to take the lead: perhaps more important is the belief shared by many governments of less developed countries that economic development requires economic planning, the effectiveness of which varies directly with public sector control over real resources. To this belief is added the pressure of popular and very often world opinion for increasing government expenditure in the traditional fields of education and social welfare, a pressure which is added to by the fact that population growth in the majority of less developed countries is very high. Finally, there is also the conviction that the vicious circle of low income-low saving-low investment-low income can only be broken, at least in the context of an acceptable distribution of income, by government and by financial tax policy aimed at raising public sector savings.

Larger government involvement in economic activity *per se* should not necessarily lead us to expect more inflation. If sufficient taxation is levied to offset the demand expansion impact of government expenditure then no inflationary pressures should arise on this score. Even if government expenditure is not fully covered by tax revenue, the government may still be able to cover its deficit by mobilizing in a non-inflationary way through borrowing in the capital market the saving of the private sector, provided it is willing to incur the market interest rate cost.

In less developed countries, however, the demand-creating impact of government expenditure may be greater than it is in developed countries; for although the share of total government expenditure in gross domestic product is not typically higher in less developed countries than it is in the developed ones, the proportion of that expenditure which falls directly on goods and services rather than on transfer payments tends to be greater. Transfer payments are of much less importance in less developed countries owing to the less developed nature of their social security systems, for example in respect of pensions, unemployment pay, family allowances and so on. Against this a much larger proportion of government revenue is raised in the form of indirect taxes than in direct taxes, a fact which in some circumstances makes the demand-reducing impact of government taxation greater. What complicates the fiscal problem of less developed countries, as against that of the more developed ones, is the fact that on the one hand, the long term pressures for increased government expenditure to satisfy the social and development needs of these countries is very severe, while on the other hand the long term elasticity of their revenue systems may be rather low. This is particularly the case if, as is usual, a large part of government revenue is derived from the taxation of foreign trade in a situation in which the growth of world demand for the country's exports tends to be rather low owing to a low income elasticity of demand.

Finally, governments of less developed countries have less chance of meeting any deficit in their fiscal account by borrowing from private capital markets. These are much less developed than in the developed countries, and, apart from the commercial banks, there are fewer lending institutions which can take up government debt on the basis of deposit and other liabilities with the general public. Thus insofar as governments of these countries cannot finance their expenditure by taxation, resort to credit creation through borrowing from the central bank and commercial banking system becomes necessary. Although there may be considerable room for financing government expenditure through the creation of money as the monetization of the economy proceeds, excessive creation of money must lead to inflation as all countries, developed or otherwise, have found to their cost.

Inflation as a means of promoting growth

It is often thought that less developed countries are more prone to inflation than developed countries because, unlike the governments of the latter, their governments see it as a way of promoting faster economic growth. The argument is that faster growth requires a higher rate of investment in productive capital than, given the level and distribution of income, voluntary saving on the part of the community can be expected to finance; inefficient fiscal systems impost a severe limit on the ability of governments to raise compulsory saving through budget surpluses: hence resort to money and credit creation to finance the excess of investment over saving is required.

Two lines of thought should perhaps be disentangled here. First, the amount of saving that a community may be willing to make depends not only on the level and distribution of income of the community, but also on the scope and range of financial institutions that exist. Where these are inadequate, channels for making profitable and safe use of saving will be consequently less than otherwise. It takes time and experience to build up an effective intermediating financial system, so that it may not be surprising if governments resort to the printing press and to the creation of credit through the existing banking system rather than restrain investment. Creation of money to finance investment, however, does not necessarily produce inflation. If monetization of the economy is taking place – as will normally be happening in the process of economic development – the community may be very willing and anxious to build up its monetary assets in the form of cash and deposits with the banking system, thereby implicitly providing the real savings to finance the higher rate of investment. Obviously, the desired build-up of such assets will be linked to the growth of real income of the community. An excessive creation of money in relation to real income growth will not meet with willing holders at an unchanged price level; and prices will, therefore, tend to rise. While some inflation is not incompatible with the continued build-up of monetary assets in real terms, if prices begin to rise very quickly in the early stages of monetization the danger would be that people would not gain confidence in monetary assets, so that the process of monetization would be inhibited. It could not then be relied upon to provide the real saving required for financing investment. On the contrary, continued credit creation at too high a rate would then lead to acceleration of inflation and possibly to a severe check to the development of a comprehensive monetary and financial system.[4]

While credit creation, coupled with the monetization of the economy, may certainly give rise to real saving even if some inflation is promoted, this is not the main mechanism through which inflation is seen to promote saving and capital formation. This mechanism takes the form of a shift in the distribution of income away from sectors with a low propensity to save towards sectors with a higher propensity to save. Thus, let us suppose that the ratio of capital formation to national product is raised from some given initial level, the increase in investment being financed by money creation. Suppose, too, that the real resources for capital formation have been diverted from the production of consumer goods, the prices of which now rise as a result. Profits of the producers of consumer goods then rise relatively to wage incomes and, assuming that profit earners have a higher propensity to save than wage earners and that money wages do not follow prices upwards, the ratio of saving to national income will rise to match the rise in capital formation. Inflation will have achieved the fall in real consumption relative to real national income that for administrative or political reasons could not have been achieved by fiscal measures, or would not have appeared voluntarily on the basis of the initial distribution of income.

Fundamentally, this manner of looking at the problem — i.e. the creation of 'forced saving' by inflation — is somewhat misleading. Obviously if an increase in real capital formation is in fact achieved, the matching real saving arises automatically at the same time (assuming for a moment a closed economy): *ex post* saving necessarily equals *ex post* investment. The fundamental questions at issue in this process are first, what determines the extent to which, and the speed with which prices will rise as a consequence of investment financed by credit creation, and, second, will the process of rising prices itself inhibit the success with which an increase in real capital formation is achieved?

As to the first question, the extent to which prices will rise depends on three elements in the situation: first, the size of the propensity to save of profit earners relative to that of wage earners; second — since the assumption that money wages will not respond to the rise in prices is clearly unrealistic — the size of the wage-price coefficient (i.e. the consequential proportionate change in money wages divided by the proportionate change in prices); and third, the amount of the increase in real capital formation relative to national output — since this will determine the rise in real saving required. Clearly, the larger is the propensity to save of profit earners relative to that of wage earners, the less prices will have to rise; but the larger the wage-price coefficient and the required rise in real saving are, the greater will be the rise in prices necessary to get the required change in distribution of income. In turn the speed of the inflation depends on the time lags between price changes and wage changes.

It is obvious that a very considerable inflation could be generated by a rise in the rate of capital formation financed by credit creation, if it provokes a serious wage-price spiral. If such a situation develops the second question referred to above becomes very relevant. If wages react quickly and fully to the rise in prices, it may become difficult to attract and mobilize the real resources required for capital formation. Bottlenecks in supply of important materials and components and in the availability of skilled labour etc. may develop, causing long delays in the starting and completion of capital projects, if not rendering their completion impossible altogether. Moreover, the character of privately financed investment may also be changed. In a very rapid inflation, saving may be increasingly directed into non-productive forms of investment, such as the hoarding of gold, precious stones, foreign exchange, securities and similar assets and into the acquisition of real estate and inventories of goods and materials. Investment in the former provides a good hedge against the depreciation of the external value of the currency which becomes inevitable if inflation proceeds very far, while investment in real estate and in the construction of luxury apartments and similar buildings is also encouraged if the inflation is producing a shift in the distribution of income and wealth in favour of upper income groups, particularly if the social groups which are obtaining most benefit from the inflation have little disposition to invest further in real productive assets. Linked to this latter point is the fact that inflation may be a socially unfair way of producing the distribution of income appropriate to the desired rate of real capital formation; for if the propensity to save of profit earners is not very much greater than that of wage earners, the distribution of income may have to shift very markedly in favour of the former before a stable price level is achieved, in which case a fall in the real consumption of the wage earner will have made possible not only the required rise in capital formation but also a substantial rise in real consumption of profit earners.

In practice, therefore, despite the theoretical advantages apparently offered by credit creation and inflation, governments will not easily resort to financing capital formation on a large scale in this way. The danger of the wage-price spiral would be too great and/or the social cost would be too high. However, if resorted to to a limited extent, inflation can be 'self-liquidating', and indeed to some extent may be inevitable if the fiscal apparatus available to a government is inadequate to finance a higher rate of capital formation necessary for faster economic growth. But certain conditions are necessary. The first is that the government should not aim at raising the rate of capital formation too quickly or too much, and the second is that the investment carried out should be of quick gestation, and yield output in the form of wage goods; for while it may be necessary to reduce the ratio of consumption to national output to achieve faster economic growth, this is easier if the total output of consumption goods is rising in absolute terms. The danger of the wage-price spiral is less if absolute consumption does not have to fall. The third condition is that inflation should redistribute income to entrepreneurs who use it to finance further productive investment or to the government in the form of increased taxation. The fourth and final condition is that the government should have sufficient control over the economy to prevent flights of capital abroad, imports of luxury type goods, speculative real estate construction and so on.

The rather moderate price inflation experienced by the great majority of the less developed countries does not suggest that their governments have in fact resorted to money and credit creation to promote the expansion of their public sectors and the rate of economic growth on any very large scale. In the case of those very few countries which have experienced fast inflation, money creation has obviously been an important element in the situation; but to what extent money creation was deliberately resorted to in these countries in order to promote growth, or to what extent it was forced on governments by other factors of a structural nature operating in the economy, cannot be decided without further examintaion. We turn now, therefore, to an examination of structural factors which are said to be a potent cause of inflation in some less developed countries, particularly countries of Latin America.

Structural inflation

Structural inflation[5] in less developed countries is associated with bottlenecks or inelasticities in supply in particular crucial sectors of the economy. It is not to be confused with inflation caused by generalized excess demand pressures or generalized cost pressures which are more typical of developed countries and which may be amenable to macroeconomic policies of the normal type. On the contrary, the attempt to deal with structural inflation by the use of conventional monetary and fiscal policies is, in the view of 'structuralists', simply to confuse the symptom of inflation with the cause and, worse still, to make the elimination of the structural causes even more difficult.

Perhaps the most important form of supply inelasticity that can cause considerable inflationary pressure in developing countries lies in agriculture, particularly in food production. The general nature of the process is straightforward: if economic growth is taking place demand for food will also be rising, although probably at a slower rate; but if food supply fails to increase to match the increase in demand, food prices will rise, causing repercussions elsewhere, and generalized inflation may well result. It is worth looking at this process in more detail, since it brings out in clear form the peculiar nature of structural inflation.

In order to simplify the analysis, suppose we have an economy assumed initially to be 'closed', composed of two sectors only, agriculture and manufacturing industry. The agricultural sector produces food while the manufacturing sector produces both capital goods and manufactured consumer goods. Capital goods are not bought by consumers and the demand for them does not depend closely on current real income. Food and manufactured consumer goods are bought by consumers and the demand for them depends on current real income and on relative prices. Let total output of the economy be initially divided between food, capital goods and manufactured consumer goods in the proportions 70 per cent, 10 per cent and 20 per cent respectively. Suppose growth now takes place as a result of rising manufactured goods output which is assumed to increase by 20 per cent in a given period of time, but agricultural (i.e. food) output remains constant.[6] What may happen to prices? There are a number of possibilities.

Suppose the rise in manufacturing output takes the form of equal *percentage* increase in the outputs of capital goods and manufactured consumer goods, so that the increase in the output of the former (i.e. investment) is one-third of the increase in total output, and the increase in the output of the latter is two-thirds of the increase in total output. Finally, to eliminate the problem of *generalized* excess demand, let us assume that the marginal saving ratio is equal to one-third so that saving rises to match investment.

There will now be excess demand for food, depending on the size of the income elasticity of demand for it, since *ex hypothesi* food output has remained constant; but this will be matched by an excess supply of manufactured consumer goods. Food prices must rise *relatively* to the price of manufactures, the more so the greater the income elasticity of demand for food and the less the price elasticity of demand. Theoretically, this relative price change can be brought about in the context of a stable *average* price level, provided manufactured goods prices are flexible in the downward direction. In practice, the situation described above is likely to result in a rise in the general price level and thus inflation, for the following reasons.

Agricultural prices tend to be much more sensitive to changes in demand than the prices of manufactured goods, so that excess demand arising in the food market is likely to push up prices there more quickly than excess supply in the manufactured good market forces prices down there. In the short run, therefore, the general price level tends to rise, the relative rise in the price of food causing a switch of demand to manufactured goods. Now a lot depends on what happens in the labour market. If money wages are sensitive to movements in prices, particularly food, then they may begin to rise with very little time lag; as a consequence money expenditure on food is maintained and the upward pressure on food prices intensified: in addition, costs of production in manufacturing will tend to rise, inhibiting the fall in the price level of manufactured goods which is required if general inflation is to be avoided.

Clearly, the government now has to choose between on the one hand, validating the inflation by creating money until the rise in food prices relative to manufactured good prices has been sufficient to eliminate excess demand for the former and excess supply of the latter, and, on the other, of restricting the inflation by appropriate monetary or fiscal means which would then leave excess supply in the manufactured goods market. In the former case, the inflation that results is not the consequence of government attempts to force saving on the community in the sense discussed earlier in this chapter, but rather the consequence of lagging agricultural output[7] in relation to the potential for growth of the rest of the economy. In the latter case, the failure of government to validate the inflationary pressure brought about by the need for a relative rise in food prices inhibits further industrial growth.

It could be argued that the constraint on growth and/or the inflationary pressure produced by a failure of agricultural output to match the increase in demand would be temporary only since the relative rise in food prices would attract resources and investment into agriculture, bringing about an expansion of supply; but there are two counter-arguments. The first is that if as a consequence of the rise in food prices a serious wage-price spiral develops, the required *relative* rise in food prices may not easily or quickly be achieved. The second is that agricultural output is not necessarily responsive to relative price changes, but rather is determined more by sociological factors bearing on land tenure systems and land utilization which make agricultural output not very responsive to economic incentives. Hence, agriculture may remain a serious problem for a considerable length of time.

Although usually cited as the most important structural factor producing inflation in less developed countries, lagging agricultural output is not the only bottleneck that may appear. Economic growth, for instance, produces an expansion of demand for many public utility services — such as power and transport — which is not quickly or easily met. Prices, therefore, rise sharply in these sectors of the economy and, given the vital nature of these services, inflationary pressures are transmitted into the economy generally. Again, the response of supply to a relative rise in price may be slow, although possibly in contrast to agriculture where non-economic factors may be significant in determining supply response, the government itself may play an important part in holding back the growth of supply by controlling the prices of public utility services in an attempt to restrain inflation. But if costs are rising at the same time, these services may be increasingly supplied at below cost, and become a charge in the fiscal budget, contributing to an overall deficit which may have to be financed by money creation.[8]

Foreign exchange bottlenecks
Inelasticities in supply of important products like food would not, however, impose a serious check to economic growth and provide a potent cause of inflation if the country had access to overseas sources of supply,

unless the export capacity and other sources of foreign exchange of the country were insufficient to pay for the necessary imports. Hence it could be argued that the fundamental cause of structural inflation is inelasticity in the supply of foreign exchange. In the absence of foreign capital inflows (aid and private investment), this reduces to inadequate and slow growth of export earnings. It cannot be denied that many developing countries do find it difficult to expand their export earnings at a sufficiently fast rate to meet their import requirements. Being predominantly exporters of primary products they come up against low income elasticities of demand and often against competition from synthetic substitutes, both of which impose a severe limit to the growth of their exports: moreover, attempts to expand exports in the short run by lowering prices come up against short run inelasticities of supply and demand. These short run inelasticities also impose further problems since fluctuations in world demand and supply of primary products may introduce large price and income fluctuations into the economies of developing countries, which complicate the task of controlling inflation.

Long and short run inelasticities in foreign exchange earnings introduce long run inelasticity and short run fluctuations in public finance. Administrative difficulties associated with imposing and collecting taxes on income and on wholesale and retail sales inevitably force less developed countries to rely heavily on taxation of the foreign trade sector – i.e. on exports and imports. Slow long run export growth and consequently slow import growth, therefore, restrict the long run growth of fiscal revenue, while short run fluctuations in exports and imports produce short run fluctuations in that revenue. Pressures on governments to increase fiscal expenditure over time are, on the other hand, enormous: population is usually growing fast and urbanization taking place as development proceeds, thus producing fast expanding requirements for public services (e.g. education and health), and social capital (e.g. roads, other transport systems), which can only be met by government. It is hardly surprising, therefore, that governments find it difficult to balance budgets. Fluctuations in revenue receipts also complicate the problem of fiscal responsibility. Governments are under great pressure and temptation to increase expenditure when revenue derived from exports is high; they find it difficult to reduce or contain that expenditure when exports and fiscal revenue fall off. Thus, even if fiscal deficits are avoided in the long run, they may not easily be escaped in the short run. Price increases generated in periods of rising exports and income are not easily reversible; nor are expectations of rising real income similarly generated. Hence, short run fluctuations in the foreign trade sector exacerbate, if not introduce, long run inflationary pressures generated by domestic structural factors referred to earlier.

The constraint on growth imposed by the export sector necessitates measures designed both to diversify exports – for example, to develop the production of and a market for manufactured goods, for which the world income elasticity of demand is substantially higher than that for primary products – and to substitute domestic production for imports. Sociological factors affecting domestic food production may inhibit substitution of food imports, but even if this is not the case, early economic development does depend to a significant extent on producing a larger share of the country's need for manufactured goods at home and importing less from abroad. A policy of import substitution, however, if pursued behind high tariff walls and pressed forward with scant regard for dynamic comparative costs can also be a potent source of inflationary pressure in developing countries. The imposition of tariffs on imported manufactured goods forces up the price level to domestic consumers as compared with the initial situation; but the bigger danger arises if a policy of hot-house import substitution encourages the establishment of industries which because of a limited market have to operate on an inefficient scale, or have to be monopolized to achieve a more efficient scale of working. Monopolies operating in a protected market are a serious source of inflationary pressure. There is no incentive for them to be 'cost conscious', and unless the government is regulating prices – which may also have its disadvantages – their control over the market permits them to cover rising costs with rising prices with little fear as to the consequences for their sales and profits.

Structural inflation is, therefore, the result of a rather complicated interaction of a number of factors, both domestic and foreign. But do these factors operate particularly strongly in Latin America, where the 'structuralist' position originated and is most heavily defended?

Inflation in Latin America

One fact should be emphasized at the outset. The view that the Latin American continent is highly inflationary is derived from the experience of four or five countries only, admittedly among the largest and most important of the countries comprising the region. As Table 1.1 (p.1) shows, most of the smaller Latin American countries have experienced very low rates of inflation, whilst at the other extreme the so-called A, B, C countries – Argentina, Brazil, Chile and Uruguay have suffered from inflation rates of the order of 30 per cent per annum or more. Colombia and Peru have had inflation rates of about ten per cent per annum, but all other countries, including Mexico, now one of the most developed countries of the region, have had five per cent or less. If, therefore, structural factors are important in producing highly inflationary situations, they have clearly not operated in all countries of the region. We would expect to find them more conspicuously apparent in Argentina, Brazil, Chile and Uruguay.

It is not obvious that this is the case. Population growth, for instance, has been a good deal slower in the A, B, C countries than it has been in the Latin American region as a whole. The commodity concentration of exports was not markedly greater in the high inflation countries than in the low ones: leaving aside Brazil and Mexico, which have succeeded in diversifying their exports substantially and have developed a significant trade in industrial goods, it is characteristic of the Latin American region as a whole that one or two commodities comprise 50 per cent or more of exports, and some very low inflation rate countries have export concentration ratios a good deal higher than this. Nor is it clear that the high inflation countries have, over the postwar period as a whole, suffered more from lagging export growth and declining terms of trade than have the low inflation countries, although it is true that Colombia and Peru and to a lesser extent Argentina did experience a substantial worsening in their terms of trade from the mid 1950s to the mid 1960s. Nor can it be said that the structural factors have been kept in the background in the low inflation countries by slow economic growth as compared with the high inflation rates. Despite rather slow population growth by Latin American standards, Argentina, Chile and Uruguay have suffered slower growth of real income per capita than have the majority of Latin American countries. Of the high inflation countries only Brazil succeeded in combining a real income per capita growth rate of more than 2½ per cent per annum, with a population growth rate also above that; and Mexico's population and real income per capita growth rates were both well in excess of 2½ per cent although its inflation was very moderate, at little more than five per cent per annum.

The one structural factor which does seem to distinguish one or two of the very high inflation countries from the slow inflation countries is the slow growth of agriculture, particularly domestic food production. Agricultural output in Argentina and Chile grew at very little more than one per cent per annum in the post Second War period, while in Uruguay it seems to have increased hardly at all. In most other countries agricultural output seems to have increased at a much faster rate. The slow growth of agriculture in Argentina and Chile is conspicuous not only in an absolute sense but also, and more relevantly for the structuralist line of argument — relatively to the growth of the rest of the economy. It would appear that manufacturing and industrial output generally grew at four or five times the rate of growth of agriculture in Argentina and Chile and ten times in Uruguay. Estimates of agricultural output growth are not available for many of the smaller, less developed Latin American countries, but where they are available they suggest that in most cases the rate of growth of manufacturing output in the low inflation countries exceeded the rate of growth of agriculture to a much smaller degree: the growth rate of the former was around twice as great as the rate of growth of the latter. This was also true of Mexico, which achieved one of the fastest rates of growth of manufacturing output in the region as a whole as well as a high rate of increase of population. It seems possible, therefore, that lagging agricultural output, both in absolute and in relative terms, may well have contributed significantly to, if not have been the main cause, of high inflation in one or two countries. An exception is Brazil, which achieved a rapid rate of increase in agricultural output in absolute terms (4½ per cent per annum) as well as in relation to population growth (2.7 per cent per annum), to industrial production growth (6 per cent per annum) and to real income per capita growth (2.6 per cent). In contrast to Argentina, therefore, the high inflation expreienced by Brazil cannot be easily explained by food supply constraints.

In general, the high inflation countries of Latin America are among the most developed countries of the region. Inflation does not seem to have been a serious problem for countries which remain relatively under-developed and largely agricultural, with low per capita real income. In a world context, the A, B, C countries of Latin America lie in the middle of the spectrum of economic development. The main characteristics of this stage of development appear to be: a relatively small subsistence sector; a substantial industrial sector producing perhaps 20 – 25 per cent of national output, which has been built up behind high import barriers and based on a policy of import substitution; concentration of population in a few large urban centres; and a number of powerful economic pressure groups with influence to affect public policy. They are economies in the phase of transition from being based largely on the production and export of primary products to economies based increasingly on the output of manufactured goods, and finding it difficult to break into world markets for these goods as a result of previous policies of import substitution behind high tariff walls. They are also substantially if not wholly monetized. These characteristics appear to render them more vulnerable to financial disturbance and monetary mismanagement than more primitive economies: moreover, the monetary consequences of structural imbalances tend to be severe and overt.

A brief account of the inflationary process in Argentina and Brazil will serve to illustrate the problems of these countries.

Inflation in Argentina

Structural inflation has probably operated most severely in Argentina and Chile, but monetary and fiscal mismanagement has greatly compounded it. Argentina has suffered from rapid inflation for virtually the whole of the post Second World War period. Between 1960 and 1966 prices rose at an average annual rate exceeding 25 per cent; they seldom rose less than 10 per cent in any one year, and in one year they rose by as much as 100 per cent. During the same period economic growth was slow, and per capita GNP rose by only 1.3 per cent annually despite a relatively slow growth of population of barely 1.6 per cent per annum.

At first sight it is possible to attribute this inflation solely to chronic government budget deficits and consequent increases in the money supply. In the ten years 1955-65 the national government budget deficit averaged about one-quarter of total government expenditure and about 3½ per cent of the country's GNP. Getting on for 50 per cent of this deficit was on average financed by recourse to the banking system, as a consequence of which the money supply rose at a fast rate throughout the years of inflation. Taken by itself however, the monetary explanation of inflation is unsatisfactory and certainly not the whole of the story. This is demonstrated by the fate of various attempts to stabilize the situation which were made by successive governments, sometimes with the support of the International Monetary Fund. Prior to 1966 the most notable attempts occurred in 1959 and again in 1962-3. In both of these periods serious attempts were made to reduce the size of the government deficit and to reduce the rate of growth of the money supply; but if the rate of inflation is anything to go by, none of these attempts had even temporary, let alone lasting success. In 1959 when, as a result of the credit policies pursued and the devaluation of the exchange rate, non-agricultural output fell by about six per cent, the rate of inflation jumped to over 90 per cent. Again, in 1962 and 1963, following two years in which output picked up and the rate of inflation slowed down, the price increase accelerated to over 25 per cent. It could be argued, of course, that the failure of both of these stabilization attempts was primarily due to the unwillingness, or inability, of the government to maintain restrictive policies sufficiently long enough for inflationary expectations to be eliminated from the economy; but the combination of faster inflation and serious recession in output made the political task of the government of the day exceedingly difficult.

In 1967 a strong military government launched yet another stabilization attempt; but on this occasion the IMF was not involved since Argentina at this time was not suffering from a current balance of payments crisis. This attempt appeared to have considerable initial success: the rate of inflation was reduced from around 30 per cent in 1965-66 to less than ten per cent in 1969. Moreover, unlike previous stabilization attempts, the economy's rate of growth accelerated to an average of 5½ per cent per annum. However, once again the stabilization programme foundered, and by the beginning of 1971 prices were rising at an annual rate approaching 40 per cent.[9]

The reasons for the breakdown of the 1967 stabilization programme are interesting and throw light on the basic structural factor underlying Argentina's long inflation.

Attention should be focused on the price of beef. This began to rise sharply in the latter part of 1969. Between November 1969 and August 1970 it rose by over 30 per cent and by a further 50 per cent in the course of the next six months. In the face of this it became impossible to continue the policy of progressive reductions in the rate of increase of money wages, which had been an essential element of the programme, and to continue with the complementary policies in the field of money and credit aimed at reducing the rate of increase of the monetary aggregates. Although the rate of increase of bank credit to the private sector in 1970 continued to decline from its high in 1968, the impact of faster rising money wages in the government sector checked the improvement that was being achieved with respect to the budget; bank lending to the government took a larger share of a faster rising money supply. Inflation in general began to accelerate, so that in the course of 1970 itself the cost of living rose by more than 20 per cent and by a further ten per cent in the first three months of 1971.

The rise in the price of beef cannot be explained by a prior breakdown in wage and monetary policies which precipitated overall excess demand in economy in the usual sense. Real incomes certainly rose in the course of 1969 as a result of the real growth of the economy, and this contributed to an increase in the demand for beef: but the main factor was clearly a decline in the supply.

The role of beef prices in Argentine inflation has long been recognized. The fact that beef is both the major export commodity and an important wage good explains for instance why large scale currency devaluation repeatedly failed to produce more than temporary improvement in the balance of payments situation, whilst at the same time more often than not accelerating the rate of domestic inflation. In a situation of inelastic domestic demand and supply, devaluation could only produce a temporary improvement in the balance of payments provided it was accompanied by other domestic policies aimed at reducing real income and output in the economy as a whole. Despite the fall in real income and output produced by the combination of devaluation and restrictive monetary policy, the burden of which usually fell most heavily on the private sector, inflation accelerated owing to the impact of rising domestic beef prices on money wage contracts. The repeated need to reduce output and real incomes in turn produced over the long run a low rate of economic growth, even though in the intervals between successive balance of payments crises the Argentine economy showed the capacity to grow at a very fast rate.

Underlying the short term situation, and indeed a basic cause of both inflation and long run growth of the economy, was the slow *long term* growth of agricultural output. Between 1945 and 1965 total agricultural output rose by barely 20 per cent, less than one per cent per annum and roughly half the rate of population growth in the same period. Admittedly, this overall performance disguises the fact that in the first decade of the period output actually fell by 10 per cent; even so, from the middle to the end of the 1950s the annual average growth rate of agriculture was only slightly above the rate of population growth, which in Argentina has been low as compared with other Latin American countries.

The fall in agricultural output in the first postwar decade was very largely the consequence of deliberate government policy aimed at the transfer of wealth and political power from rural to non-rural sectors and at the promotion of industrialization. Later efforts to promote agricultural growth were hindered by a legacy of problems generated by these past policies which have contributed to inflation and made it difficult to control. These include the creation of uneconomic state enterprises, a weakening of public finances and a lack of confidence on the part of the rural sector.

Although it was the failure of agriculture to grow in line with the rest of the economy which caused both the balance of payment difficulties and the slow growth of the economy as a whole, a vicious cycle was in operation: the repeated use of exchange rate depreciation, aimed at improving the balance of payments, and the consequential accelerated domestic inflation, combined with a far from consistent export retention tax policy produced wide short run fluctuations in agriculture's terms of trade which offset the gradual long term improvement which admittedly took place following 1960. It is clear that wide short-run fluctuations are inimical to long term agricultural development since investment with long pay-off, such as that in equipment, permanent pasture and on-farm storage capacity, is discouraged by them.

Of course, despite the slow growth of agriculture, substantial industrial development has taken place in Argentina in the post Second World War period, and a more complex and developed industrial sector now exists than can be found in most countries with comparable population size and per capita income level. Indeed, the share of manufacturing production in GDP was almost one-third in 1966 which, given its per capita real income, makes Argentina one of the most industrialized countries in the world; the per capita production of industrial products was about two-thirds of that in Italy in the same year. However, the process of industrial development through import substitution in an environment of almost complete protection against imports has led to high costs of production which in large part reflect excessive product differentiation and inability to take advantage of economies of scale. Because of its high costs, industry is almost entirely domestically oriented; only a few industries (for example, railway cars, calculators, pharmaceuticals, tyres, etc.) have been successful in selling their products abroad. The industries that were expanded or created were not such as to raise Argentina's export capacity; nor did they in the long run significantly reduce the ratio of imports to national product. Instead, highly capital intensive local monopolies catering solely for the domestic market have been created behind high tariff walls and until very recently these worked well below full capacity. Moreover, being capital intensive, this development has not created employment on the same scale, as a consequence of which the public sector has been put in the position of absorbing large amounts of inefficiently used labour. Inflation has exacerbated the problem of obtaining industrial financing, and this helps to explain the prominent place which subsidiaries of foreign firms occupy in the Argentine economy by virtue of their access to external sources of capital. Indeed, recent industrial development has been based to an important extent on foreign capital, a large part of which has taken the form of supplier's credits contracted on expensive terms.

The character of Argentine industrial development has in turn affected the growth of agriculture and Argentina's balance of payments. On the one hand, the high prices of industrial consumer goods relative to the domestic price of meat has encouraged the Argentine consumer to spend a larger part of his budget on meat and foodstuffs in general than would normally be expected given his per capita level of income. On the other hand the high price of industrial inputs to agriculture has delayed the mechanization of the industry and has therefore operated to hold back the growth of output. Both factors, of course, have operated to maintain a tight balance of payments restriction on Argentina's overall economic growth.

The failure of the 1967-69 stabilization measures because of the short and long run reasons referred to above appear to support the structuralist position against that of the monetarist (i.e. the position of those who hold that Argentina's inflation was due to over-expansion of the money supply), in the sense that it demonstrates very clearly that short run stabilization measures and long run development strategy are intimately related to each other. It is clearly not possible at present to prevent inflation in Argentina by monetary measures alone, no matter how well they are designed. But it must also be admitted that without appropriate monetary measures of the kind discussed earlier which are aimed at slowing down the rate of inflation, it may in fact be difficult to produce the long run structural changes and long run improvements in agriculture which are required if Argentina is to succeed in obtaining faster economic growth with more price stability.[10]

Paradoxically, too, it might be argued that the character of economic development that has taken place in Argentina over the last 30 years – resulting in the present restricted situation that Argentina now finds itself in – reflects more the structuralist position than the orthodox monetarist one, which usually embraces the virtues of freer trade. The structuralist position has tended to support a policy of long run development based on import substitution and a switch of resources from primary production towards industry; certainly there is reason to believe that post-war Argentine economic policy was influenced in some degree by the early views of the Economic Commission for Latin-America in this respect. In retrospect, however, it must surely be obvious that the pattern of economic development that has taken place in Argentina during the last 30 years has resulted in the country benefiting far less from international trade than would have been possible given her natural resources and export potential. As a consequence of this, real income per capita in Argentina has lagged well behind that of other countries with similar resource endowments (Australia, for example), while a depressed agricultural sector and low rural income have created increasingly serious social problems and political tension.

Inflation in Brazil

Unlike that of Argentina, Brazil's inflation cannot be said to be rooted in a fundamental structural cause. In the postwar period inflation in Brazil has averaged over 30 per cent per annum with inflation rates peaking to well above 50 per cent in the early and mid-1960s. All the expected characteristics associated with high inflation were evident: a substantial government deficit, rapid increases in the money supply, an endemic wage-price spiral and a depreciating exchange rate. But structural factors are not so easy to identify. As indicated earlier in this chapter, agricultural production and in particular food supply seemed to be rising at a satisfactory rate relative to population growth and to the growth of manufacturing output and real income per capita. Export growth was rather slow, but despite the rather heavy concentration on coffee Brazil did not suffer substantially from adverse terms of trade. The substantial balance of payments current account deficit throughout the 1950s and 1960s was covered by substantial inflows of foreign capital. Moreover, in strong contrast to Argentina Brazil's inflation was accompanied by very high rates of economic growth. In the 1950s GNP grew at an annual rate of over six per cent per annum, although there was some slowing down in the early 1960s.

Brazil's inflation during the 1950s has been cited as an example of inflation forcing saving and thereby stimulating economic growth. Throughout this period wages lagged behind prices and the share of profits tended to rise. A high rate of capital formation averaging about 15 per cent of GDP was sustained and this was financed by domestic savings which never provided less than about 80 per cent of total capital formation. During the early part of the period it was the private sector that benefited mainly from the lags inherent in the process, while towards the end of the 1950s and early 1960s it was mainly the government that succeeded in financing its increased investment expenditures through inflationary methods of finance. Inflation was successful in forcing saving due to the general lack of sophistication of workers in protecting themselves against it and by the weakness of trade unions — both factors accentuated by the low urbanization of the Brazilian economy. It could be expected that neither of these factors would remain constant as urbanization and economic growth proceeded, and by the early 1960s trade unions encouraged by a government favourable to their aspirations began to be a much more powerful force in wage bargaining. As a consequence wage demands became much more frequent and the wage-price spiral much more violent. Inflation accelerated and in 1963 and 1964 it reached an annual rate of over 70 per cent.

A new government launched a stabilization programme in 1964. The main element in this was a rigorous incomes policy, the main aim of which was to keep wage increases below the rise in the cost of living. At the same time, however, the attempt was made to eliminate the price distortions that had been introduced by previous governments in the interests of slowing down inflation and bringing about an increase in real wages.[11] The exchange rate was devalued and the subsidized rates that had applied to certain imports were abolished. Controls over agricultural prices and rents were relaxed and the prices of public services, notably transport and electricity, were sharply increased. The government also adopted a more flexible exchange rate policy to protect exports from the effects of rising internal costs and prices, but imports were kept under control by surcharges and other restrictive measures. The government also took steps to slow down the rate of growth of the money supply, and credit to the private sector was sharply contracted. These restrictions, plus others the government adopted, produced a steep decline in production and employment in the consumer durables and textile industries, and a rather severe recession affected the Brazilian economy during 1965 and 1966. The rate of inflation was reduced from its high of over 80 per cent in 1964, but even so the inflation rate remained at over 60 per cent in 1965 and over 45 per cent in 1966. Further improvement took place in 1967 and 1968, and by 1969 inflation had been reduced to 23 per cent. Some relaxation in policy constraints was made in 1966 and the growth of the Brazilian economy began to pick up and achieved above eight per cent again in 1968. However, the inflation rate remained high and it is clear that overall the stabilization attempt only had very limited success. Moreover even this was only achieved by the ability of the government to enforce a fairly rigorous incomes policy which had the effect of holding back real wages, the level of which remained constant between 1965 and 1969.

The Brazilian experience, and indeed that of the Argentine, demonstrates quite clearly that it is extremely difficult to halt a rapid and prolonged inflation within a short period of time even if a country has a strong militaristic government. Inflationary expectations are built into the economy and it is extremely difficult to reverse them without producing severe industrial recession which is as politically unacceptable as is the inflation rate itself. However it is evident from the case of Brazil that the problem is a good deal easier if the country has the advantage of abundant resources and does not suffer from constraints of a structural nature which inhibit growth. It remains to be seen whether the richer countries of the O.E.C.D. will prove to have more success in defeating inflation now that it has reached Latin American proportions.

10
Acceleration of World Inflation after 1968

After 1968 inflation began to accelerate in virtually all O.E.C.D. countries and throughout the world generally. The average annual rate of increase of the price level in the O.E.C.D. area as a whole was over six per cent from 1969 to 1972, nearly double its rate over the previous 15 years (see Table 10.1). By 1973 the inflation rate had risen to over eight per cent, over two and a half times what it had been in 1968, and it rose further and even more strongly in 1974. The acceleration was particularly great in the U.K., the U.S., Japan, Italy and Ireland. By 1973, Japan and the U.K. had displaced France and Denmark as the most inflationary countries in the area. Despite the sharp acceleration in the inflation rate, the U.S., together with Germany and Belgium, remained the least inflationary ones.[1]

Table 10.1. O.E.C.D. INFLATION RATES 1969-73

(GDP Deflator; per cent increase per annum)

	Average 1954-68	1969	1970	1971	1972	1973	Average 1969-72
Belgium	2.5	4.3	4.7 (4.0)	5.7 (4.4)	5.9 (5.4)	(7.0)	5.1
Canada	2.4	4.5	3.7 (3.4)	3.3 (2.8)	4.4 (4.8)	(7.6)	4.1
Denmark	4.5	5.1	8.1 (6.5)	6.0 (5.9)	8.8 (6.6)	(9.3)	7.0
France	4.8	6.6	5.5 (5.9)	5.2 (5.6)	5.7 (5.8)	(7.1)	5.7
Germany	2.6	3.5	7.1 (3.8)	7.7 (5.1)	6.1 (5.8)	(6.9)	6.0
Ireland	3.4	8.1	9.6 (8.2)	10.3 (8.9)	14.3 (8.7) (11.3)		10.7
Italy	3.4	4.3	7.4 (4.9)	7.6 (4.8)	5.7 (5.7) (10.8)		5.8
Japan	3.7	4.2	6.7 (7.2)	4.4 (6.3)	4.9 (4.8) (11.2)		5.2
Netherlands	4.2	6.2	5.4 (3.6)	8.1 (7.5)	9.3 (7.8)	(7.9)	7.2
Norway	3.5	3.0	− (10.6)	6.0 (6.3)	4.3 (7.2)	(7.5)	3.9
Sweden	3.8	3.4	7.1 (6.2)	7.3 (7.7)	6.2 (6.2)	(6.8)	6.0
U.K.	3.2	5.6	7.3 (6.4)	8.8 (9.5)	7.8 (7.1)	(9.2)	7.3
U.S.	2.2	4.9	4.7 (5.9)	4.7 (4.3)	3.3 (3.3)	(6.2)	4.3
O.E.C.D. Average	3.3	4.7	6.4 (5.8)	6.4 (6.1)	6.5 (6.1)	(8.4)	5.9

Note: The numbers in brackets refer to Consumer Prices.

Table 10.2 provides some broad indicators of the anatomy of inflation after 1968, comparing it with the earlier period. As one would expect, the rate of increase of money wages in manufacturing industry showed a

Table 10.2. INDICATORS OF INFLATION 1954-68 AND 1969-73
(Percentage increase per annum)

	Inflation rate (GDP deflator)		Money wages (hourly earnings)		Productivity (manufacturing)		Export prices (national currency)		Import prices (national currency)		Money supply	
	1954-68	1969-72	1954-68	1969-73	1954-68	1969-73	1954-68	1969-73	1954-68	1969-73	1954-68	1969-73
Belgium	2.5	5.1	6.4	12.4	4.7	3.2	-0.1	2.0	-0.1	1.5	5.3	8.3
Canada	2.4	4.1	4.4	8.3	3.8	3.9	1.4	4.5	1.5	3.8	7.5	12.0
Denmark	4.5	4.7	8.3	12.2	3.0	5.6	0.6	5.7	0.5	4.3	9.5	12.0
France	4.8	5.7	8.2	11.5	6.1	7.6	2.3	6.8	2.1	5.6	10.5	7.7
Germany	2.6	5.8	7.4	10.5	4.5	4.5	0.3	1.6	-0.8	0.5	9.0	9.6
Ireland	3.4	10.7	6.3	14.7	3.4	4.6	1.3	8.6	1.3	7.5	6.4	7.5
Italy	3.4	5.8	5.5	10.8	7.3	2.6	-0.9	5.8	-0.4	7.0	12.5	17.6
Japan	3.7	5.2	7.7	15.8	9.7	9.7	-0.7	3.3	-0.7	2.1	15.5	18.9
Netherlands	4.1	7.2	8.1	11.7	5.3	7.5	0.1	3.0	-0.1	4.2	6.2	12.4
Norway	3.5	4.4	6.5	10.7	4.1	?	0.4	4.0	0.2	4.2	5.7	12.8
Sweden	3.7	6.0	7.0	9.8	5.1	4.4	0.8	5.2	0.7	5.2	4.4	6.3
U.K.	3.2	7.3	4.5	11.5	3.0	4.0	2.0	7.5	1.1	7.9	3.4	9.6
U.S.	2.2	4.6	3.7	6.1	3.4	3.2	1.2	6.2	0.1	8.2	3.1	6.1
Average	3.3	5.9	6.7	11.2	4.9	5.1	0.7	4.9	0.4	4.8	7.6	10.8

similar acceleration to the price level, although it is noteworthy that the average annual rate of increase for the period 1969-73 accelerated by about 70 per cent as compared with 90 per cent for the annual rate of increase of prices. Productivity growth in manufacturing industry also seems to have risen somewhat, from about 4.9 per cent per annum in 1954-1968 to 5.1 per cent in 1969-73. The rate of increase of the money supply increased sharply — from an average annual increase of 7.8 per cent in the earlier period to over 10 per cent in the later one.

A significant difference between the earlier and later period however lies in the behaviour of foreign trade prices. Both import and export prices of most of the O.E.C.D. countries remained virtually stable in the period 1945-68, but after 1968 they began to rise quite strongly, at nearly five per cent per annum for the area as a whole. As one would expect, foreign trade prices rose most strongly in those countries (U.S., U.K) whose currencies had been significantly devalued just prior to or during the period. Other countries whose currencies had appreciated, in particular Belgium and Germany, continued to enjoy relative stability in their foreign trade prices. On the other hand Japan's export and import prices, which had tended to fall in the 1950s and 1960s, rose quite quickly after 1968.

Rising export prices of industrial countries after 1968 largely reflect the behaviour of manufactured and semi-manufactured good prices in these industrial countries. It will be recalled that in the 1950s and 1960s manufactured good prices tended to lag well behind the rise in prices generally. The price level of services and construction took the lead in the pre-1968 inflation with food prices keeping roughly in line with the average price level. This pattern seems to have broken down after 1968, particularly in the three years 1969-71. The price level of manufactured goods rose sharply, and in many countries the rate of increase of manufactured good prices was higher than that of prices in general. Industrial prices in general do, of course, tend to reflect the cyclical behaviour of the economy, and it is typical for the prices of manufactured goods to rise more sharply in the later stages of the upswing in the economy due to rising costs of production and pressure on capacity. But the rise in these prices appears to have been significantly greater than was the case earlier.

The reasons for the acceleration of world inflation after 1968 are undoubtedly complex: it is doubtful whether the acceleration can be attributed to any one cause, the removal of which would enable the world once again to enjoy the relatively moderate inflation of the 1950s and 1960s. This chapter will confine itself to discussing a number of possible causes and their interaction. Policy issues will be left for Chapter 11.

Some explanations of the acceleration

In earlier chapters of this book we attributed inflation in industrial countries to a combination of demand and cost pressures bearing directly and indirectly on the price level. It was argued that prices would be likely to rise at a faster rate when the pressure of demand in the economy was high and rising, and we indicated the possibility of a trade-off between unemployment and inflation. In Chapter 7 some econometric evidence was presented to show the nature of that trade-off in O.E.C.D. countries. However, it was also stressed that absence of a level of aggregate demand in excess of full employment capacity output was no guarantee of price stability. Provided unemployment is not very high, organized labour can and has exerted an autonomous upward pressure on money wages and labour costs, causing prices to rise even when demand was not excessive in relation to output. In practice, at any rate throughout the 1950s and 1960s, this pressure manifested itself in a tendency for the average level of money wages across the economy as a whole to rise at a rate geared more closely to the rate of increase of productivity in the more technologically advanced and faster labour productivity growth industries than to the average rate of increase of labour productivity across the economy as a whole. As a consequence, although the rate of increase of money wages was not excessive in relation to productivity growth in the advanced sectors of the economy, it was excessive as far as many other sectors of the economy were concerned. Labour costs tended to rise in these industries, forcing a rise in prices to maintain profit margins. Despite price stability in important sectors of the economy, the general price level therefore tended to rise, albeit, as we have seen, at a moderate rate. Some econometric evidence was presented in Chapter 8 to suggest that the different rates of inflation suffered by different O.E.C.D. countries could be partially but by no means wholly explained by differences in the relative rates of productivity growth in different sectors of the economy.

How far can the acceleration of inflation in the O.E.C.D. area after 1968 be explained in terms of the analysis of inflation which we have developed earlier? Did the pressure of demand increase year by year, thus producing a steady acceleration in the rate of increase of prices between 1968 and 1973? Did the productivity gap between key sectors of the economy widen in O.E.C.D. countries after 1968?

Econometric predictions
Some light on these questions is thrown by the fact that the econometric equations derived in Chapter 7 to explain annual variations in O.E.C.D. country inflation rates substantially underpredict the post 1968 inflation. It will be remembered that the independent variables which proved to be significant causal factors determining variations in the inflation rate prior to 1968 were the unemployment rate (which in general was a proxy for the pressure of demand), import prices and indirect taxes.

Table 10.3. O.E.C.D. ACTUAL AND PREDICTED RATES 1969-1973
(GDP Deflator)

	1969		1970		1971		1972		1973		AV	
	a	c	a	c	a	c	a	c	a*	c	a	c
Belgium	4.3	2.6	4.7	4.4	5.7	4.7	5.9	4.6	7.0	6.5	5.5	4.6
Canada	4.5	3.8	3.7	3.0	3.3	2.8	4.4	2.3	7.6	3.8	4.7	3.1
Denmark	5.1	2.3	8.1	6.4	6.0	7.1	8.8	4.5	9.3	6.2	7.5	5.3
France	6.6	2.8	5.5	3.1	5.2	3.4	5.7	2.1	7.1	1.4	6.0	2.6
Germany	3.5	2.9	7.1	4.8	7.7	4.1	6.1	4.5	6.9	3.8	6.3	4.0
Ireland	8.1	5.5	9.6	6.6	10.3	5.2	14.3	4.4	11.3	11.0	10.7	6.5
Italy	4.3	2.4	7.4	4.8	7.6	5.8	5.7	6.2	10.8	4.1	7.2	4.7
Japan	4.2	3.4	6.7	5.2	4.4	4.1	4.9	1.4	11.2	7.1	6.3	5.2
Netherlands	6.2	5.8	5.4	8.7	8.1	8.1	9.3	4.2	7.9	10.0	7.4	7.3
Norway	3.0	4.6	10.6*	10.2	6.0	5.9	4.3	4.6	7.5	5.9	6.3	6.2
Sweden	3.4	2.2	7.1	3.3	7.3	8.7	6.2	4.2	6.8	3.1	6.2	4.3
U.K.	5.6	3.9	7.3	2.7	8.8	1.3	7.8	0.4	9.2	1.4	7.7	2.0
U.S.	4.9	3.8	4.7	4.1	4.7	2.3	3.3	1.5	6.2	1.8	4.8	2.7
Average	5.0	3.5	6.6	5.2	6.4	4.9	6.5	3.5	8.4	5.1	6.7	4.4

Notes: a = actual   c = calculated   * = consumer prices

Functions Used For Predictions 1969-1973

B $p = -0.71 + 0.39p_{-1} + 17.23\,(u_{-1}^{-1} - 0.5\,u_{-2}^{-1}) + 0.79\,(\bar{p}_m - 0.5\bar{p}_{m-1}) - 0.79\,(\Delta\tau - 0.5\Delta\tau_{-1})$

CA $p = -1.69 + 16.78u_{-1}^{-1} + 0.40p_{US}$

DK $p = 1.99 - 0.54p_{-1} + 20.61u_{-1}^{-1} + 0.98\bar{p}_m + 0.45\Delta\tau$

F $p = -1.61 + 0.37p_{-1} + 6.42\,(u_{-1}^{-1} - 0.5\,u_{-2}^{-1}) - 2.50\,(\Delta\tau - 0.5\Delta\tau_{-1})$

G $p = 0.98 + 0.48p_{-1} + 2.50\,(u^{-1} - 0.8u_{-1}^{-1}) + 0.73\,(\bar{p}_{m-1} - 0.8\bar{p}_{m-2})$

IR $p = -0.92 + 27.46u^{-1} + 0.94\bar{p}_m + 1.14\Delta\tau$

I $p = 0.20 + 0.55p_{-1} + 24.66\,(u_{-1}^{-1} - 0.80u_{-1}^{-1}) + 1.17\,(\bar{p}_{m-1} - 0.8\bar{p}_{m-2}) + 0.04\,(\Delta\tau - 0.80\Delta\tau_{-1})$

J $p = 2.78 + 0.94u^{-1} + 3.26\bar{p}_m - 2.33\Delta\tau$

NL $p = 1.49 + 0.24p_{-1} + 3.03\,(u_{-2}^{-1} - \tfrac{1}{3}u_{-3}^{-1}) + 1.26\,(\bar{p}_m - \tfrac{1}{3}\bar{p}_{m-1}) - 0.28\,(\Delta\tau - \tfrac{1}{3}\Delta\tau)$

N $p = 2.31 + 0.11p_{-1} + 0.96u^{-1} + 0.91\bar{p}_m + 1.18\Delta\tau$

S $p = 3.18 - 0.25p_{-1} + 1.77u_{-1}^{-1} + 1.38\bar{p}_{m-1} + 1.53\Delta\tau$

UK $p = -1.87 - 8.34u_{-1}^{-1} + 0.49\,(\bar{p}_{m_1} + \bar{p}_{m_2}) + 1.02\Delta\tau$

US $p = -1.85 + 20.40u_{-1}^{-1} + 0.27\Delta\tau$

In Table 10.3. we compare the annual rates of inflation which would have been predicted by these equations on the basis of changes in the independent variables that took place after 1968 with the rates of inflation that actually occurred. The 'statistically best' equation for each country was used to make the predictions and these are listed in the lower half of the table, along with the annual changes in the relevant independent variables.

It will be seen that the equations do in general predict a rise in the rate of inflation after 1968. Taking the O.E.C.D. area as a whole, the equations predict an average annual inflation rate of 4.4 per cent for the five years 1969-73, as compared with an average O.E.C.D. inflation rate of about 3.4 per cent during the previous 14 years. Even so, the equations underpredict the inflation that actually occurred. The actual average annual inflation in 1969-73 was greater than six per cent. Moreover, whereas our equations predict lower inflation rates in 1971-73 than in 1970 the actual inflation rate rose fairly steadily from five per cent in 1969 (about three per cent in 1968) to over eight per cent in 1973.

Looking at the individual countries it is evident that the underprediction for the O.E.C.D. area as a whole stems from a major underprediction for some countries, in particular the U.K., the U.S., France and Germany. The equations did not predict badly for a number of others. The equation for the U.K. predicts less inflation after 1968 than before, while the predicted average annual inflation rate for the period 1969-73 was barely one-fourth of what actually occurred, the discrepancy being particularly wide in the years 1971-3. The discrepancy between predicted and actual was also great for these years in the case of France, while the equation for the U.S. predicted steadily worse as the period evolved. If we relate the structure of the country equations to their predictions, and observe the contribution of the independent variables to the predicted inflation rates (see Table 10.4.), we note that the equations predict best in the case of countries for which the coefficient attached to the import price variable tends to be high relatively to the average — Japan, Netherlands, Norway and Sweden for example. They do less well, indeed badly, for the countries in which the reverse is true — for instance the U.S., U.K., Italy and France. It seems clear that the higher unemployment rates found in the U.K. and the U.S. in the post-1968 period explain why the equations for these countries predict such low inflation rates. In other words the inflation rates that were actually experienced by these countries after 1968 were much higher than would have been expected on the basis of the unemployment rates which ruled, assuming that the same trade-off relationships had held as in 1954-68. The difference cannot be explained by the behaviour of import prices, for although in most (but not all) countries the behaviour of import prices after 1968 would have produced higher domestic inflation rates as compared with 1954-68, the rise in the import prices of the U.K. and the U.S. cannot by itself explain why inflation rates in these countries were high relative to the unemployment which

Table 10.4. CONTRIBUTION OF THE INDEPENDENT VARIABLES
TO THE PREDICTED INFLATION RATE

BELGIUM

Function: $p = -0.71 + 0.39p_{-1} + 17.23\,(u_{-1}^{-1} - 0.50u_{-2}^{-1}) + 0.79(\overline{p}_m - 0.50\overline{p}_{m-1})$

$$- 0.79\,(\Delta\tau - 0.50\,\Delta\tau_{-1})$$

	Constant term	p_{-1}	Unemployment	Import prices	Indirect taxes		Total
1969	−0.71	1.05	1.50	0.87	−0.12	=	2.6
1970	−0.71	1.68	2.88	0.43	0.12	=	4.4
1971	−0.71	1.83	3.55	−0.16	0.20	=	4.7
1972	−0.71	2.22	2.97	−0.47	0.63	=	4.6
1973	−0.71	2.30	1.95	3.00	n.a	=	6.5
Average	−0.71	1.82	2.57	0.73	0.21	=	4.6

CANADA

Function: $p = -1.69 + 16.78u^{-1} + 0.40p_{US}$

	Constant term	Unemployment	US inflation rate	Total
1969	−1.69	3.57	1.88	3.8
1970	−1.69	2.84	1.88	3.0
1971	−1.69	2.62	1.88	2.8
1972	−1.69	2.66	1.32	2.3
1973	−1.69	3.00	2.48	3.8
Average	−1.69	2.95	1.89	3.1

DENMARK

Function: $p = 1.99 - 0.54p_{-1} + 20.61u_{-1}^{-1} + 0.98\overline{p}_m + 0.45\Delta\tau$

	Constant term	p_{-1}	Unemployment	Import prices	Indirect taxes		Total
1969	1.99	−4.32	4.12	0.29	0.18	=	2.3
1970	1.99	−2.75	5.28	1.76	0.15	=	6.4
1971	1.99	−4.37	7.11	2.45	−0.05	=	7.1
1972	1.99	−3.24	5.57	0.00	0.13	=	4.5
1973	1.99	−4.75	5.73	3.72	−0.45	=	6.2
Average	1.99	−3.89	5.56	1.64	−0.04	=	5.3

Note: for p_{-1} we always use the *observed* inflation rates, not the calculated ones. If we had used the latter, the average would have been 6.10 instead of 5.26.

FRANCE

Function: $p = -1.61 + 0.37p_{-1} + 6.42\,(u_{-1}^{-1} - 0.50\,u_{-2}^{-1}) - 2.50\,(\Delta\tau - 0.50\,\Delta\tau_{-1})$

	Constant term	p_{-1}	Unemployment	Indirect taxes		Total
1969	−1.61	1.78	1.70	0.88	=	2.75
1970	−1.61	2.55	3.31	−1.13	=	3.12
1971	−1.61	2.18	1.99	0.88	=	3.44
1972	−1.61	1.96	1.29	0.50	=	2.14
1973	−1.61	1.96	1.30	−0.25	=	1.40
Average	−1.61	2.09	1.92	0.18	=	2.58

Table 10.4. Cont.

GERMANY
Function: $p = 0.98 + 0.48p_{-1} + 2.50\,(u^{-1} - 0.8u_{-1}^{-1}) + 0.73\,(\bar{p}_{m\text{-}2} - 0.8\,\bar{p}_{m\text{-}2})$

	Constant term	p_{-1}	Unemployment	Import prices		Total
1969	0.98	0.72	1.44	−0.26	=	2.9
1970	0.98	1.58	1.35	0.86	=	4.8
1971	0.98	3.55	0.27	−0.70	=	4.1
1972	0.98	3.65	−0.23	0.09	=	4.5
1973	0.98	2.74	0.27	−0.18	=	3.8
Average	0.98	2.45	0.62	−0.04	=	4.0

IRELAND
Function: $p = -0.92 + 27.46u^{-1} + 0.94\bar{p}_m + 1.14\Delta\tau$

	Constant term	Unemployment	Import prices	Indirect taxes	Total
1969	−0.92	4.29	1.79	0.34	5.5
1970	−0.92	3.81	3.10	0.57	6.6
1971	−0.92	3.81	2.44	−0.11	5.2
1972	−0.92	3.39	1.88	0.00	4.4
1973	−0.92	3.81	7.99	0.11	11.0
Average	−0.92	3.82	3.44	0.18	6.5

ITALY
Function: $p = 0.20 + 0.55p_{-1} + 24.66\,(u^{-1} - 0.80\,u_{-1}^{-1}) + 1.17\,(\bar{p}_{m\text{-}2} - 0.8\,\bar{p}_{m\text{-}2})$

$$+ 0.04\,(\Delta\tau - 0.8\Delta\tau_{-1})$$

	Constant term	p_{-1}	Unemployment	Import prices	Indirect taxes		Total
1969	0.20	0.83	1.62	−0.22	−0.01	=	2.4
1970	0.20	2.31	1.90	0.36	0.01	=	4.8
1971	0.20	3.63	1.54	0.44	−0.02	=	5.8
1972	0.20	3.69	0.69	1.66	−0.02	=	6.2
1973	0.20	3.30	1.57	−0.96	+0.02	=	4.1
Average	0.20	2.75	1.46	0.26	−	=	4.7

JAPAN
Function: $p = 2.78 + 0.94u^{-1} + 3.26\bar{p}_m - 2.33\Delta\tau$

	Constant term	Unemployment	Import prices	Indirect taxes		Total
1969	2.78	0.86	−	−0.23	=	3.4
1970	2.78	0.79	1.63	−	=	5.2
1971	2.78	0.79	0.33	0.23	=	4.1
1972	2.78	0.67	−2.28	0.23	=	1.4
1973	2.78	0.72	3.59	−	=	7.1
Average	2.78	0.77	1.57	0.05	=	5.2

Table 10.4. Cont.

NETHERLANDS

Function: $p = 1.49 + 0.24p_{-1} + 3.03\,(u_{-2}^{-1} - 0.33\,u_{-3}^{-1}) + 1.26\,(\bar{p}_m - 0.33\,\bar{p}_{m_{1-1}})$

$$-0.28\,(\Delta\tau - 0.33\,\Delta\tau_{-1})$$

	Constant term	p_{-1}	Unemployment	Import prices	Indirect taxes	Total
1969	1.49	0.91	0.60	2.47	0.33	= 5.8
1970	1.49	1.49	1.09	4.87	−0.29	= 8.7
1971	1.49	1.30	1.64	3.68	−0.05	= 8.1
1972	1.49	1.94	2.04	−1.25	0.01	= 4.2
1973	1.49	2.23	0.98	5.13	0.12	= 10.0
Average	1.49	1.57	1.27	2.98	0.02	= 7.3

NORWAY

Function: $p = 2.31 + 0.11p_{-1} + 0.96u^{-1} + 0.91\bar{p}_m + 1.18\Delta\tau$

	Constant term	p_{-1}	Unemployment	Import prices	Indirect taxes	Total
1969	2.31	0.11	0.96	0.73	0.47	= 4.6
1970	2.31	0.33	1.20	2.91	3.40	= 10.2
1971	2.31	1.17	1.20	1.73	−0.47	= 5.9
1972	2.31	0.65	0.96	0.91	−0.24	= 4.6
1973	2.31	0.47	1.20	2.37	−0.47	= 5.9
Average	2.31	0.55	1.10	1.73	0.54	= 6.2

SWEDEN

Function: $p = 3.18 - 0.25p_{-1} + 1.77u_{-1}^{-1} + 1.38\bar{p}_{m-1} + 1.53\Delta\tau$

	Constant term	p_{-1}	Unemployment	Import prices	Indirect taxes	Total
1969	3.18	−0.65	0.89	0.41	−1.68	= 2.2
1970	3.18	−0.85	1.04	0.55	−0.61	= 3.3
1971	3.18	−1.78	1.26	2.48	3.52	= 8.7
1972	3.18	−1.83	0.89	1.93	n.a.	= 4.2
1973	3.18	−1.55	0.89	0.55	n.a.	= 3.1
Average	3.18	−1.33	0.99	1.18	0.25	= 4.3

UNITED KINGDOM

Function: $p = -1.87 + 8.34u_{-1}^{-1} + 0.49\,(\bar{p}_{m\,-1} + \bar{p}_{m\,-2}) + 1.02\Delta\tau$

	Constant term	Unemployment	Import prices	Indirect taxes	Total
1969	−1.87	3.34	1.13	1.33	= 3.9
1970	−1.87	3.34	1.52	−0.31	= 2.7
1971	−1.87	3.21	0.88	−0.92	= 1.3
1972	−1.87	2.45	0.78	−0.92	= 0.4
1973	−1.87	2.19	1.03	n.a.	= 1.4
Average	−1.87	2.91	1.07	−0.16	= 2.0

Table 10.4. Cont.

UNITED STATES
Function: $p = -1.85 + 20.40\, u_{-1}^{-1} + 0.27\Delta\tau$

	Constant term	Unemployment	Indirect taxes		Total
1969	−1.85	+ 5.67	0.03	=	3.84
1970	−1.85	+ 5.83	0.11	=	4.09
1971	−1.85	+ 4.16	0.03	=	2.34
1972	−1.85	+ 3.40	− 0.08	=	1.47
1973	−1.85	+ 3.64	n.a.	=	1.79
Average	−1.85	+ 4.54	0.02	=	2.71

existed. The behaviour of import prices as well as that of unemployment should have caused a fall in Germany's inflation rate, instead of the rise that actually occurred.

The fact that our equations tend to underpredict the actual rate of inflation after 1968 suggests that the acceleration of inflation which took place cannot be explained solely in terms of a higher pressure of demand than typically ruled in the 1950s and 1960s. However, in common with all equations of this type the unemployment rate serves as a proxy for the pressure of demand. It could be that the relationship between unemployment and demand pressure changed significantly in the late 1960s and early 70s as compared with the earlier period. Some studies by the Economic Secretariat of the O.E.C.D. suggest that this might well have happened.[2] In 1972, for example, the unemployment rate in a number of member countries (Canada, France, Belgium, Netherlands, U.K.) was about one per cent above the rate prevailing at a similar stage of the previous cycle of economic activity as measured by other indicators of demand. This was particularly true of the U.K. − a country for which the econometric equation greatly underpredicts the post-1968 inflation: unemployment rose much more than might have been expected on the basis of the behaviour of other indicators. It appears that a substantial 'shake-out' of labour occurred in the U.K. in 1971, possibly due to rather pessimistic entrepreneurial expectations as to the growth of economic activity, and perhaps also to the fast rise in labour costs during the 1971 recession in activity. On the other hand, there does not seem to have been a corresponding 'shake-in' in 1973 when output was rising fast.

The O.E.C.D. studies suggest that longer term structural factors, operating on both the demand and the supply side of the labour markets, may also have affected the relationship between the pressure of demand in the economy and the level of unemployment. On the supply side, it could be that an increasing proportion of workers losing their jobs actually registered as unemployed (and were, therefore, measured in the statistics) rather than, as was the case earlier, dropping out of the labour force altogether. Such a development could be associated with a changing attitude of women towards full time work and increased female participation in the labour force which has undoubtedly occurred in both the U.S. and Europe in recent years. It could also be that more generous unemployment benefits have encouraged registration as unemployed as well as reducing the urgency with which the unemployed look for new jobs. Finally, there have been marked signs of increasing job dissatisfaction, on the part of the young in particular, and an unwillingness to work which has led to more rapid job turnover in recent years.

The possibility that structural demand factors, leading to significant imbalances between the demand and supply of particular types of labour, may be operating as well is suggested by the growing disequilibrium between unemployment and job vacancies in many countries. The underlying factors suggested by the O.E.C.D. could include a rise in female participation, which is concentrated in sectors of the economy whose rate of growth has been too low to provide sufficient employment opportunities; regional imbalances, which have certainly assumed greater importance in a number of European countries (for instance, Belgium and Italy); the substitution of capital for labour in some countries, owing to the accelerated rise in labour costs after 1968; too slow an increase in the capital stock relative to the increase in labour supply in others;[3] and finally improvements in statistical coverage of unemployment.

While many or all of the factors mentioned above may have contributed to some change in the underlying relationship between aggregate demand in the economy and the level of unemployment, the O.E.C.D. studies do not suggest that the factors assumed sufficient importance after 1968 to warrant the conclusion that unemployment was no longer a reliable indicator of the pressure of demand. Hence part at least of the explanation of the changed relationship between inflation on the one side of the pressure of demand and unemployment on the other must be looked for elsewhere.

Rising foreign trade prices

The fact that on the basis of a rise in import prices in most O.E.C.D. countries our equations correctly predicted a rise in the inflation rate after 1968, but at the same time underpredicted the rate of inflation that actually occurred, suggests that in looking for an explanation of the acceleration we should focus attention on two issues. First, why did import prices rise? Second, even allowing for the rise in import prices, why did the trade-off between unemployment and inflation appear to get worse?

One preliminary comment should be made with respect to import prices. It should be noted that in large part the import prices of O.E.C.D. countries are also the export prices of the same group of countries. This implies that the rise in import prices is very largely an endogenous factor in the O.E.C.D. inflation, not an exogenous one. Only in so far as the rise in import prices applied to imports coming from countries outside the O.E.C.D. area (largely the less developed primary producing countries) can this be regarded as an exogenous element underlying the rise in the O.E.C.D. inflation rate. Even then the question would arise how far the rise in the export prices of the suppliers of goods to O.E.C.D. countries stemmed from autonomous demand pressures arising in the O.E.C.D. area itself. In other words we are faced with the problem of explaining part at least of the rise in foreign trade prices generally as an integral element of the post-1968 acceleration of inflation. In fact, as Table 10.2. shows, export prices of the O.E.C.D. area as a whole (unweighted average) generally rose at about the same rate as, or a little faster than O.E.C.D. import prices, at any rate up to 1972. It wasn't until 1973 that the rise in import prices significantly exceeded the rise in export prices.

The experience of the various O.E.C.D. countries with respect to their foreign trade prices (measured in national currencies) was not at all similar, except in 1973 when virtually every country's import and export prices — particularly the former — rose substantially. In 1968, the U.K.'s foreign trade prices rose strongly, along with those of Ireland. U.S. export prices which had been rising fairly steadily from the mid-1960s until 1969, rose sharply in 1970, as did import prices. France's import prices fell in 1968 but then, with export prices, rose strongly in 1969 and 1970. Germany's export prices rose through 1968-73 while its import prices fell until 1973 when, along with other industrial countries, they rose significantly. Japan's and Italy's prices were stable in 1968 and 1969 but tended to rise in 1970 and 1971.

This pattern of price behaviour is clearly quite different from what happened prior to 1967. As far as this earlier period is concerned it is possible to relate the behaviour of individual countries' export prices (domestic currency) and overall inflation rates to the behaviour of the world price level of traded manufactured goods. The latter, in turn, seemed to be substantially determined by rapidly rising labour productivity and falling labour costs in Japan and Italy which were able to exert a price leadership role in world trade. But the modified Scandinavian structural model developed in Chapter 8 to explain relative country inflation rates loses much of its usefulness when large and repeated changes in exchange parities are taking place, as was the case from the end of 1967 on.

Whereas in the period 1955-67 the exchange rates of the major industrial countries had remained virtually fixed, in the following five years substantial changes in parities took place. The first major change was a 14 per cent devaluation of sterling against the dollar and other currencies generally in November 1967. The French franc was devalued by about 11 per cent in August 1969, and this was shortly followed by an upward float of the Deutschemark in September of the year which three weeks later was consolidated into a ten per cent revaluation against the dollar. The Canadian dollar was floated in mid-1970, and this was followed by a further upward float of the deutschemark and Dutch guilder in May 1971. By this time the currency crises had become acute and the position of the U.S. dollar was under severe attack. Following a suspension of the gold convertibility of the dollar in August 1971, a realignment of currencies took place at the Smithsonian monetary agreement in December 1971: the U.S. dollar was formally devalued and other currencies, including the deutschemark and the yen but not sterling or the French franc, were revalued. The realignment did not survive long. Sterling was floated in June 1972; there was a further devaluation of the dollar in February 1973 when the Italian lire and the yen were also floated. Finally, further revaluations of the Deutschemark and Dutch guilder were forced in the second half of 1973.

FIGURE 10.1

FOREIGN EXCHANGE RATES OF MAJOR CURRENCIES

(Percentage deviation with respect to dollar parities of October 1967)

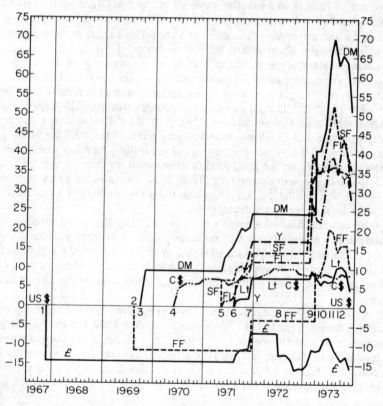

By the end of 1973 every major currency apart from sterling had risen in value against the dollar as compared with the parities of October 1967. The revaluation of the deutschemark amounted to over 50 per cent (at one time 70 per cent: see Figure 10.1.), while that of the yen, the Swiss franc and Dutch guilder amounted to over 30 per cent. Sterling, however, remained devalued by about 15 per cent as compared with the October 1967 parity. Foreign trade prices measured in national currency of the various O.E.C.D. countries were bound to be affected by such massive changes in exchange parities.

Large changes in exchange rates can be expected to result in a rise in the domestic currency price of traded goods in countries whose currencies have depreciated relative to the average and a fall in these prices in countries whose currencies have appreciated against the average. One would also expect that the domestic price level would be affected most in countries with the largest trade sectors, existing inflation being accelerated in the depreciating countries and decelerated in the appreciating countries: in theory, the domestic price level could even fall in the latter countries, although in practice the downward rigidity of domestic costs will tend to prevent or limit it. In a situation in which one or two large countries are in deficit and one or two in surplus, which was the case in the late 1960s and early 1970s, the required change in relative prices to correct the situation can be brought about either by a devaluation of the deficit country's exchange rate relative to the rest or by an appreciation of the surplus country's exchange rate, or, of course, both. In all cases existing inflationary pressures will be given a boost in the deficit countries and moderated in surplus countries. The effect on third countries will generally depend on whose exchange rate is changed. Owing to the different effect on the import prices and to a lesser extent export prices of the third countries, a revaluation of the surplus country's currency is likely to result in a greater upward pressure on the price level of these countries than is a devaluation of the deficit country's currency. Thus, third countries are likely to find their domestic inflation exacerbated more by revaluations of other major currencies than by devaluations.

We can conclude that, given some downward rigidity in industrial costs and prices, a major alteration of exchange parities is likely to produce some rise in the general world price level, the more so the more the adjustment takes the form of an appreciation of surplus countries' currencies against the rest than a depreciation of the deficit countries' currencies against the rest.

Evidently, sterling devaluation of November 1967 was the major factor causing the sharp rise in U.K. foreign trade prices in 1968 and the following acceleration in the domestic rate of inflation. Ireland, whose currency was devalued with sterling, was similarly affected. But non-devaluing countries received stabilizing influences, and in most cases their import and export prices fell in domestic currency terms. The French franc devaluation in

August 1969 made possible the sharp rise in French export and import prices in 1969, but the direct price-stabilizing impact on third countries' foreign trade prices may have been offset by the immediately following appreciation of the Deutschemark.[4] The further revaluations of the Deutschemark and other currencies against the dollar which took place in the course of 1971 were accompanied by a rise in export and import prices in nearly all O.E.C.D. countries, revaluing ones as well as non-revaluing ones. Although the successive revaluations of the Deutschemark which took place did cause a fall in Germany's import prices, it is significant to note that export prices did not fall but continued to rise at about the same rate as in the early part of the 1960s.

The major realignment of currencies under the Smithsonian agreement of December 1971 had further effects on foreign trade prices. In this realignment the U.S. dollar was effectively devalued against currencies in general while the Deutschemark and the Japanese yen were effectively revalued. Import and export prices rose sharply in countries whose exchange rates had been effectively devalued[5] under the agreement (for example, the U.S.), but they did not fall much if at all in countries whose exchange rates had been effectively revalued; even then import prices were more affected than were export prices. Despite the very substantial appreciation of the Deutschemark and the Yen, German and Japanese export prices were very little affected. Foreign trade prices were roughly stabilized in countries whose effective parities had changed rather little. It appears therefore that as far as third countries were concerned the inflationary effects of German and Japanese revaluation were roughly offset by the deflationary effects of U.S. devaluation.

Underlying these movements in foreign trade prices was a steady rise in U.S. export prices which commenced in the mid 1960s and accompanied the steady acceleration in the U.S.'s own inflation rate. It has been argued[6] that the acceleration of inflation in the U.S. was the prime cause of the acceleration in the world's inflation rate in the late 1960s. Given that U.S. output contributes about one-third of the total output of the Western World, there is obvious considerable force in this argument, although it should be noticed that the world price level (measured in U.S. dollars) lagged well behind U.S. export prices up to 1968.[7] It does not seem sufficient by itself to explain what happened to the world inflation rate without reference to what happened to exchange parities. U.S. export prices in fact rose much less rapidly than U.S. domestic prices, at any rate up to the end of 1971 when the U.S. dollar was devalued. However, as will be argued later, the massive acceleration which occurred in the world inflation in 1973-4 certainly had its origins in the U.S. balance of payments.

It is interesting to note that country inflation rates rose less over the years 1968-72 than could be expected on the basis of 1954-67 experience; given the rise in domestic currency export prices that took place. The Scandinavian structural model which is described and tested in Chapter 8 would predict inflation rates in O.E.C.D. countries 0.8 per cent above what actually occurred. However, the overprediction may simply be due to time lags between the very sharp changes in national export prices produced by the exchange rate changes and the consequential impact on the general price level.

A Commodity Boom of 1973

If the rise in foreign trade price level of the O.E.C.D. area as a whole in the years 1968-72 can reasonably be attributed to the sharp changes in exchange parities between industrial countries which took place, the very large rise which took place in 1973 and 1974 cannot be. This is not to say that changes in exchange rates had no effect on foreign trade prices in these years. The downward float of the sterling exchange rate after June 1972 clearly contributed to the continued rise in U.K. sterling import prices in 1972 and 1973. But, as indicated earlier, what was significant about 1973 and 1974 is the fact that O.E.C.D. import prices rose much faster than O.E.C.D. export prices. It was the sharply rising price of commodities produced *outside* the O.E.C.D. area which produced the rise in the cost of imports to the area as a whole.

Here again, however, we must distinguish between various countries of the O.E.C.D. The import prices of some countries rose much more strongly than did those of others. The U.K., Italy and the U.S. were most afflicted, import prices rising by around 20 per cent or more. Japan's import prices also rose considerably — by over 12 per cent. At the other end of the scale Germany's import prices rose by only 3½ per cent.

O.E.C.D. export prices also rose considerably but for most countries in less proportion than import prices. Conspicuous exceptions to the latter generalization are Canada, France and the U.S., whose terms of trade either did not suffer or improved. This latter group of countries, being significant exporters of temperate climate food products, benefited from the steep rise in primary product prices which was the most significant feature of world inflation in 1973. Between 1972 and 1973 the world price index of primary products rose by about 50 per cent and by a further 25 per cent in 1974. It is not surprising that inflation rates throughout the world, which had shown some tendency to stabilize in 1972, received a further boost.

There were a number of special factors underlying the rise in primary product prices in 1973. *Per capita* world agricultural production declined in 1972. The U.S.S.R., in particular, suffered a bad grain harvest in 1972-3 and became a net importer of grain on a massive scale in 1973. Grain prices on world markets more than doubled as a consequence. There were signs too of a secular upturn in primary product prices generally, following a long relative decline that began in the mid 1950s. The major international currency crisis of 1971, and distrust in the U.S. dollar and in the value of currencies generally, also clearly provoked speculative and precautionary demands for many commodities. But the main factor was a coincident upturn during 1972 in rates of economic expansion in the main countries of the O.E.C.D. Real GDP of the O.E.C.D. area grew nearly 6 per cent in 1972 and by a further 6¾ per cent in 1973 as compared with average rates of economic expansion in the 1960s of less than 5 per cent per annum. The upturn seems to have begun in North America – the U.S. and Canada enjoyed very high rates of growth in 1972 – and then spread to Europe and Japan in 1973. The coincidence of the timing of the economic booms in the major countries of the Western World was unprecedented in the post Second World War era. It led to early and widespread capacity bottlenecks in many basic industries which could not, as in earlier years when there were always some countries not enjoying boom conditions, be met by any country by importing from others. Shortages of many basic industrial raw materials developed, as a consequence of which their prices quickly rose to very high levels. It has been estimated by O.E.C.D. Economic Secretariat that the rise in commodity prices accounted for virtually the whole of the rise of the O.E.C.D. area GDP deflator between 1972 and 1973. Moreover, rising food prices contributed about half of the rise in consumer prices in 1973 and were clearly an important factor in the acceleration of inflation everywhere, including countries which were protected by currency revaluation, or by agricultural self-sufficiency or by price control (see Table 10.5 and Figures 10.2 and 10.3.).

O.E.C.D. countries were afflicted by the rise in primary product prices in different degrees. The impact on any one country clearly depended on the commodity composition of its imports. It also depended on what happened to its exchange rate. Germany's national currency import prices were clearly held down by the strong appreciation of its currency in 1973. So were the import prices of France, Belgium and Japan although to a lesser extent. The import prices of the U.S., the U.K. and Italy rose massively since their currencies showed no appreciation against the dollar in which most primary products are priced. It is not surprising therefore that inflation accelerated more rapidly in these three countries than it did in Germany or France. The acceleration was also great in Japan despite the appreciation of the yen, owing to the greater sensitivity of the Japanese price level to import prices.

Table 10.5. CONSUMER PRICES: PERCENTAGE CHANGES FROM PREVIOUS PERIOD AT ANNUAL RATES

	Average 1959-60 to 1970-71	1971	1972	1972 II s.a.	1973 I s.a.	Three months ending October 1973 s.a.	n.s.a.
Canada	2.6	2.9	4.8	5.6	7.6	11.4	11.2
United States	2.8	4.3	3.3	3.4	6.2	11.4	11.1
Japan	5.7	6.1	4.5	5.9	11.8	13.0	13.5
Australia	2.7	6.1	5.8	4.9	10.5	16.3[b]	15.3[b]
France	4.1	5.5	5.9	7.8	5.7	10.6	9.8
Germany	2.8	5.2	5.8	7.5	7.1	5.5	2.5
Italy	3.9	4.8	5.7	8.2	11.6	8.9	8.2
United Kingdom	4.2	9.4	7.1	8.9	8.4	12.0	8.3
Belgium	3.0	4.3	5.5	6.8	7.3	6.6	6.0
Netherlands	4.4	7.6	7.8	7.6	8.2	6.1	6.0
Denmark	5.7	5.8	6.6	6.5	9.7	9.0**	9.9**
Ireland	4.7	8.9	8.7	8.9	12.8	11.0**	9.2**
Austria	3.6	4.7	6.3	8.0	8.0	6.3	6.7
Finland	5.0	6.1	7.4	8.8	10.0	21.1	20.8
Greece	2.1	3.0	4.4	4.4	13.7	31.6	26.1
Norway	4.4	6.2	7.2	8.6	6.6	6.4	4.9
Spain	5.9	8.3	8.3	9.1	9.9	17.8	19.8
Sweden	4.2	7.4	6.0	6.7	5.9	6.1**	5.5**
Switzerland	3.4	6.6	6.7	6.9	9.0	10.0	8.2
OECD total*	3.4	5.3	4.7	5.5	7.5	10.9	10.2
Of which: Food*	3.3	4.3	5.4	6.9	13.4	19.1	19.3
Non-food*	3.5	5.6	4.5	4.9	5.7	7.8	6.8
OECD Europe*	3.9	6.6	6.5	8.1	8.2	9.6	8.1
Of which: Food*	3.7	6.0	7.1	9.6	9.9	8.5	7.0
Non-food*	4.1	6.9	6.2	7.1	7.1	9.8	8.5

* 1970 private consumption weights and exchange rates.
** 1973 third quarter over second quarter.
Note: s.a. seasonally adjusted; n.s.a. not seasonally adjusted.

Source: O.E.C.D. Economic Outlook, Dec. 1973.

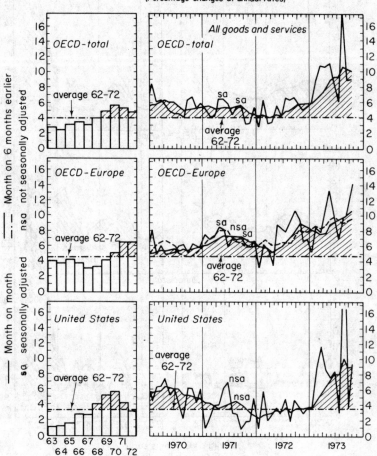

CHANGE IN CONSUMER PRICES
(Percentage changes at annual rates)

Source: O.E.C.D. Economic Outlook, Dec. 1973

FIGURE 10.3

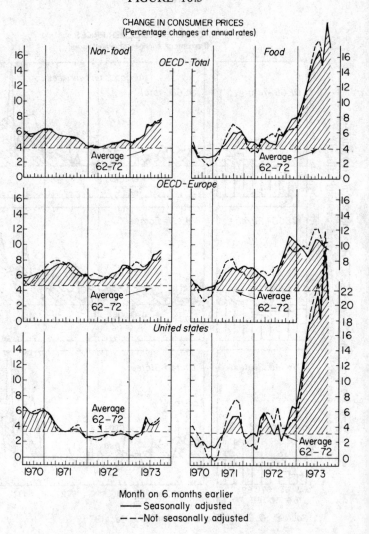

CHANGE IN CONSUMER PRICES
(Percentage changes at annual rates)

Month on 6 months earlier
—— Seasonally adjusted
----Not seasonally adjusted

Source   O.E.C.D. Economic outlook   Dec. 1973

The question that arises at this point is: what caused the coincident boom in economic activity in the Western World in 1972-3? Was it a coincidence? or was there some underlying cause which operated in all countries simultaneously?

Table 10.6. COMPOSITION OF CHANGES IN INTERNATIONAL LIQUIDITY
(SDR billion; not seasonally adjusted)

	Amounts outstanding			Changes			
	End-1969	End-1972	End-June 1973	Annual average 1970-72	Q1	1973 Q2	Q3[a]
Gold	39.1	35.8	35.8	−1.1	0	0	0
SDRs	−	8.7	8.8	2.9	−	0.1	−
Reserve position in the IMF	6.7	6.3	6.2	−0.1	−0.1	0	0
Currency assets	33.5	97.7	103.3	21.4	2.6	3.1	3
Total countries' recorded reserves	79.3	148.5	154.0	23.0	2.5	3.2	3
Memorandum item:							
Total countries' recorded reserves (US $)	79.3	161.3	186.1	27.4	21.0	3.9	4

Source: O.E.C.D. Economic Outlook, Dec. 1973.

It is difficult to dismiss a purely monetary explanation of the upturn. It is a stark fact that the volume of international liquidity − i.e. international money − more than doubled in the three years 1970-72. The figures are given in Table 10.6., while Figure 10.4. brings out very clearly the tremendous rise in the amount of world official reserve assets which took place after 1969. The underlying cause was a massive deterioration in the U.S. balance of payments on the official settlements basis which, in part at least, had its roots in growing fiscal deficits (see Chapter 6). The U.S. had experienced increasing difficulty with its balance of payments throughout the 1960s and surplus countries had become increasingly unwilling to go on financing the U.S. deficit by accumulating dollars in their reserves. Even so they were reluctant to appreciate their exchange rates against the dollar. When it was forced on them, as it was on Germany in 1969 and again in 1970, the changes were not sufficient to correct the situation. Distrust in the U.S. dollar began to mount in 1970 and reached a climax in 1971. Speculation against the dollar took place on a massive scale, and central banks abroad, particularly those of Germany and Japan, were forced to take in vast quantities of dollars in an effort to prevent the appreciation of their exchange rates. The realignment of exchange rates in the Smithsonian agreement of December 1971 reduced speculative pressure against the dollar; even so, inflow of dollars into central banks reserves continued on a substantial scale into 1972. At the same time, the Euro-currency market expanded enormously, in part due to the growing practice of central banks depositing excess dollars in the market. Central banks in Europe and elsewhere found it difficult to neutralise the domestic monetary effects of the massive dollar inflow. They were reasonably successful in 1969 and 1970 but, as Table 5.12. (p.95) shows, domestic money supply in many O.E.C.D. countries began to rise very fast after 1969.[5]

FIGURE 10.4

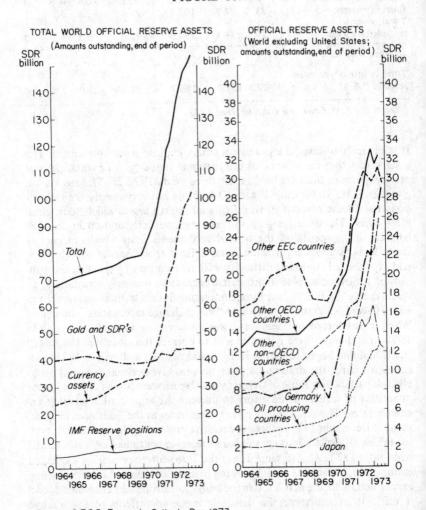

Source: O.E.C.D. Economic Outlook, Dec. 1973

FIGURE 10.5

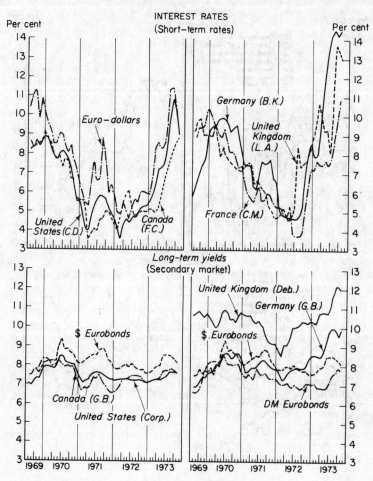

INTEREST RATES
(Short-term rates)

Euro-dollars

United States (C.D.)

Canada (F.C.)

Germany (B.K.)

United Kingdom (L.A.)

France (C.M.)

Long-term yields
(Secondary market)

$ Eurobonds

Canada (G.B.)

United States (Corp.)

United Kingdom (Deb.)

Germany (G.B.)

$ Eurobonds

DM Eurobonds

Source: O.E.C.D. Economic Outlook, Dec. 1973

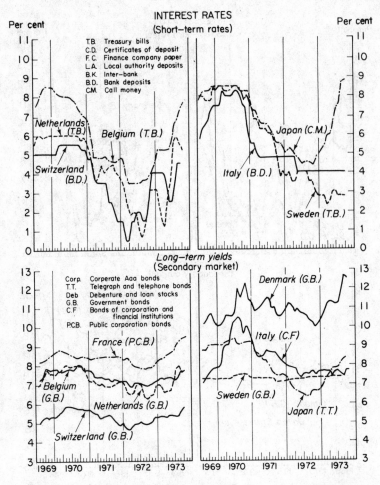

INTEREST RATES
(Short—term rates)

TB. Treasury bills
C.D. Certificates of deposit
F.C. Finance company paper
L.A. Local authority deposits
B.K. Inter—bank
B.D. Bank deposits
CM. Call money

Long—term yields
(Secondary market)

Corp. Corperate Aaa bonds
T.T. Telegraph and telephone bonds
Deb Debenture and loan stocks
G.B. Government bonds
C.F Bonds of corporation and financial institutions
P.C.B. Public corporation bonds

Source: O.E.C.D. Economic Outlook, Dec. 1973

One does not have to be a monetarist to believe that the rapid rise in money supply in the O.E.C.D. area as a whole had something to do with the subsequent rise in economic activity. Keynesians would point to the fall in world interest rates that took place at the same time. It can be seen from Figure 10.5. that Euro-dollar rates fell from a peak of over 11 per cent in mid-1969 to about five per cent in mid-1972, and similar falls took place in short term interest rates in virtually all O.E.C.D. countries. Long term interest rates also tended to fall after the middle of 1970 although less than short rates. By 1972 long rates in many countries were one or two per cent below what they had been in 1970. Given this interest rate scenario, it is hardly surprising that investment expenditure was stimulated almost everywhere.

The trade-off between unemployment and inflation

Although O.E.C.D. countries enjoyed a substantial economic boom in 1972-3, it should be noted that unemployment rates did not fall to excessively low levels as compared with the previous decade or so. Unemployment rates did fall in some countries in 1973 but the trend was by no means universal. In many countries unemployment was beginning to rise again towards the end of the year. This, plus the fact that with the exception of 1973 rising import prices cannot by themselves explain the rise in O.E.C.D. inflation rates after 1968, still leaves us with explaining why the trade-off between unemployment and inflation worsened, taking the five-year period 1969-73 as a whole.

Three explanations may be advanced: first, the development of inflationary expectations; second, a greater degree of structural inflation, in particular an increase in the productivity gap between key sectors of the economy; and third, increased trade union militancy, in a general climate of political unrest and dissent.

Inflationary expectations

The expectations explanation is the one favoured by monetarists. The essence of the explanation is that although the connection between demand pressure (i.e. the unemployment rate) and the inflation rate certainly remains, it has become increasingly modified by inflationary expectations. In terms of the Phillips Curve analysis, the curve describing the short run relationship between unemployment and the rate of change of money wages and the price level shifted upwards after 1968, so that at any given level of unemployment (and import price change) the actual rate of inflation became greater.

If people do anticipate a significant and continuing rise in prices, clearly they have an incentive to accelerate their purchases at existing and lower price levels. This would add to pressure of demand at the lower price level, thereby helping to produce the further rise in the price level that had been expected. However, it is not through this chain of causation that inflationary expectations alter the *relationship* between a given level of demand pressure and the consequent behaviour of the price level; for although actual inflation would have been increased by such expectations, one would expect this to be associated with a lower level of unemployment and greater output owing to the higher level of demand.

Hence, if inflationary expectations are to alter the trade-off between unemployment and inflation they must do so through their direct influence on wage and price determination independent of the effect on the pressure of demand. This is not impossible. Trade unions may base their claims for higher wages in the coming period on expectations of higher prices in that period as well as on other factors; similarly, firms in setting their prices for the coming sales period will take into account the expected rise in the wage and price level. In a very real sense, the rate of inflation becomes autonomously determined and independent of the level of demand, and although it can perhaps be reduced by reducing the pressure of demand and raising the unemployment level, the trade-off between inflation and unemployment has worsened. The former relationship between unemployment and the rate of inflation can only be restored by an elimination of the inflationary expectations which initially worsened that trade-off.

Why should inflationary expectations have become so important around 1968 that they caused a significant shift in the relationship between the existing pressure of demand and the current inflation rate? Did they become important in all O.E.C.D. countries simultaneously? If so, why?

Prior to 1968, O.E.C.D. countries had experienced more than 15 years' moderate inflation varying from about two per cent per annum in the U.S. to over four per cent per annum in France and one or two other countries. It is possible to believe that there had been a gradual but cumulative build-up of inflationary expectations which finally, in the later 1960s, became so firm among wage-and price-decision makers that the actual behaviour of money wages and prices began to reflect it; but it seems unlikely, and in any case it is difficult to demonstrate by reference to evidence which is independent of the behaviour of wages and prices itself. However, the behaviour of exchange rates in the late 1960s and early 1970s which we have just been discussing may have produced inflationary expectations in at least one or two countries.

A clear case seems to be provided by the U.K. The devaluation of sterling in November 1967 clearly set up expectations of faster inflation in the U.K. All the means of communication – newspapers, television, etc. – dwelt at length on the inflationary implications of a decline in the sterling exchange rate, often drawing false parallels with earlier devaluation in 1949. Moreover, opposition political leaders in particular were not slow to make statements that could hardly fail to influence the attitudes of wage bargainers and others involved in wage and price determination. On the other hand there was no immediate explosion of wage demands or increases: it wasn't until 1970 that the rate of increase of money wages rose significantly, and this appears to have followed rather than preceded an acceleration in the rate of increase of consumer prices.[9]

Inflationary expectations produced by exchange rate depreciation may have had something to do with the rise in the inflation rate and worsening in the unemployment trade-off relationship in Ireland and Denmark, which devalued with sterling in November 1967, and may also have been generated in France by the franc devaluation of August 1969. But they cannot have been relevant in those countries whose currencies showed substantial appreciations of their exchange rates in 1969 and following years — Germany, Japan, Italy and other countries of the E.E.C. Inflationary expectations cannot be dismissed as a cause of the shift in the unemployment-inflation trade-off relationship after 1968, but it is difficult to establish the independent evidence which would prove it. If they were operating at all, it seems more likely that they only became significant in 1973 when the worldwide commodity boom we have referred to earlier caused a very sharp rise in inflation rates everywhere, in devaluing and revaluing countries alike.

Productivity inflation and structural factors

A second factor which may have caused a worsening in the unemployment-inflation trade-off relation after 1968 is an exacerbation of the structural causes of inflation in industrial countries in the postwar period, namely productivity or wage-transfer inflation, the nature of which was described in Chapter 2. In Chapter 8 we provided some econometric evidence to suggest that comparative inflation rates in O.E.C.D. countries were related in some degree to differences between countries in the size of the productivity gap between important sectors of the economy. Productivity or wage transfer inflation could have got worse in the O.E.C.D. area after 1968 as a result of a widening gap between productivity growth in the manufacturing sector of the economy and productivity growth in other sectors of the economy.

It is certainly clear that in recent years governments of the major industrial countries have become increasingly concerned to promote productivity growth. They have encouraged mergers and takeovers on technological and efficiency grounds, often at the expense of increasing the monopoly power of the firms concerned; and in many countries they have actively played a part in promoting the application of science and advanced technology. Moreover they have also attempted to pursue incomes policies which, although aimed at limiting wage increases overall, have often tied wage increases to concessions on productivity gains. Although such policies may well have encouraged the increase in labour productivity desired, they may also have tended to widen the dispersion of rates of productivity growth in industry generally and have set up pressures for wage increases which could not be met in many sectors of the economy without substantial rises in prices.

The spread of U.S. technology and U.S. wage bargaining practices into Europe, largely as the result of the growing influence of U.S.-owned and controlled multinational corporations, which has been a feature of the 1960s and early 1970s, has also probably accelerated labour productivity growth and increased labour's bargaining power. Here again only some sectors of the economy (notably the production of automobiles), have benefited from the increase in productivity whilst consequential wage demands in industry have been more widespread. Moreover, it seems evident that the spread of the multinational corporation is tending to bring in its train the spread of multinational or international trade unionism which, once fully developed, must substantially increase labour's bargaining power.[10] In brief, the technological and organizational developments which appear to have taken place at a rapid rate throughout the 1960s have significantly increased the size and influence of the 'administered price' or 'non-competitive pricing' sector of the modern economy, so making wage and price determination less influenced by short run demand and market considerations.

While it is possible that the structural factors referred to above may have operated more intensively after 1968 than before, it is evident that their contribution to the acceleration of inflation in industrial countries must be relatively minor when compared to the effects of exchange rate changes and money supply factors discussed earlier.

Political and sociological factors

Finally, political and sociological factors may well have contributed to a significant change in wage determination and to more union agressiveness in recent years. In many countries, for instance, trade unions have succeeded in getting cost of living clauses built into their wage agreements which protect them against price inflation. This development tends to increase the downward stickiness of rates of wage increase, rendering them even less sensitive to the state of demand in the labour market and the level of unemployment.

More important, however, is the spread of left wing, anti-capitalist ideology which, even if not fully embraced by the typical trade union leader, has produced an increase in union aggressiveness. Signs of this occurred in France in 1968 when student-worker demonstrations forced the government to concede massive wage increases to all workers. Both the devaluation of the franc and the sharp rise in the inflation rate in France in 1969 (when unemployment was by no means excessively low) were clearly the direct consequence of the events of 1968. Similar pressure arose in Italy in 1969 and 1970; and in a smaller, but no less significant way, the success of the militant coalminers' strike in the U.K. in 1972 and again in 1974, under a leadership which made no bones about its determination to end the capitalist system, was indicative of a change in the political environment. The striking fall in the share of companies' gross trading profits in U.K. total domestic income, particularly in the years 1968-70 (despite sterling devaluation which could have been expected to raise profits)[11] is evidence of the pressure which organised labour has been able to exert on capitalism, and evidence also of the fact that inflation in the U.K. in 1968-70 had much more of a cost-(largely wage) push character than demand-pull.

The direct cost and price raising pressures produced by inflationary expectations and political and sociological factors were by the end of

1973 operating largely independently of the pressure of demand. At the same time, in the interest of slowing down inflation, governments were increasingly moving towards more restrictive monetary and fiscal policies. In the short run, these bore more on output and employment than on the price level so that continuing high rates of inflation were associated with growing unemployment.

Conclusions

It is evident that the acceleration of inflation after 1968 was due to a complex set of forces. Indeed, the period can probably be divided into two: the years 1968 to mid-1972, during which an acceleration in the U.S. domestic inflation rate and large changes in exchange parities appear to have been the main factors underlying both the rise in domestic inflation rates and the tendency for foreign trade prices to rise after a decade of so of virtual stability; and the years 1972 to 1974, during which the world experienced a very sharp and dangerous jump in its inflation rate as a result of a rise in economic activity in all major industrial countries simultaneously. Largely as a result of this but also because of a few special factors mentioned earlier, primary product prices skyrocketed, injecting massive cost inflationary pressures into industrial economies. Although most industrial economies were also experiencing some inflationary demand pressures at the same time, these do not appear to have been excessive as compared with what many had experienced in certain earlier years of the postwar period. What was unprecedented about the 1972-3 situation was the coincidence of booming activity in all major countries of the O.E.C.D. It was this that was responsible for the boom in commodity prices.

In a fundamental sense the acceleration of inflation after 1968 can perhaps be said to have one basic cause — the massive and fundamental balance of payments disequilibrium which had been allowed to develop between the U.S. on the one hand and the rest of the world (excluding of course the U.K.) on the other during the 1960s. Unwillingness of governments to change their exchange parities during the early part of the 1960s meant that when the changes eventually became unavoidable they had to be large ones, thus compelling large changes in relative prices which had to be compressed in a short period of time in all trading countries. Given a degree of downward inflexibility of prices in industrial countries, the inevitable result was a sharp rise in the world price level. Moreover, the eventual devaluation of the U.S. dollar was so long delayed that it did not take place until massive speculation against the dollar had produced an equally massive rise in world money supply and fall in real interest rates. Economic activity was stimulated throughout the world, producing a shortage of many basic raw materials and foodstuffs whose supply had perhaps been constrained by the preceding long decline in prices of these commodities relative to manufactures. A rise in the world inflation rate was inevitable. Certainly other factors of a domestic nature, such as the autonomous wage pressure exerted by militant labour organizations, were also operating: indeed, these factors are likely to prove to be a potent source of inflationary pressure in the future. But they were not the main factor underlying the rise in the inflation rate after 1968. Unfortunately, the combination of all the factors involved had by 1974 produced a situation in which inflation had derived its own internal dynamic.

At the end of 1973, the world suffered another blow which at least initially tended to compound its inflationary problem: the fourfold rise in the price of oil. In addition to adding to the inflationary fire that was already raging in the Western World in the second half of 1973, the rise in oil prices complicated an already difficult payments imbalance between industrial countries, and, paradoxically, at the same time it injected a massive degree of demand deflationary pressure into these economies.[1 2] Thus by the second half of 1974 governments were faced with the difficult choice of allowing the deflationary impact of the oil producer surpluses to produce falling real income and rising unemployment in their economies, or of offsetting this impact by demand expansionary measures which would tend to exacerbate the existing rate of inflation. To the extent that this dilemma remained unresolved, the world faced the danger in 1975 of having both inflation and economic recession at the same time.

11
Economic Policy and Inflation

Between the mid 1950s and the end of the 1960s the Western industrial world experienced a period of moderate inflation, averaging about three per cent per annum. This was both preceded by and followed by years of very much higher inflation rates, characterized by steeply rising primary product prices throughout the world. The earlier period of high inflation rates was associated with the outbreak of the Korean War and with consequent precautionary stockpiling of strategic materials and foodstuffs by governments in anticipation of a spread of the conflict. The Third World War did not materialize, and within a year or two of the outbreak of the war primary products began to return to their prewar levels; worldwide inflation subsided. The decline in primary product prices continued throughout the rest of the 1950s and early 1960s, contributing significantly to the very moderate character of inflation in industrial countries of that period. The later period of high inflation rates, which at the time of writing of this book were still apparant, appeared to be the direct consequence of a coincident boom in all major industrial countries; and this can be attributed primarily to the massive deterioration in the U.S. balance of payments in 1970-71 and the consequent increase in international liquidity and domestic money supplies. Underlying this development was a worsening in the U.S.'s fiscal position and an acceleration in its own inflation rate. Acute shortages of some basic materials including foodstuffs developed in 1972-3, and bottlenecks in many sectors of the industrial countries themselves appeared. Rising material prices pushed up industrial production costs and forced up the cost of living. As a consequence, money wages began to rise at a much faster rate than in the preceding 15 years, pushing industrial costs and prices up further. The process was then given additional momentum at the end of 1973 by a quadrupling of oil prices imposed by O.P.E.C. countries.

By mid-1974 world commodity prices had begun to level out and in some cases were beginning to fall sharply; but whether world inflation will, after a time lag, subside, as it did after the Korean War boom, remains to be seen. By the second half of 1974 rapidly rising money wages had taken over from rising commodity prices as the main engine of continued high inflation; moreover, unlike the Korean War period, inflationary expectations were clearly influencing price and wage determination on a significant scale. Thus even by the end of 1974 it could not be said with any degree of assurance that inflation in the Western industrial world would return to the more moderate levels of the previous decade. One element in the situation which seems to suggest that it will not is the more aggressive stance adopted by organized labour in virtually all countries of the capitalist world. In bidding for a larger share of the national product, unions appear to be making it more difficult for the capitalist system to generate without inflation the saving required to maintain the rate of capital formation necessary to sustain high rates of growth, which, in turn, are necessary to satisfy expectations of fast-rising living standards held by the mass of the population in industrial countries.

The urgent question facing the Western industrial world in 1974 was whether their economic and democratic political systems could survive a continuance of very high inflation rates which, in the absence of a successful counter-inflation policy, appears to be the prospect for some time to come, if not permanently. If the experience of the semi-industrialized, high-inflation countries of Latin America — Argentina, Brazil, Chile — is anything to go by, countries can live with high inflation over a long period without its becoming hyper; and if we take Brazil, although not Argentina and Chile, as our example, high rates of growth can be achieved at the same time. But it cannot escape notice that in these countries, as well as in others where inflation rates have been consistently high, democratic regimes have failed to survive or take root: military governments have been the order of the day. It is true that in neither Argentina nor Brazil, where military governments took over from more democratic regimes owing to the social conflicts and other economic problems generated by inflation, was the rate of inflation permanently brought down to levels which in the 1950s and 1960s the major O.E.C.D. industrial countries would have thought acceptable, although in Brazil the regime did succeed in reducing the inflation rate from well above 50 per cent per annum in the early 1960s to closer to 15 per cent at the end of the decade. Perhaps the main contribution of the military regimes was to contain the social conflicts generated by stabilization policies, although not necessarily in a desirable or acceptable way.

The problem of high inflation rates
What can be done about the high inflation rates presently afflicting the O.E.C.D. industrial countries? Of course, it would have been better to have avoided the initial conditions which generated the acceleration of inflation in the first place. While it is not within the grasp of economic policy *per se* to prevent outbreaks of war such as the Korean War in 1950, it is in principle within the grasp of policy to avoid massive commodity booms of the 1972-3 type which triggered off the recent bout of high inflation. It seems reasonably clear that if during the 1960s governments had taken earlier action with respect to their exchange rates in the face of obvious and growing fundamental disequilibrium in their balances of payments (particularly between the U.S. and other major industrial countries), then both

the very large and sudden changes in exchange rates and the massive speculation against the U.S. dollar which introduced the 1973 boom could
have been avoided. As we have seen, the former imposed on the international economy the need for very large relative price changes which
could not easily take place except in the context of a rise in the general
price level, and the latter brought about massive increases in international
and domestic money supplies which triggered off worldwide demand
pressures to add to cost pressures already existing in many countries.[1]

Given the worldwide boom in commodity prices in 1972-3 and its
inflationary consequences, what policy action is now open to governments
of countries afflicted by high and apparently rising inflation rates?

The choice lies between, on the one hand, a severely deflationary
monetary and fiscal policy aimed at quickly breaking the inflationary
expectations underlying the strong wage and other income demands which,
following the levelling out of world commodity prices in mid-1974, have
taken over in virtually all countries as the main inflationary pressure
behind the continuing and fast rise in prices; and on the other, a more
moderate policy aimed at a progressive slowing down in the rate of
inflation over a number of years whilst maintaining a moderate rate of
growth of national product and a continuing high level of employment.
Owing to the need to convince price setters and wage bargainers that prices
and wages will not go on rising in the future at as fast a rate as in the
immediate past, the former policy would almost certainly involve creating
temporary and probably substantial excess supply conditions in product
and labour markets. It would therefore involve a substantial cost in terms
of a steep rise in unemployment and a fall in real product and real wages
as well, especially in those countries most afflicted by inflation and
inflationary expectations. It is by no means clear that such a development
would be any more compatible with democratic institutions and processes
than a continuation of inflation at very high rates. An essential element in
the latter policy would be a progressive improvement in the fiscal budget
and a progressive reduction in the rate of increase of money supply; but
the success of the policy in achieving both a progressive reduction in the
rate of inflation and continued growth of real output and real wages
would depend crucially on whether trade unions would accept a wage
policy under which money wage increases would be linked at most to past
increases in the price level rather than to anticipated ones. Without such
agreement, even a moderately restrictive monetary and fiscal policy would
involve serious unemployment. The combination of the latter and continuing high wage and price inflation would sooner or later force governments
to impose a statutory wage and price freeze.

Monetary correction

Since present high inflation rates in the Western World are already creating
social conflict and injustice, any policy aimed at a slowing of inflation over
time rather than at a precipitate decline would probably have to be accom-

panied by various forms of 'monetary correction', The introduction of such measures would indeed become inevitable if reduction in present high rates of inflation proved impossible.

By monetary correction is meant the deflation of nominal money values of transactions by a price index to arrive at the underlying real values; the application of monetary correction measures to transactions involving income and capital would ensure that the transactors deal in real values rather than in misleading monetary ones. The object of introducing such measures would be to prevent or limit the changes in the distribution of income and wealth which tend to accompany inflation when this is not being correctly anticipated, or when some groups have inadequate political or economic power to defend their particular interests. In principle, therefore, the measures would have to be wide-ranging and include the application of price escalation clauses to wage and salary agreements (so that wages and salaries would be automatically adjusted in line with the inflation rate) and to all financial transactions involving borrowing and lending (so that payments of money interest and capital values would be adjusted in line with the inflation rate). Many forms of government expenditure and taxation would also have to be subject to price correction. The practical difficulties would clearly be immense.

In many countries price escalation clauses are already attached to most wage and salary agreements, and as a result of the experience of 1973-4, other countries are rapidly moving in this direction. But few if any countries have as yet adopted measures applying to borrowing and lending. Governments, so far, have not been willing to give a lead by applying monetary correction to taxation of public sector borrowing, partly because of the nominal cost to fiscal budgets but mainly because of the fear that an acceptance of the principle of monetary correction would intensify inflation itself.

Whether or not the universal adoption of monetary correction would exacerbate inflation is a complex question; but in the last resort the answer depends on what the basic cause of inflation is. If excessive creation of money is the cause of prices rising, then linking wages and salaries to prices cannot exacerbate inflation; in this case the rate of increase of money wages depends on the rate of increase of prices, so that if the latter depends only on the rate of increase of the money supply, inflation cannot be affected unless money supply itself is affected by monetary correction. Indeed, monetarists such as Professor Friedman believe that far from exacerbating inflation, the adoption of monetary correction would make it easier to slow it down, since it would reduce the adverse side effects that policies aimed at reducing inflation necessarily have an output and employment.[2] The basic argument here is that if inflation has continued for some time so that, increasingly, inflationary expectations are reflected in interest rates and wage and other long term monetary contracts, a decline in the inflation rate which was unexpected by all the transactors must involve substantial windfall gains and losses. For instance, borrowers who had agreed to pay high nominal rates of interest in expectation of continuing high inflation would suffer badly if the rate of inflation turned out to be much lower than they had anticipated: they will be against stopping inflation. So will employers who have conceded large wage increases on the basis of similar expectations: a fall in the inflation rate would involve them in losses. Moreover, in the latter case unemployment and output would also suffer, since employers would be forced to cut their losses by reducing production. If wages, salaries and interest payments were indexed to the price level, unexpected losses and consequential side effects on employment and output would be avoided as inflation is reduced.

To those who believe that rising costs of production stemming from autonomously generated money wage increases in excess of productivity, or from rising material prices, are a root cause of inflation (which in an effort to avoid unemployment and falling output governments are forced to validate by creating money), indexation of money wages to prices must keep the inflationary fires burning. If rising money wages cause rising prices, and rising prices cause rising money wages, a wage-price spiral is the inevitable consequence, the speed and life of which depends on the nature of the interactions and the underlying growth rate of labour productivity. According to this view of the causes of inflation, it could be slowed down more rapidly if percentage increases in money wages agreed on for the coming period were smaller than the percentage increase in the price level over the preceding period.

In the context of the very high inflation rates afflicting the international economy in 1974, monetarists and non-monetarists are not far apart in their attitude to monetary correction and wage and salary indexation. Given the elastic inflationary expectations that have been generated, perhaps the best that can be hoped by non-monetarists is for a wages policy under which money wage bargains do not exceed the current rate of inflation: normal productivity growth can then be relied upon gradually to reduce the rate of inflation. From the monetarist's point of view, any policy which successfully lowered the anticipated inflation rate or made it irrelevent in wage and income bargaining, would reduce the adverse employment side effects of a progressive reduction in the rate of growth of the money supply.

However, there are circumstances in which the indexation of money wages and other income to prices would clearly be inappropriate or indeed ineffective. If, for example, inflation is accompanied (perhaps caused) by an autonomously caused absolute fall in the aggregate real income of an economy, an attempt to employ indexation to prevent a fall in real income of every group or person in that country must clearly fail, as well as exacerbate the inflation. A number of countries were in this position in 1973-4 — the U.K. and Japan were conspicuous examples. Being substantial importers of basic materials and foodstuffs, these countries were badly affected by the commodity boom of 1973. The U.K.'s commodity terms of trade probably worsened by 16 per cent in the course of less than 12 months. In effect, this meant that the U.K.'s real income per capita declined four per cent in the same period. For a time the effect on living standards could be offset by borrowing abroad, i.e. allowing the current account of the balance of payments to deteriorate by a corresponding amount, but unless the terms of trade showed subsequent improvement, the effect on domestic real consumption and investment could not be avoided. An attempt to avoid such a cut in living standards by tying wages to prices can only lead to more inflation.

In general, wage and income indexation clearly does not deal with the problem if inflation is at root the result of a basic political struggle for shares of the national cake. If, as there is every reason to believe, inflation is the outcome of labour's attempt to increase the share of wages and salaries in national income at the expense of profits and rentier income, indexation of wages to prices is clearly besides the point: it does not meet the objectives of the major participant in the struggle. The point is conceded by Professor Friedman in the following terms:

'An objection of a very different kind (to escalator clauses) is that inflation serves the critical social purpose of resolving incompatible demands by different groups. In this view, the participants in the economy, to put it crudely, have "non-negotiable demands" for more than the entire output. These demands are reconciled because inflation fools people into believing that their demands have been met when in fact they have not been. Escalator clauses, it is argued, would bring the inconsistent demands into the open. Workers who would accept a lower real wage produced by unanticipated inflation will not be willing to accept the same real wages in explicit negotiations. If this view is correct on a wide enough scale to be important, I see no other ultimate outcome than either runaway inflation or an authoritarian society ruled by force. Perhaps it is only wishful thinking that makes me reluctant to accept this vision of our fate.'[3]

If 'wishful thinking' is rejected, so must be the monetarist view that at root inflation is solely caused by excessive creation of money. If, on the contrary, "inflation serves the critical social purpose of resolving incompatible demands by different groups", the remedy can hardly be a technical one, namely controlling the supply of money. Political problems require political solutions, not technical ones.

Social benefits and costs of inflation

Suppose that governments generally are successful in reducing inflation rates from the high levels of 1974 to the more moderate rates that ruled throughout the second half of the 1950s and most of the 1960s. Would it be possible to go further and eliminate price inflation altogether? Would it be desirable to do so and aim at virtual price stability? It will be convenient to answer the second question first.

In posing the question we are obviously not referring to the kind of self-destroying hyper-inflation which has inflicted some countries in the immediate aftermath of wars, for example Germany and Hungary after both world wars. But high, although not hyper, inflation rates have occurred in a number of countries, particularly in Latin America; and in one or two cases, at least, these inflations have clearly been compatible with fast economic growth and fast rising living standards. Hence the answer to the question — does inflation matter and should anything be done about it — is by no means self-evident. It is by no means clear that going all out for a policy to stop moderate inflation would necessarily be in the best interests of the mass of the population. It is obvious that in most inflations, as actually experienced, some people gain and some people lose: but it is by no means obvious that the redistributions of income and wealth which do take place can, on normal value grounds, be regarded as undesirable.

Balance of payments argument

One argument which is quite often advanced as a reason for stopping inflation can be rejected straight away. This is the balance of payments argument, which says that as a result of rising domestic prices exports will be discouraged, imports encouraged and the balance of payments will therefore fall into disequilibrium. It is obvious, however, that in a world in which inflation is occurring generally that there is no reason why the balance of payments of any individual country should be worsened by its own domestic rate of inflation. In fact it is quite possible that a country may suffer from inflation and yet its balance of payments improve owing to higher inflation rates in the rest of the world. But even if this is not the case, even if it is the case that only one country is suffering from inflation, it does not follow that its balance of payments will necessarily fall into disequilibrium and become unviable. Provided the exchange rate is allowed to adjust to the domestic rate of inflation, thereby stabilizing the real terms of trade, then exports need not become uncompetitive, nor need home production against imports. Of course, as a consequence of the rate of exchange being adjusted downwards to offset the rise in the domestic price level, the rate of inflation itself may be exacerbated since import prices will be pushed up. Moreover, expectations of faster inflation may develop which become self-fulfilling. But whether faster inflation is a good or bad thing must be judged in relation to other considerations and not the balance of payments alone since, as we have just said, no matter how high the rate of inflation becomes, the exchange rate can always adjust to offset its impact on the balance of payments.

We must focus attention on two interconnected aspects: first, the effect of inflation on the output of the economy and its real rate of growth over time, and second, on the social and wealth distribution effects internally. As to the first aspect, we need to ask whether inflation provides an encouragement to real capital formation and investment, or, on the other hand, whether it leads to a misallocation of what real capital formation is in fact carried out. We need also to ask what will be the effect on the economic efficiency with which the economy operates. As to the second aspect, we are concerned with the income distribution effects of inflation and also the changing relationship between debtors and creditors.

It is not easy on *a priori* grounds alone to say what the nature of these effects will be; nor does the available evidence throw much light on them. It is evident that countries have been able to enjoy rapid growth rates whether they have had negligible or moderate inflation or, on the contrary, have experienced very fast inflation rates. Moreover, it is possible that income distribution and social effects in general can be offset by an appropriate combination of domestic economic and social policies. However, it seems likely that the social costs and benefits of inflation will depend on whether inflation is in some general sense unexpected or whether it has become fully anticipated so that society as a whole — consumers and producers, debtors and creditors — has become fully adjusted to it. Also, given the evidence that, until recently at any rate, inflation rates have been negatively associated with unemployment rates, we need to take into account the efficiency and distributional consequences of having less unemployment even though more inflation.

Unexpected inflation
Although the natural rate of unemployment hypothesis discussed in Chapter 3 is not necessarily acceptable, it provides a convenient starting point to examine the general efficiency and social effects of inflation. According to this hypothesis, unemployment below the natural rate is only compatible with inflation which is unexpected. Once inflation has become fully anticipated, the level of unemployment will return to its natural level. What can be said about a situation in which unemployment is lower and unexpected inflation is higher as compared with a situation in which the former is higher and the actual inflation is lower?

Considering first the effects on efficiency and output of unemployment being below its natural level, there are clearly a number of pressures pulling in opposite directions. In a situation in which unemployment is being maintained at a lower than natural level, such that vacancies and job opportunities far exceed unemployed workers available to fill them, it might be expected that firms would have difficulty in recruiting and keeping labour, particularly of the skilled sort. Thus it could be argued that production difficulties will arise, quality will fall, firms will fail to make delivery dates, bottlenecks will appear in other industries, people will waste time looking for alternative sources of supply, and, in general

economic efficiency will suffer. Moreover, in the labour market in particular, since search unemployment will be low and workers will not be
encouraged or forced to seek those jobs in which their marginal productivity is highest, the allocation of labour becomes less efficient and output
per worker becomes consequently lower than it would be at higher levels of
unemployment.

Against this line of argument it could be said that when demand for
labour is very high a larger labour supply is then induced. More job
opportunities encourage entrance to the labour market — people reduce
their leisure time which, in the past, has often been forced on them —
and labour moves from producing for home consumption (home decor-
ating, gardening, handicrafts, etc.) to producing for the market, as a
consequence of which society's overall economic demands are met more
efficiently. Firms, too, are enabled to use their capital equipment more
intensively, which may offset any disadvantage arising from a shortage
of labour of particular skills.

Taking an overall view, there must be some presumption that larger
employment does result in larger output; even if the marginal product
of labour falls quite rapidly as employment rises, it is hardly likely that
it would become negative. Also, since the unemployed are involved in
psychic costs derived from being unemployed, they also gain from a
widening of employment opportunities.

Unexpected inflation can, if excess demand is the basic cause of
inflation, shift the distribution of income towards profits with beneficial
effects on investment and saving and, therefore, on the growth of output
in the longer run. This consequence is not so likely if the inflation is the
consequence of cost-push rather than demand-pull, since in this case,
profits are in danger of being squeezed. Both the source of saving and
the inducement to invest then suffer.

Distributional effects are not easy to analyse or assess in unexpected
inflation. If inflation is associated with a lower level of employment than
would occur if there were no inflation, there is some presumption that
lower paid unskilled workers gain at the expense of their more highly paid
and skilled fellows. Unemployment tends to be concentrated in the
unskilled group, and a recovery in employment is therefore likely to
benefit the unskilled, not only because of the fact that more jobs are
available but also because the wages of the unskilled are likely to rise
relatively to those of the skilled. Older people in the work force, normally
less mobile than younger people, are more likely to lose jobs when
employment falls, and are therefore correspondingly likely to gain from
high employment; on the other hand, they may lose more than do younger
workers from adverse wealth distribution effects produced by inflation
itself.

In an unexpected inflation, creditors tend to lose out to debtors
since the real rate of interest received by the former and paid by the

latter tends to be below its equilibrium level. The mortgage housing market is an important illustration of this. Clearly, the owners of net monetary assets (monetary assets less monetary liabilities) lose in unexpected inflation, while owners of real capital and equity claims on real capital goods gain. But do the poorest of our society necessarily lose in unexpected inflation? The poor certainly tend to hold most of their assets in monetary form, but they also tend to have offsetting monetary liabilities in the form of, for example, outstanding hire purchase debt. Richer income groups tend to be the owners of real capital, i.e. productive capital and property, but they also hold substantial monetary assets. The ratio of net monetary wealth to total wealth is usually higher for upper income groups than it is for the lower, so that there is some presumption that taking the employment situation into account as well as inflation, the poor lose less, even if they do not positively gain, from unexpected inflation than do the middle class even though the latter are usually substantial property owners. A proximate gainer in the situation is usually the government, since in most countries it is a substantial net debtor with respect to the private sector of the economy: the ultimate gainer however depends on government fiscal and monetary policy.

The poor may gain from unexpected inflation due to the response of government in making and receiving transfers from the private sector. There is usually greater pressure on governments to keep social benefits etc. in line with the price level so as to maintain their real value than there is on it to allow for inflation in fixing tax rates. With a progressive tax system, inflation tends to cause tax payments to rise in greater proportion than money incomes and the price level. Tax rates would have to be adjusted downwards in inflation to prevent the real take of the government from rising in inflation. But if tax rates are not lowered or not lowered sufficiently, the taxpayer is being subjected to an inflation tax which is more likely to fall on higher than lower income groups.

In sum, there is some presumption that the poorer income groups of modern industrial societies are likely to benefit from moderate unexpected inflation, provided this is associated with a high level of demand for labour in relationship to the available labour force.

Anticipated inflation

In the case of inflation which has become fully and universally anticipated, wealth distribution effects are, in principle at any rate, virtually ruled out by the assumption: nominal interest rates become adjusted to the anticipated rise in the price level so that neither debtors nor creditors gain at the expense of each other. Moreover, if the natural rate of unemployment hypothesis is accepted, unemployment will be at its natural level. Probably in a fully anticipated inflation the rich, having access to or being able to pay for information, are more able to protect themselves from inflation by investing more in those assets on which the nominal rate of interest has been adjusted to the inflation rate. The poor, on the other hand, hold monetary assets, a substantial part of which may be in the form of fiat money on which interest cannot easily be paid. There is, of course, still the inflation tax on the higher income groups which governments may be able to employ to protect the lower income groups, depending on the balance of political forces ruling.

Although wealth distribution effects within the private sector are less likely to appear in the case of anticipated inflation, other effects may still be apparent, bearing on the efficiency of operations of the economy and its rate of growth. These relate to the function of money as the medium of exchange and as a store of value. In a modern monetary economy money, that is, the acceptable medium of exchange, derives its utility from the fact that its use in exchange reduces frictional costs. Transactors can seldom synchronize the timing of their receipts and payments in a manner that would make it unnecessary for them to hold an asset generally accepted as the medium of exchange. Of course, they can attempt to hold this purchasing power in the interval before it is required in the form of some interest bearing asset which, when the time for payment arrives, can be converted into money itself; but brokerage costs are usually involved in shifting between money and the asset on which interest is paid. Interest payable on the asset will offset these costs so that the higher the interest paid, the more incentive there is to hold the asset when money itself is not immediately required. Brokerage costs tend to have a threshold character with some minimum expense involved which is independent of the smallness or largeness of the size of the transaction itself. This is a disincentive to small shifts between the asset and money for any given rate of interest, and it generally tends to lead to some money always being held.

The marginal social cost of producing money is, however, very low, if not negligible. Hence, it would seem that money should be created in amounts that would reduce the marginal social benefits of extra amounts of it being created to virtually zero; in other words, the interest cost on alternative assets should be reduced to levels which fail to cover the threshold brokerage costs of holding an interest-bearing asset instead.

It is clear that inflation, when anticipated, reduces the marginal social benefit of holding money owing to the implicit tax which is placed on monetary holdings. It becomes difficult to persuade people to hold money in a quantity at which its marginal social benefit would be zero, and transactors would prefer to bear the frictional and brokerage costs involved in holding purchasing power in a non-monetary form until required. From this point of view, the ideal quantity of money is best achieved in an economy in which the anticipated rate of inflation is very low, perhaps even negative. Thus exchange efficiency appears to require stable, if not falling prices. Gains on the side of exchange efficiency, however, may be bought at the expense of a rise in the real rate of interest if measures to accommodate the increase in the demand for money involves a windfall rise in the real wealth of the private sector and a consequent fall in the propensity to save.[4] Moreover, although inflation does impose a capital loss on the holders of money, the gain in the case of fiat money accrues to government which can use it to finance capital formation or other social objectives. Thus there is a case for not allowing negative inflation and a case for permitting some moderate rate of positive inflation. But the rate of inflation must not be pushed too high, since it would cause a flight from money and a growing inefficiency of the market exchange system. Banks' would respond by paying interest on inside money, namely bank deposits, but it would be difficult for the government to do so on fiat money. The composition of the society's stock of money would be shifted from outside to inside money, which would involve higher marginal social costs of production as well as probably lower marginal social benefits.

The case for moderate rather than high inflation is strengthened by the need to maintain money as a useful unit of account, and to keep down the costs of decision-making. High inflation makes accounting difficult and also forces entrepreneurs to give excessive attention to the financial side of their businesses and insufficient attention to the production side. Minimizing real costs of production becomes less important than financial programming, and the economy can become progressively less efficient as a consequence.

If, as appears to have become true in recent years, high inflation is associated with a higher level of unemployment rather than a lower one so that the costs of inflation are not offset by the gains of higher output and employment, it is clear that there is no presumption that the poorer and weaker sectors of the society will be advantaged by inflation. Gains from higher employment are not available to offset possible losses from inflation. Highly paid workers remaining in employment may gain substantially, as will, unless inflation becomes fully anticipated, property and real capital owners. But saving and investment may be discouraged, and as a consequence the performance of the economy may suffer. Thus, although it should not be the object of the policy to prevent all inflation, it should be the object at any rate to prevent inflation from exceeding moderate levels. What moderate means in this context is difficult to say *a priori*; it depends very much on the circumstances; but in most modern industrial economies a three per cent inflation rate would appear to be a not unreasonable objective. It is perhaps not surprising that Western governments did not give any real priority to containing inflation in the 1950s and 1960s when inflation rates averaged just over three per cent. But suppose that three per cent inflation was unacceptable to them, as some economists argue that it should be? Can complete price stability be achieved?

Policies against moderate inflation

Price control

Since inflation is a situation in which prices are showing a continuous tendency to rise, it might be thought that the obvious way to stop it would be for the government to impose price control. A government decree that firms should not raise prices would put an effective end to inflation. A similar decree concerning wages would not seem to be necessary: first, because even if prices are prevented from rising, rising labour productivity would permit some rise in money wages without producing difficulties for firms, and second, because firms would not be in a position to raise wages at a faster rate than productivity is rising since their profits and, therefore, their incentive to go on producing, would suffer. Pressure from the side of labour to obtain wage increases in excess of the increase in labour productivity would be met by resistance from firms which in the last resort would have to cease production.

If the imposition of a price ceiling would be a simple method of stopping inflation why do not governments in general resort to it? Of course, many governments have imposed some form of price control or regulation on a temporary basis, but none of the free market economies has resorted to it as a permanent or regular method of containing inflation, except in wartime. There are good reasons for this.[5]

In a situation of general excess demand price control would simply cope with the symptom and not the cause. A rise in the price level is the way in which demand and supply is encouraged. If prices are prevented from rising by controls but no other methods are used to reduce demand or increase supply, supply would remain inadequate to meet the demand. The inflationary pressure would be repressed rather than eliminated. By definition, demand could not be satisfied in the markets subject to price controls, and sellers would be forced to sell to first-comers or ration their customers on an informal basis. Queues and waiting lists would appear. Worse still, black markets would be encouraged in which goods would be sold at higher than controlled prices. Inflation would not be prevented, even though official prices did not rise. The scarcity profits would be taken by the unscrupulous rather than by the legitimate producer, and the *de facto*, if not *de jure*, rise in prices would fail to induce the increase in production which is the function of a rise in price. The distribution of the available supply of goods among persons would not necessarily be more equitable than would be the case if prices were allowed to rise to equate supply and demand. Those who had time to queue or were on intimate terms with suppliers would be better off than those without such advantages. The rich would be in a position to pay others to queue for them or to bribe sellers, and in any case would do better in black markets.

The application of price control would be even more difficult in an open economy which imports a substantial proportion of the goods it consumes at home. If the foreign price level rose relative to the controlled home price level, foreign suppliers would not find it profitable to sell in the price controlled economy so that, far from rising, supply would decline. Governments may try to meet the difficulty by subsidising the home consumer – i.e. pay a subsidy to importers to allow them to pay the world price but sell to domestic consumers at a controlled lower price; but the subsidies would have to be financed. If financed from higher taxation, people would benefit from the controlled prices as consumers but they would lose as taxpayers; if financed from an increase in the money supply, aggregate demand would be further increased, leading to greater pressures on the price level of the kind indicated earlier.

It follows from the foregoing that in a situation of general excess demand, extensive price control cannot be relied upon to contain inflation; for even though official prices may be prevented from rising, the actual (black market) prices of many goods will rise, and many, if not most, of the evils associated with inflation will still be experienced. There would seem to be more rationale for imposing price control, or regulation in a situation in which rising costs rather than excessive demand is the cause of inflation.

Prevention of excess demand

If the inflationary situation is characterized by a general excess of demand over supply, the elimination of this is obviously a necessary condition for stopping inflation. Governments of mature developed economies have a range of financial measures available to them to bear on aggregate monetary demand. As indicated in an earlier chapter, government is a major spender in any developed economies, and changes in government expenditure have a major impact on aggregate demand, both directly and indirectly through multiplier effects. In addition, governments can influence private sector spending through changes in taxation and through changes in money supply and interest rates.

Although in principle governments are in a position to regulate aggregate demand so as to keep it in line with supply, thereby preventing demand pressures on the price level, in practice control over demand, whether exercised directly through the budget or indirectly through money supply, is by no means as precise as theory would suggest. Moreover, even if it were, there would still be the problem in a dynamic growing economy of estimating the growth of supply potential with which aggregate demand must be kept in line. Keeping demand and supply in balance is at best no more than a rather rough and ready operation; so that at times aggregate demand can be expected to exceed the capacity of the economy to produce while at other times it will fall short of it. Which side of the line aggregate demand can most often be expected to lie depends very much on the political complexion of the government and on its assessment of the attitude of the electorate. In the early part of the post Second World War period, many governments placed the maintenance of a high and stable level of employment very high on their list of economic objectives. Hence they preferred to err on the side of permitting excessive demand rather than deficient. This preference undoubtedly contributed to inflation, although as we have said, throughout most of the 1950's and early 1960's its rate was rather moderate and caused little or no political difficulty. In the latter part of the 1960's, inflation has obviously become a more serious problem and its containment has been pushed higher in the list of economic priorities. As a consequence, governments have generally aimed at keeping aggregate demand somewhat lower in relation to potential capacity to produce than was the case earlier.[6]

There is little evidence to suggest that willingness to permit higher unemployment rates could eliminate inflation. Econometric evidence presented in Chapter 7 certainly suggests that a 'trade-off' between unemployment and inflation existed in O.E.C.D. countries during 1954-68; but it is not possible to infer from this evidence what the level of unemployment would have had to have been to obtain complete price stability. As unemployment rises the sensitivity of the rate of inflation to changes in unemployment falls, and it would appear that there is a broad band of unemployment over which price inflation is broadly unaffected. The policy aim of combining 'full' employment (when this is defined with reference to objective labour market conditions and not tautologically with reference to price stability itself) with absolute price stability is therefore not easily, if at all, achieved by simply controlling the level of demand.

Monetarist solution

The monetarist solution, as propounded by Professor Friedman and others, is to allow the money supply to grow at a constant rate, over time, the desired rate being a function of the potential rate of growth of output, as determined by the availability of factors of production and the state of technology, and the real income elasticity of demand for money balances. Leaving aside the question whether the monetary authorities do have the ability to determine within narrow limits the growth of the money supply, and ignoring the problem of measuring and indeed forecasting the real income elasticity of demand for money, it still seems unlikely that the monetarist solution could produce long run price stability.

Monetarists do not deny that the velocity of circulation of money can vary in the short run, i.e. that the rate of spending can vary relatively to any given money stock; and although they affirm that in the long run only prices and not output are determined by the money stock, they do not deny that output and employment can be affected by the latter in the short run. Thus it is possible, even with a stable rate of increase of the money supply, for the rate of monetary spending to depart from its longer run equilibrium relationship with the stock of money. Owing, for example, to a fall in the community's propensity to save or a burst of investment expenditure, the rate of monetary spending could be temporarily lifted with respect to the monetary stock, and excess demand for goods and labour could appear. Additional employment and output could be stimulated, and, as a consequence money wages and prices bid up above the long run equilibrium level. The monetarist's position is that if the rate of increase of the nominal money stock remains unchanged, a fall in the rate of increase of the *real* money supply (i.e. nominal money supply increase deflated by the price level) will pull the growth of output down to its equilibrium level and eventually pull the price level down as well. Such an outcome however depends on prices being as flexible in the downward direction as in the upward direction, and on money wages being principally determined by demand for labour rather than by the monopoly power of trade unions. Monetarist solutions apply to a world in which money wages and prices are market rather than administratively determined, and equally flexible in both directions. It may be doubted whether the real world corresponds or can be made to correspond to this image. Indeed, there are good reasons for believing that the search for complete price level stability (i.e. no inflation) is a chimera in modern industrial economies.

Given the inevitability of relative price changes in a dynamic economy, stability of the general price level would imply that some prices at least would have to fall; moreover, in many sectors of the economy labour would have to be willing to accept money wage increases that were smaller than the corresponding increase in their productivity; trade unions would have to accept the fact that increases in the standard of living of their members would depend more on the pricing decision of employers than on their own success in wage bargaining. The oligopolistic character of much of modern industry and the interests and power of trade unions do not suggest that downward flexibility of manufactured good prices can be relied on to offset the rise in labour costs and price levels in more labour intensive sectors of the economy. Empirical evidence presented in Chapter 8 suggested that differences in country inflation rates could be at least partly explained by the size of the productivity gap between the competitive sectors of their economies (in the main, manufacturing industry) and the sheltered sectors (in the main, construction and services), and it therefore gives indirect support to the view expressed in Chapter 2 that moderate inflation in industrial countries in the period 1954-68 was largely the consequence of significant differences between productivity growths in different sectors of the economy, in other words, that it was of the 'productivity-gap' or 'wage-transfer' kind.

Of course it could be argued that the downward inflexibility of industrial prices and wages is itself the direct consequence of government full employment policies. During the nineteenth century, cyclical downswings in economic activity put considerable pressure on price and wage levels in the afflicted economy, making it possible for *relative* price changes to be brought about in the context of a generally stable or even falling price level. But in the post Second War period, government commitment to full employment has provided entrepreneurs with the assurance that declines in economic activity significant enough to force them into a radical re-appraisal of their pricing policies will be prevented; and it has also strengthened the power of trade unions and increased the power of labour generally by significantly reducing the fear, prevalent in earlier times, that too much pressure to get money wages raised would create unemployment. In this respect, trade unions seem to be on particularly strong ground in bargaining with public sector industries since, in contrast to private sector industry, the fear, even threat, of bankruptcy is largely absent.

As indicated earlier (in Chapter 6) there is controversy as to the actual contribution of government policy to the maintenance of a high level of employment in industrial countries since 1945; but it cannot be denied that the general level of economic activity in capitalist countries has been considerably more stable during the last 25 years than it was during the previous 100. If this was the consequence of basic changes in the technological and economic characteristics of capitalist economies and not due to government, then clearly the inflationary consequences cannot be blamed on the latter. Leaving this possibility aside, and assuming that government full employment policies were an important element, our previous discussions of the social costs and benefits of inflation do not suggest that governments were wrong. The benefits of stable economic activity and a high level of employment most certainly outweighed any net costs of moderate inflation.

Long term measures for dealing with productivity inflation
Given success in keeping the growth of aggregate demand approximately in line with the growth of potential supply, governments could aim at reducing or eliminating 'productivity-gap' inflation by long term measures. These measures would be designed to narrow or close significant productivity gaps and to increase downward flexibility of prices. They would have have to be complemented by a marked change in the attitudes of trade unions in such a way that wage bargaining in the high productivity growth industries did not aim at capturing the full increase in labour productivity in the form of increased money wages. A form of incomes policy may well have to be entertained, although this would not be a simple one.

Since 'productivity gap' inflation is the result of money wages growing at a faster rate than labour productivity in some sectors of the industry, it might be said to contain the seeds of its own long term correction: rising labour costs in these sectors should lead to the substitution of capital for labour and a higher rate of productivity growth. The substantial structural changes which have taken place in some service industries in recent years are indicative that this process is happening. The growth of supermarkets and progressive disappearance of many small shops in the richer industrial countries are the result of labour-saving innovations in the retail distribution industry. But if governments are maintaining a relatively tight monetary policy with the aim of containing the rate of this inflation, profits may be squeezed in these industries, holding back such innovations. Innovation in labour intensive public service industries, such as postal services and telephones, is indeed often held back by constrained government expenditure policies, themselves aimed at containing inflation. Positive policies aimed at raising the rate of investment and introducing more modern technology in backward industries, including public services may be a more relevant, if long term, policy for reducing inflation. Such policies may involve the closing down of smaller units of production or their consolidation into larger units.

Measures to obtain greater downward price flexibility in industry are also obviously long term. They must include measures, such as anti-monopoly legislation, to increase the degree of competition in broad sectors of industry. Such measures could in some cases conflict with the need to consolidate smaller units of production into larger ones so as to facilitate the introduction of more modern technology. Tax measures could also be introduced to encourage price competition and discourage non-price competition such as advertising. Until trade unions can be confident that the benefits of rising productivity will be transferred to consumers in the form of falling prices, they are hardly likely to acquiesce in a wage policy under which workers in the high productivity growth industries forego the full benefit of rising productivity in the form of rising money incomes.

Incomes Policy

Incomes policies attempt either to remove wage and salary determination from the market place altogether or to provide guidelines for the collective bargaining over incomes that normally takes place in it. The policy can be statutory, i.e. supported by the force of law, or it can be voluntary; in practice there is not a great deal of difference since, in a democracy at any rate, the statutory form must be acceptable to the majority of income earners if the law is to be successfully enforced. Incomes policy can not be expected to be successful, except very temporarily, when excessive demand for goods and labour are pulling up wages and prices: the failure of a number of attempts to introduce incomes policies in Western countries in postwar years is largely due to its inappropriate use in such circumstances: but it has its rationale when prices and wages are being forced up by factors working on the side of supply in circumstances when excessive demand is not apparent.

Ostensibly, incomes policy aims at preventing the sum total of money incomes rising at a faster rate than total real output; in practice the policy is directly applicable to wages and salaries only, it being left to monetary and fiscal policy to influence profits, and to taxation to keep disposable money income in line with the available supply of consumption goods. The policy may be implemented either by the authorities setting a total amount of money income which is fixed in the light of the anticipated available consumer goods, to be divided up among the mass of the participants in the labour market through the mechanism of collective bargaining, or by laying down that wage and salary increases should be linked partly or wholly to real productivity increases. In principle, incomes policies do not aim at determining wage and salary relativities which should respond to changes in the demand and supply pattern for particular types of labour and skill; but when in use, it is difficult for an incomes policy not to have undesigned effects on wage and salary differentials, effects which in the past have contributed to the eventual breakdown of the policy.

Fundamentally, the case for an incomes policy arises when inflation stems from incompatible demands for income shares which cannot be reconciled by monetary and fiscal policy without reducing the bargaining power of at least some participants in the struggle by creating unemployment. There is then an undesirable loss of real income to the community as a whole, so that every participant can be worse off than he need be. The problem of reconciling incompatible demands on the nation's total real product becomes particularly acute if the latter is reduced owing to factors outside its own control. A country which suffers a substantial deterioration in its commodity terms of trade, as happened to the U.K., Japan and some other countries in 1973-4, finds its real income declining relatively to existing monetary demand. Although these countries can resort to temporary foreign borrowing or utilize foreign exchange reserves to maintain domestic consumption for a time, the burden of the real income loss must eventually be borne by the population at large in the form of falling real wages and consumption. If the allocation of the burden among income earners is left to the market place, participants try to avoid their share either by refusing to accept cuts in money income or by bidding up their money incomes in line with prices. Inflation is the inevitable result.

Economists who believe that at root inflation is simply a monetary phenomenon naturally deny both the need for and the effectiveness of incomes policy; but they also have to deny that inflation can result from competition for income shares or from declining real income due to adverse terms of trade when this, as it usually does in industrial countries, takes the form of a steep rise in a country's import prices. A denial that steeply rising import prices and an adverse movement in the terms of trade need affect the domestic price level necessarily involves 'monetarists' in arguing that restriction in money supply growth will cause domestic costs and prices, including money wages, to fall, thus offsetting the rise in import prices. The behaviour of prices and money wages in no major industrial country of the Western capitalist in the postwar period supports the view that money wages and the prices of industrial goods generally are sufficiently flexible in the downward direction. Restriction of the money supply in the face of sharply rising import prices would be likely to force rising unemployment rather than falling money wages. The real burden of the adverse shift in the terms of trade would then of course be borne in large part by the unemployed. The case for incomes policy in such circumstances is to enable this burden to be shared more equitably, and with both less inflation and less unemployment.

In practice, the problem of devising and implementing an incomes policy is formidable, as is witnessed by the failure of many attempts to do so. Nonetheless, continuing attempts must be made to introduce one[7] since it is becoming increasingly clear both that inflation is by far the most serious economic and social problem facing the democratic countries of the Western world, and that the form it now takes is not amenable to orthodox monetary and fiscal policy. Inflation is more a political problem than an economic one, and it requires political solutions.

Political factors underlying inflation

Unfortunately there are signs that inflation is more than a symptom of incompatible demands for the nation's product which could in principle at any rate be handled in a democratic way through an agreed incomes policy. It cannot be overlooked that strong political forces are also at work, which will become increasingly important in the future. The capitalist system itself is under attack from within as well as from outside itself, and it will be surpirsing if it does not undergo substantial modification in Western Europe, even if it is not completely replaced, during the next two or three decades. The overt form which the attack is taking is clearly an attack on profits. Labour movements everywhere are seeking a larger share of the national income and are conducting wage bargaining accordingly: profits are being squeezed.[8] The capitalist is seeking to maintain the share of profits which indeed is necessary in a capitalist economy if investment is to be financed: inflation results. The attempt of government to restrain inflation by means of holding back demand contributes more to the squeezing of profits than it does to restraining of wage demands, which in many cases are motivated by political considerations – that is, by the explicit desire to replace the capitalist system.

Since Keynes, the capitalist system is less likely to succumb to a failure to generate sufficient demand to keep capital employed, as orthodox Marxist theory would have it, than to a failure to generate sufficient saving to finance the investment necessary for a rate of economic growth that will satisfy the real consumption expectations of the mass of the people. Inflation is the result, not the cause; but it no longer, as it once did, forces saving to match investment.

If the pressures of wage demands result in profits being insufficient to finance the required rate of capital formation, real saving clearly has to be generated through other channels, most probably in the public or government sector of the economy. Political pressure from the left is forcing all governments to adopt more active interventionist roles, including the takeover of many forms of industrial activity. But the squeezing of profits *per se* cannot permit a significant increase in real wages or real consumption of the mass of the people. Even if all economic activity were completely state controlled and financed, the avoidance of inflation would still require restraint on *money* wages. In a socialist state an incomes policy would be inevitable, although perhaps more acceptable in the context of a possibly more egalitarian society. But the incomes policy that would evolve would not be compatible with free trade unions and free collective bargaining as Western democracies recognize them, nor perhaps with political democracy itself.

Notes

Chapter 1: *Introduction*

1. See Table 5.2, Chapter 5, for O.E.C.D. G.D.P. growth rates in the postwar period.
2. See M. Bronfenbrenner (ed.), *Is the Business Cycle Obsolete?*. Wiley 1969.
3. Some countries experienced more serious recession in 1974/5 following the collapse of the industrial boom in 1973 and steep rise in the price of oil at the end of that year. See Chapter 10.
4. See E. Lundberg, *Instability and Economic Growth*, Yale U.P., 1968.
5. Organization for Economic Co-operation and Development.
6. Other explanations are also available. See for instance, Phelps-Brown and Ozga, Economic Growth and the Price Level', *Econ, Journal*, March 1955, and G. Maynard, *Economic Development and the Price Level*, MacMillan, 1962. A. Schwartz: "Secular Price Change in Historical Perspective" Journal of Money, Credit and Banking, February 1973.
7. Some economists take the view that the quantity of money (i.e. the acceptable medium of exchange) is not something that can be exogenously controlled: rather it is an endogenously determined quantity that adjusts to expenditure decisions. See N. Kaldor, 'The New Monetarism' *'Lloyds Bank Review*, July 1970.
8. For a brief outline of the analytical basis of the monetarist position see, for example, H.G. Johnson, 'A Survey of Theories of Inflation" in *Essays in Monetary Economics*, Unwin University Books 1967 or *Inflation and the Monetarist Controversy*, North-Holland Publishing Company 1972.

Chapter 2: *The Nature and Causes of Inflation in Industrial Countries*

1. The Literature on inflation is voluminous and no attempt will be made in this or later chapters to provide footnote references to all sources, but it is obvious that we have drawn on the literature or at any rate, on as much as we have been able to read! Readers who wish to obtain familiarity with what has been written on the subject could refer to R.J. Ball and P. Doyle (eds), *Inflation*, Penguin.
2. The attitude of trade unions reinforces this. See later discussion.
3. There is evidence that in the late 1960s and early 1970s U.K. firms were forced to concede wage increases which, owing to the market

situation, they were unable to recoup fully in higher prices, as a result of which profits were squeezed.

4. See R.J. Ball, *Inflation and the Theory of Money*, Allen & Unwin, 1964.

5. See C.L. Schultz, 'Recent Inflation in the United States' in *Employment, Growth & Price Levels* (Hearings before the Joint Economic Committee, 86 Congress, 1st Session, May 25-28 1959), pp. 4-10.

6. A study of international productivity and wage data by Turner and Jackson suggests that it is generally true in most countries that wages tend to rise in line with output per head in the fastest productivity growth industries. See H.A. Turner and D.A.S. Jackson 'On the Determination of the General Wage Level – a World Analysis', *Economic Journal*, December 1970.

7. It is worth noting, however, that if this productivity disparity-type inflation is important, it is not easy to draw conclusions about inflation and country comparisons of international competitiveness. One country may have a higher rate of inflation than another, yet its international competitiveness may be greater than that of the second country. This will occur if productivity in its export sectors was growing faster than productivity in the export sector of the second country, and fast relative to productivity in another sector of its own economy. Export prices would be kept very stable provided money wages did not rise in excess of productivity in the export sector, whilst the rise in the average domestic price level might be taking place at a fast rate. This situation may well explain why Japan has such a favourable export performance, although its domestic rate of inflation has been considerably higher than most, if not all, of its competitors in the postwar period.

8. From the policy point of view, the important question relates to the degree of unemployment that would be necessary to reduce the power of trade unions to force up the money wages and prices. See Chapters 3 and 7 for further discussion.

9. This conclusion is implied by the Equation of Exchange $MV = PO$, where M is the money stock, V is the income velocity of circulation of money, P is the average price level and O is the level of real output.

10. However, it is not always the case that equity prices will rise in inflation. If profits are being squeezed as a result of cost inflation, wealth-holders will have to look elsewhere for protection.

11. If expectations of continuing inflation have become firm, an initial fall in output and employment may be unavoidable in stopping inflation, whatever its underlying cause.

Chapter 3: *Inflation and Unemployment: Theoretical Considerations*

1. Lord Beveridge, *Full Employment in a Free Society*, Allen & Unwin, 1944, pp. 198-201.

2. A.J. Brown, *The Great Inflation 1939-1951*, O.U.P. 1955, pp. 88-103. See particularly Diagram 13 on page 99. Reference is also made in A. Lerner, *The Economics of Employment*, and in A.C. Pigou, *Lapses from Full Employment*.

3. A.W. Phillips, 'The Relation between Unemployment and the Rate of Change of Money Wage Rates in the United Kingdom 1861-1957', *Economica*, (n.s.) vol. 25, November 1958. An extensive literature on the Phillips Curve has subsequently developed. An Appendix at the end of this chapter lists some of the main references. See also *The Current Inflation*, ed. H.G. Johnson and A.R. Nobay, MacMillan 1971 and *Inflation*, ed. R.J. Ball and P. Doyle, Penguin, 1969.

4. Phillips, op. cit., Figure 12. Most recently: R.G. Lipsey: "The Micro Theory of the Phillips Curve Reconsidered: A Reply to Holmes and Smyth" Economica, February 1974.

5. R.G. Lipsey, 'The Relation between Unemployment and the Rate of Change of Money Wages in the United Kingdom 1862-1957', *Economica*, (n.s.) vol. 27, Feb. 1960, pp. 1-31.

6. See Phelps *et. al.*, *Microeconomic Foundations of Employment and Inflation Theory*, Macmillan, 1971, especially Part I.

7. See J.C.R. Dow and L.A. Dicks-Mireaux, 'The Excess Demand for Labour: a Study of Conditions in Great Britain 1946-56', Oxford Economic Papers, February 1958. Also C.C. Holt, 'Job Search, Phillips' Wage Relation and Union Influence: Theory and Evidence' in Phelps, op. cit.

8. Professor Friedman has described the 'natural rate of unemployment' in the following terms: 'The "natural rate of unemployment . . . is the level that would be ground out by the Walrasian system of general equilibrium equations, provided there is embedded in them the actual structural characteristics of the labour and commodity markets, including market imperfections", stochastic variability in demands and supplies, the cost of gathering information about job vacancies and labour availabilies, the cost of mobility, and so on.' Milton Friedman, 'The Role of Monetary Policy', *American Economic Review*, March 1968, pp. 1-17.

9. See Chapter 7 for further empirical evidence concerning the relationship between unemployment and inflation in OECD countries.

10. See A.G. Hines, 'The Determinants of the Rate of Change of Money Wage Rates and the Effectiveness of Incomes Policy' in H.G. Johnson and A.R. Nobay, *The Current Inflation*, Macmillan, 1971.

11. This seemed to be the situation in a number of industrial countries in latter half of 1974.

Chapter 4: *The International Transmission of Inflation.*

1. See Chapter 5, Table 5.6.
2. G. Edgren, K.O. Faxén and Clao-ErikOdhner, 'Lönebildning och samhalls-ekonomi', S.A.F., LO and TCO, Rabén and Sjögren, Stockholm 1970. A shortened version of this study was published in English in the Swedish Journal of Economics, 1969, under the title 'Wages, growth, and the distribution of income'.
3. See Chapter 10 for a discussion of the causes of inflation in this period.
4. SDRs were first allocated to members of the International Monetary Fund in January 1970. For an interesting and perceptive account of the events leading up to the creation of the new SDR facility and a description of the facility itself see F. Machlup, *Remaking the International Monetary System*, Johns Hopkins Press, Baltimore, 1968.
5. See Chapter 10.
6. Devaluation by the deficit country would also reduce the competitiveness of exporters in the surplus country, but this can be blamed on the government of the deficit country.
7. This is not necessarily true since even in a floating rate system, speculators could prevent the rate from depreciating; but if the domestic rate of inflation remained higher than elsewhere, it is doubtful whether they would do this for long.
8. See Chapter 2, pp. 22-25.
9. See Chapter 10.
10. The nature and growth of the multinational corporation is well documented. See, for instance, J.N. Behrman, *Some Patterns in the Rise of the Multilateral Enterprise* and J.H. Dunning, *The Multinational Enterprise*, Allen & Unwin 1970. Only a brief account is, therefore, given here since we are only concerned with its implications for the rate and transmission of inflation.
11. J.N. Behrman, op. cit., p. 61.
12. See Gennard, John, *Multinational Corporations and British Labour: A Review of Attitudes and Responses*, British North American Committee, 1972.
13. See Levinson, C., 'The Answer to the Giant Company', *Voice of the Unions*, May 1970 (published at 73 Ridgeway Place, London S.W.19.).
14. Geoffrey Maynard 'Monetary Policy' in J. Dunning (Editor) *Economic Analysis and the Multinational Enterprise*, Allen & Unwin 1974.

Chapter 5: *The Anatomy of Inflation in O.E.C.D. Countries*

1. The choice of the year 1968 is rather arbitrary, although significant events occurred around this time which were clearly related to the acceleration of inflation.
2. Between the mid 1950s and the latter part of the 1960s commodity export prices (excluding oil) fell by about eight per cent.

3. Unfortunately this coincided with a worldwide boom in commodity prices which together with the devaluation of sterling produced a massive deterioration in the U.K.'s terms of trade, largely against primary producer countries. This contributed to a further worsening, not an improvement, in the U.K.'s balance of payments.

4. The different behaviour of the velocity of circulation of money in the different countries reflects, in part at least, the different income elasticities of demand for *real* money balances; but we have no independent estimates of the latter.

Chapter 6: *The Contribution of Government to Aggregate Demand and Inflation in the O.E.C.D. Countries*

1. See, for instance, J.C.R. Dow, *Management of the British Economy*, Cambridge University Press, 1964; Martin Bronfenbrenner (ed.), *Is the Business Cycle Obsolete?*, Wiley-Interscience, 1969; E. Lundberg, *Instability and Economic Growth*, Yale University Press, 1968; G.D.H. Worswick, 'Fiscal Policy and Stabilisation in Britain' in A. Cairncross (ed.), *Britain's Economic Prospects Reconsidered*, Allen & Unwin, 1971.

2. R.C.O. Mathews, 'Why has Britain had Full Employment since the War?, *Economic Journal*, September 1968.

3. See p. 122 for a discussion of this concept.

4. See Chapter 7.

5. See Chapter 2.

6. E. Lundberg, *Instability and Economic Growth*, Yale University Press, 1968.

7. We must also take into account the possibility of a wage-price spiral being triggered off by a rise in indirect taxes. For a full discussion of the complexities of indirect taxation see A. Peacock and G.K. Shaw, *The Economic Theory of Fiscal Policy*, University of York Studies in Economics.

8. See Peacock and Shaw, op. cit.

9. There is some justification for doing this if, for instance, the government is pursuing a monetary policy which is rather independent of its fiscal policy e.g. if it is taking decisions about the desired money stock independently of the fiscal balance. Moreover, in recent years, it is clear that international capital movements have become very interest elastic. Also, given the values of the domestic propensities to consume, save, tax etc., typical of developed countries, the size of the multiplier does not seem to be greatly different in an open economy from what it is in a closed one — i.e. the rise in exports induced by a rise in imports goes some way to offsetting the leakage effect of the latter.

10. See C.V. Brown and D.A. Dawson, 'Personal Taxation, Incentives and Tax Reform', P.E.P. Broadsheet 506, January 1969.

11. The net primary impact of government expenditure and taxation is indicated by equation (iv) .a. on page 123.

$$Np = G (g + tc') - T (u'c'' + u'')$$

$$= vY [(g + tc') - \alpha(u'c'' + u'')]$$

If $\bar{\alpha}$ is the ratio T/G which makes N equal to zero while α is the *actual* ratio of T to G, the actual net primary impact of expenditure and taxation will be measured by:

$$vY [(g + tc') - \alpha (u'c'' = u'') - (g + tc') + \bar{\alpha} (u'c'' + u'')]$$

which equals

$$vY [(\bar{\alpha} - \alpha) (u'c'' + u'')]$$

The total impact (primary plus secondary) N_T

$$= \frac{vY [(\bar{\alpha} - \alpha) (u'c'' + u'')]}{1 - c(1 - r) + m}$$

12. Owing to 'rounding' at various stages of the calculations, neither these estimates nor the charts should be taken too literally.

13. Of course, this is not the normal concept of the multiplier: it is not the number which, say, an autonomous rise in private investment has to be multiplied in order to get the total effect on income.

14. Assumed values entering into the calculation of k and n_p and n_p^* are:

	c	c'	c''	m	r
U.S.	.94	.95	.85	.05	.09
U.K.	.94	.95	.80	.24	.10
Germany	.86	.90	.80	.21	.10
France	.90	.95	.85	.16	.09
Italy	.84	.95	.80	.16	.05
Austria	.91	.95	.85	.29	.13
Belgium	.88	.95	.80	.38	.05
Denmark	.90	.95	.80	.36	.10
Netherlands	.86	.95	.80	.52	.13
Sweden	.88	.95	.80	.27	.10
Canada	.91	.95	.80	.24	.10

15. Note that while the net primary impact appears to have been highest in Netherlands, its high import coefficient holds down the total net impact.

16. In 1958 government expenditure rose by about 11 per cent whilst tax revenue showed little change; in 1959 revenue rose by over 12 per cent and expenditure by less than 3 per cent. Corresponding figures

for 1967 are expenditure up 14 per cent and revenue up 7 per cent, while in 1968 revenue rose by 16 per cent and expenditure by 11 per cent.

17. Table 6.5. is not continued beyond 1968 since some changes in national income accounting data would make post-1968 calculations not completely comparable with earlier ones.

Chapter 7: *The Inflation – Unemployment Trade-Off in O.E.C.D. Countries*

1. E.g. when $\tau = 0.1$ and $p = 0.05$, $\tau p = 0.005$.
2. R.J. Wonnacott, 'Canadian-American Dependence. An Interindustry Analysis of Production and Prices', North Holland, 1961, p. 121. Wonnacott found a coefficient of 0.36.
3. For a contrary view, see R.C. Geary and J.L. Pratschke, 'Some Aspects of Price Inflation in Ireland', Paper No. 40, The Economic and Social Research Institute, Dublin, 1968.
4. See W. Galenson and A. Zellner: "International Comparison of Unemployment Rates" in "The Measurement and Behaviour of Unemployment", NBER, Princeton, 1957.
5. M.E. Streit: 'The Phillips Curve: Fact or Fancy? The Example of W. Germany', *Weltwirtschaftliches Archiv*, 1972, p. 628: 'The initial distortions in the locational distribution of labour when compared to employment opportunities were slowly removed, at first primarily by migration of labour. The labour markets became more transparent with a continuous improvement of labour exchanges, reducing the search costs and fostering mobility. Mobility was further increased by the reduction of housing shortages and the introduction of retraining schemes and financial support by the labour exchanges.'

Chapter 8: *Structural Factors in O.E.C.D. Inflation*

1. G. Edgren, K.O. Faxen, ·C.E. Odhner, '*Wage Formation and the Economy*', Allen and Unwin, London, 1973. This book is a translation of the original report in Swedish, a summary of which appeared in the *Swedish Journal of Economics* in 1969. The Swedish report was itself based on an official Norwegian report, the so-called *Ankunstreport*, which appeared in the series of the Norwegian Central Statistical Office in 1970.
2. This process was analysed in more detail in Chapter 2, pp 18-20.
3. The breakdown is reminiscent of the classification by Harrod of products in A, B and C-goods (*International Economics*), Cambridge Economic Handbooks, 1939. The price of A-goods is entirely determined by the world market (raw materials, e.g.). The price of C-goods, which cannot be traded on the world market, depends on domestic conditions only (constructions, services). The price of B-goods depends on both influences (manufactures mainly).

4. It is not strictly necessary that the rate of wage inflation in the lagging sector be equal to the corresponding rate in the advanced sector, only that it should be determined more by that than by physical productivity growth in the lagging sector.

5. For a recent such example, see S-Ch. Kolm, 'Note sur l'inflation de productivité' Revue *Economique*, 1970, pp. 1006-11.

6. Strictly speaking this is only true for the Swedish model. The Norwegian study, which uses a six-sector input-output framework, does incorporate import prices and indirect taxes, as well as intersectoral relations.

7. In the Swedish study, the competitive sector is relatively small (less than 30 per cent of GDP) and includes the following branches; competitive production of raw materials, intermediate products for export, import competing production and finished goods industry.

8. See especially D.A. Worton, *The Service Industries in Canada, 1946-66* and the comments by N.E. Terleckyj in V.R. Fucks, (ed.) *Production and Productivity in the Service Industries*, Studies in Income and Wealth No. 34, NBER New York, 1969, pp. 237-68.

9. J. Eatwell, J. Llewellyn and R. Tarling in "Money Wage Inflation in Industrial Countries" (The Review of Economic Studies, October 1974) found a close relationship between wage inflation and productivity growth in the top three sectors of manufacturing. This may help explain why in our results w_c must have been greater than q_c, since the latter refers to a much wider grouping of sectors.

10. During the period 1954-68 the average growth rate of the world price level was 0.6 per cent per annum, so that if we accept the estimate of 2.5 for p_c as mentioned above the condition $p_w < p_c$ was certainly satisfied, at least on the average.

11. This refers to export prices expressed in the different national currencies. If we measure the growth rate of the world price level expressed in a common currency, say the U.S. dollar, we also find a (weighted) average of 0.6 per cent. This is the estimate of p_w used above. (For an index of export prices of industrial countries see *International Financial Statistics*, I.M.F.)

12. See Chapter 5.

13. We are here referring to the 1954-68 period.

Chapter 9: *Inflation in Less Developed Countries*

1. See Chapter 4.

2. H.A. Turner and D.A.S. Jackson, 'On the determination of the General Wage Level — A World Analysis', *Economic Journal*, December 1970.

3. Beef in Argentina is a very good example: see later discussion.

4. See R.I. KcKinnon, *Money and Capital in Economic Development*, Bookings Institution, 1973.

5. The concept of structural inflation originated in Latin America and was

extensively employed by the Economic Commission for Latin America for analysing the inflationary problems of that region. An early article on the subject is O. Sunkel, 'La Inflacion Chilêna: Un Enfoque Heterodoxo', *El Trimestre*, XXV, 4 Mexico, oct-dic 1958, págs 570-599.

6. It is assumed that labour productivity in agriculture is rising sufficiently to offset a loss of labour to the manufacturing sector.

7. It is not necessary to assume that agricultural output cannot expand at all but simply that food supply *per capita* does not increase at a rate appropriate to the increase in real income *per capita* and the income elasticity of demand for food.

8. We return to this point later on.

9. For an analysis and appraisal of the 1967-71 stabilization programme see G. Maynard and W. van Ryckegham, 'Stabilization Policy in an Inflationary Economy: the case of Argentina' in G. Papanek, *Development Policy: Theory and Practice*, Harvard University Press, Cambridge, Mass., 1968, pp. 207-235, and 'Argentina 1967-70: A Stabilization Attempt that Failed', Banca Nazionale del Lavoro, *Quarterly Review*, No. 103., December 1972.

10. As professor W.A. Lewis has argued, while structural factors may explain why some moderate inflation cannot be avoided as economic growth proceeds, they cannot explain why the inflation rate should be 25 per cent or more. This requires a wage-price spiral and chronic budget deficits.

11. Agricultural prices and rents had been controlled and public utility rates, particularly in the transport sector of the economy, had been prevented from rising to offset the increased costs; as a consequence public enterprises tended to run up large deficits which limited the ability of certain private enterprises to finance their investments and hence expand their capacity. Also the previous governments had been reluctant to adjust the exchange rate in line with the domestic inflation, and subsidized exchange rates were provided for imports of wheat, petroleum products, newsprint and other products with the aim of limiting the rise in the price level. However, this policy in common with the holding down of public utility prices, contributed to monetary expansion and, therefore, added to inflationary pressure in this direction.

Chapter 10: *The Acceleration of World Inflation after 1968*

1. After 1968 there was a marked discrepancy between the behaviour of the GDP deflator and the behaviour of the consumer price index in a number of countries. This was due to substantial changes in exchange rates which, initially at any rate, could be expected to affect the behaviour of import prices in national currency relatively to the behaviour of domestic costs. Thus the 4 per cent fall in Germany's

import prices after 1969 held down consumer prices although domestic factor costs, including profits, rose faster than before.

2. See O.E.C.D., *Economic Outlook*, 14 December 1973, 'Recent Labour Market Developments'.

3. Contrary to textbook theory, an increase in the supply of labour relative to capital does not readily lead either to a fall in wages or to using capital saving technology.

4. 1970 was in any case a year in which demand pressures picked up in a number of European countries and unemployment fell, an exception being the U.K.

5. U.S. export prices however did not rise at a faster rate after the devaluation of the dollar than they did before, although import prices rose quite sharply.

6. See for instance R. Hinshaw (ed.), *Inflation as a Global Problem*, John Hopkins Press, 1972, p. 2.

7.

	World Price Level (U.S. dollars)	U.S. Export Prices
1953	100	100
1958	103	105
1963	104	108
1968	109	119
1973	156	161

8. However, there is no close correlation between the extent to which a country's foreign exchange reserves increased and the rate at which its money supply subsequently expanded. Germany's foreign exchange reserves increased more than most other countries, yet the expansion in its money supply was less than that of most other countries.

9. Between the end of 1967 and the beginning of 1970 weekly wage rates rose by about 10 per cent: in the following year they rose by nearly 8 per cent.

10. See Chapter 4 for a discussion of this point.

11. The share of non-nationalized companies' gross trading profits, less stock appreciation, in total domestic income (after stock appreciation) fell from 15 per cent in 1960 to little more than 10 per cent in 1972 (*Short Term Outlook for Company Profitability, Cash Flow and Investment*, Confederation of British Industry, June 1974).

12. The rise in oil prices meant an improvement in the terms of trade of oil producers and a shift in the distribution of world income in their favour. However, owing to the fact that they are unable to translate, at least in the immediate future, the rise in their real income into a demand for the real output of the rest of the world, a deflationary impact is imposed on the world economy generally. This can of course be offset by demand expansionary measures in the industrial countries which would be 'financed' by borrowing the unspendable

financial surpluses of the oil producers. Technical difficulties arise in the intermediation process of transferring the financial surpluses of the oil producers to the oil-consuming borrowers: but the main problem which faced the world in 1974 was a lack of agreement among the governments of the West as to the degree of priority to be given to offsetting the deflationary impact of the oil price rise as against reducing the rate of inflation.

Chapter 11: *Economic Policy and Inflation*

1. It is an interesting question whether, given the basic initial condition which produced the worldwide industrial and commodity boom, any individual country could have contracted out of its inflationary repercussions. It appears to be the view of some economists that this would have been possible. Thus, in an open letter addressed to the U.K. Prime Minister in July 1974, a group of British economists appear to have argued that U.K. inflation in 1974 had nothing to do with the rise in world commodity prices but only to do with the massive increases in U.K. domestic money supply in the two preceding years. Of course, there can be little doubt that the U.K.'s tremendous budget deficit in 1972-3, which was the outcome of the Conservative Government's desire to stimulate economic growth and which was largely financed by an equally large increase in the money supply, contributed to the U.K.'s very high domestic inflation rate. The steady depreciation of sterling from mid-June 1972 anticipated the world commodity boom and then added to the cost inflationary effects of the latter on the U.K.'s price level. The U.K.'s inflation rate in 1974 was higher than that of many other countries, and there were signs that it would continue to remain high when other countries' inflation rates showed signs of falling. But this being admitted, can it really be argued that the U.K.'s domestic rate had nothing to do with the worldwide boom in commodity prices?

Presumably, it could be argued that a tight monetary policy in the U.K. would have permitted an appreciation of the U.K. exchange rate which would have stabilized U.K. import prices in domestic currency. But what would have been the implications for U.K. export prices? Assuming that other industrial countries were allowing the rise in primary product prices to feed through into their industrial costs and prices, some rise in the foreign currency price of U.K. exports would be possible without U.K. exports becoming unprofitable. But the industrial countries as a group were experiencing a worsening in their real terms of trade against primary producers. Could the U.K. have prevented a worsening in its own terms of trade against primary products? It seems unlikely, given heavy U.K. reliance on imported raw materials and foodstuffs. Hence, an appreciation of sterling sufficient to prevent a rise in U.K. import prices and costs in terms of national currency would have implied a substantial fall in U.K. export prices in terms of national currency and therefore in manufactured good prices generally. One can reasonably doubt whether such an outcome would have been possible, at least without substantial unemployment, given downward inflexibility of wage and other domestic costs in the U.K.

Perhaps the group of economists in question had in mind joint action on the part of all industrial countries together. If all such countries had appreciated their currencies against primary producing countries together, (if that were possible), each would have had less fear that the competitive position of its exports would be adversely affected. However, given that conditions had been created to bring about a substantial improvement in the terms of trade of primary producing countries against industrial countries, an appreciation of industrial countries' currencies against primary producing countries' currencies would have implied a fall in the domestic currency price level of manufactured good output generally. No doubt the monetary stringency necessary to produce such a development would have prevented the industrial and primary product boom in the first place; but this is no more than saying what has been admitted earlier, namely that if the tremendous monetary expansion of 1970-71 had been avoided, so would a substantial part of the acceleration of world inflation. This is a far cry from the proposition that the U.K. or indeed any other country could have completely contracted out of the worldwide increase in inflation rates. It is instructive. to note that countries whose currencies did appreciate over the period and/or which pursued relatively tight monetary policies — for instance, Japan and Germany — nonetheless suffered from a sharp rise in their inflation rates. Indeed, Japan's rate of inflation increased more than the U.K.'s.

2. See Milton Friedman, 'Using Escalators to Help Fight Inflation' *Fortune,* July 1974.

3. Friedman, op.cit.

4. See E.S. Phelps *Inflation Policy and Unemployment Theory* Macmillan 1972, Chapter 6, pp 183-197.

5. Temporary price control may be imposed to help break price expectations in a situation of high inflation and rising unemployment.

6. This was probably true even in 1972-3 when inflation rates throughout the world became very high, for the higher rates of inflation experienced were less due to each country working closer to its full employment productive capacity as compared with earlier years than to the fact that all major countries were booming together, so forcing up world primary product prices.

7. For a discussion of incomes policies, see A. Jones, *The New Inflation,* Penguin, 1972, and H. Clegg, *How to Run an Incomes Policy,*

Heinemann, 1971.

8. The process has probably gone further in the U.K. than in many other industrial countries. Between 1948 and 1972 the share of wages and salaries rose from 65 per cent to over 68 per cent. Between the early 1950s and the early 1970s, the share of non-nationalized company gross trading profits (excluding stock appreciation) fell from over 15 per cent of total domestic income to less than 10 per cent. The relatively low rate of growth of the U.K. economy may have been in part the consequence.

Authors Index